Preston Manning
and the
Reform Party

Murray Dobbin

James Lorimer & Company, Publishers
Toronto, 1991

Canadian Cataloguing in Publication Data

Dobbin, Murray, 1945 -
    Preston Manning and the Reform Party

Includes index.
ISBN 1-55028-359-6 (bound) ISBN 1-55028-357-X (pbk.)

1. Manning, Preston, 1942-   .   2. Reform Party of Canada.
3. Canada - Politics and government - 1984-   .*   I. Title.

JL197.R4C8 1991   324.271'0983   C91-095506-9

Cover photo: Canada Wide Photo

James Lorimer & Company, Publishers
Egerton Ryerson Memorial Building
35 Britain Street
Toronto, Ontario
M5A 1R7

Printed and bound in Canada.

CONTENTS

ACKNOWLEDGEMENTS

As with any such project, this one was accomplished with a lot of assistance from others — friends and colleagues who were willing to take time from their busy lives to help me with this book.

Harold Bronson alerted me to the importance of the Reform phenomenon, and his insights into the party started me on the path to writing this book. Other friends helped in a variety of ways, each of them important to the final product: I thank John Warnock, Don Kossick, George Manz, Anne Smart, Ellen Gould, Larry Haiven, and new friends Richard Sherbaniuk and Howard Goldenthal.

Mark Bidwell did research for me with an enthusiasm which took him beyond what I had expected. Others helped in critical areas of research which I simply would not have had time to do myself. I am grateful to Ian Bullock, Rita Feutl, and Keith Rimstad for their work. Other friends and colleagues helped me with certain parts of the book which required their special knowledge: Ben Smillie for his insights on Christian fundamentalism; Howard McConnell for his advice on constitutional matters; Ron Fisher for his expertise on conflict resolution; and David Laycock for his reading of parts of the manuscript relating to Social Credit political reforms. I thank them.

Of course, in thanking all these people I do not wish to burden any of them with responsibility for any shortcomings in this book. I have myself to thank for those.

I am grateful to the Douglas-Coldwell Foundation for their timely and generous contribution of a grant to help research this book.

The Reform Party staff was friendly and helpful when responding to my requests for material.

Many people gave freely of their time and their thoughts in interviews I did in researching this book. Without their co-operation, it simply couldn't have been done.

PREFACE

Nineteen ninety was an extraordinary year for Canadian politics and democracy. The enormous outpouring of anger and frustration that the country witnessed had not been seen in decades. There were many issues at the root of this anger — thousands of jobs lost to free trade, the gutting of VIA Rail, Meech Lake, the closing of yet more rural post offices, legislation that would lead to an end to federal funding of medicare. The list seemed endless.

While not everyone was angry over all these issues, almost everyone was angry about the GST. Yet even with this issue, on which people had very different ideas about what the alternative to the tax should be, there was an almost unprecedented agreement that it had to go. More important, the sentiment that Brian Mulroney had to go became overwhelming.

Hatred of Brian Mulroney and the desire to get rid of him was almost a national obsession. As much as the issues themselves, people were exercised over how the country was being run. Not only was the country being transformed, it was being transformed by a man and a government that seemed to believe that once it got a majority in the House of Commons, it could do anything it pleased, the people be damned.

The prime minister, saying that he would always "choose the right thing for the country, not the popular thing," elevated contempt for the popular will to a governing principle. With 80 per cent of the population against the GST, Mulroney appointed twenty-four Tories to the Senate to get his bill passed.

In his actions on the GST, in his rolling of the dice on Meech Lake, and in his contempt for the feelings of Canadians, Brian Mulroney accomplished something he had not intended: he created a national political party out of a western protest party.

The Reform Party was originally cast very much in the mould of the prairie populist party, including advocacy of American-style political reforms: referenda, plebiscites, recall and free votes in Parliament. In fact, it was these radical ideas for reforming the system which had so often doomed Alberta-based parties to regional obscurity.

Brian Mulroney changed all that. By the end of 1990, the issue was no longer just the GST or the other policies of the Conservative government. The issue, in a phrase which was repeated across the country, was "How do we get rid of this man?" There was a passion for democracy in the country — but it found its expression in the profoundly negative sentiment of hatred for the prime minister.

The defeat over the GST took the fight out of a lot of people. They had used the institutions they were supposed to use to register their dissatisfaction, but nothing had happened. Mulroney had just laughed in their faces. And Jean Chrétien and Audrey McLaughlin couldn't do anything about it — and were thus blamed for the result, too. There was a perceptible shift in the focus of people's political attention. What was wrong with a political system that allowed this man to do what he was doing?

The frustration with the failure of the system to deliver democracy was a gift to Preston Manning. He stood to gain not only because his party advocated political reforms which seemed to hold promise for more democratic control over governments, but also because many people were looking for someone who was not part "of the system." They were looking for someone unsullied, untainted by its failure. Somebody new. And here was Preston Manning, presenting himself as just that person.

I had heard about the Reform Party, like everyone else. But it hadn't really registered with me as an important political phenomenon. I was vaguely aware that it was a right-wing party, if only because it was advocating the traditional right-wing democratic reforms. But I was like most Saskatchewan people: we are rarely attracted by Alberta-based movements and generally pay them little attention.

But this one seemed, on the surface at least, to be different. It was gaining strength on the basis of genuine, mass discontent. It had fought against the GST and was clearly in tune with people's pro-democracy sentiment. It was a western party which seemed to speak to many national concerns.

When I moved back to Saskatchewan after a year in Ontario, a friend and former political science professor drew my attention to Reform Party policy. It was contained in the party's newspaper, *The Reformer*, in the form of sample resolutions for debate at the party's annual assembly to be held in Saskatoon in April, 1991.

Three policies in *The Reformer* struck me immediately and started me on the course of writing this book. The first was on agriculture. I have an urban background, but no self-respecting student of politics in Saskatchewan is unfamiliar with the issues facing farmers. The farm-policy resolution which startled me stated that the party's policy was not guided by the interests of producers, but by the "demand of consumers for ... secure supplies of food at the lowest competitive prices."

While this resolution might not cause alarm at the dinner tables of urban Canada, it is tantamount to a declaration of war on the family farm. It was a cheap food policy. If actually carried out it could wipe out half the farmers in western Canada. Farmers, today, are in greater danger of bankruptcy than at any time since the 1930s: grain prices are actually comparatively lower than they were then. If Reform was a populist party, what explained a farm policy that would reverse sixty years of populist reforms?

The second surprise was medicare. Not only was the policy one of eliminating the nation-wide health care system, but it was phrased in such a way that the impact of the policy was obscured. The resolution called for the "provincialization" of medicare, an odd way of saying that the National Health Act would be rescinded. But rescinding the Health Act is what "provincialization," with "unconditional" funding from Ottawa would mean. Its implications were enormous: it could and probably would mean the balkanization of medicare and, eventually, one system for the rich and another for the poor. There was no popular outcry for changing the medicare system, so why was this populist party calling for this radical change?

Perhaps the most surprising resolution was on the GST. There was a resolution from a constituency association calling for the repeal of the tax. But there was another, from the Party's Policy Committee, declaring that the Reform Party only opposed the GST "in its present form" and suggesting a Reform government would keep the tax. Here was a party which had jumped to the national stage, from relative obscurity, on the basis of its uncompromising opposition to the GST. How would Preston Manning justify to Reform supporters keeping a tax they believed he was committed to cancelling?

What struck me first was the consistency of the right-wing message in these policy examples. They were uniformly free-market policies, not the sort of eclectic mix of policies one would expect of a populist party responding to people's grievances. I was also struck by the fact that these policies were all put forward by a party committee, not the constituencies. I obtained a copy of the party's policy booklet. Policies in other areas were also uniformly conservative, though many were vague or short on detail. The book also contained a foreword by Preston Manning in which he declared that the old "left-right-centre" politics were no longer adequate.

There seemed to be little public awareness of Reform policies, yet a great deal of interest in the party and Preston Manning. This could simply be explained by a lack of real media scrutiny of a relatively new party. But with the party's big national assembly coming in April to my home town, Saskatoon, and the national media paying them a lot more attention, these policies and their implications were, I thought, bound to be discussed and reported.

It didn't turn out that way. The media, with some important exceptions (such as Jeffrey Simpson, who compared Preston Manning and Reform to the Republican Party in the U.S.), focused on what they said they would: the party's decisions regarding running in provincial elections and expanding eastward and its hard-line on Quebec. While some did tag the party as "right- wing," Preston Manning's description of his party as "populist" went unchallenged.

Meanwhile, though little was being said about the substance of Reform Party policies, Preston Manning was rapidly gaining support from a broad spectrum of Canadians. Many people, including friends and acquaintances, were declaring support for this new party — along the lines of "I'm mad as hell and I'm going to vote Reform." Many readily admitted that they did not know what Preston Manning actually stood for, but firmly believed he couldn't be as bad as Brian Mulroney.

Like Preston Manning, I am a student of western politics and democratic movements. I remember the Depression stories told by my grandfather who was one of the first grain elevator agents for the farmer-owned Saskatchewan Wheat Pool. And as a student at university, I studied the populist politics of the prairies. Later, I focused my attention on the popular movements of the Métis in the 1930s and 1960s. When the Reform Party was first emerging as a national force, I was immersed in writing a book on the Métis movement.

I decided to postpone my work on the Métis to find out more about Preston Manning and his party. This book describes what I have learned about the man, the party, and their policies. The first chapters focus on Manning, who continues to have an enormous influence on the party's character and direction. I examine the early influences which shaped Preston Manning, his fifteen years as a business consultant, and his early efforts to form a conservative political party.

Then, I look at the Reform Party itself: its origins, the background and beliefs of its membership, the role of Preston Manning and the party headquarters in directing the party, and the evolution of Reform policy since it was founded in 1987. I also examine the connections the party has with other groups — formal and informal — that finance it, share its political objectives, and identify it as a vehicle for their particular issues.

The last chapters examine the party's actual policies. I look at Reform's social and economic policies first and discuss the common thread that binds them together. I analyze the party's constitutional reforms and its policy towards Quebec. I then examine its political and parliamentary reforms in the context of the political crisis believed by many Canadians to be at the heart of the country's problems.

In the final chapter, I draw my own conclusions about Preston Manning and the Reform Party of Canada. I attempt to judge the party on its own terms, on the basis of the standards it has set for itself: its claim to be a populist party, created and directed by its grassroots; its claim to be something genuinely new — taking us beyond the old "left-right-centre" politics; its claim to speak to the discontent Canadians have expressed over what is happening to their country and the party's claim that its democratic reforms will effectively address the crisis in democracy.

In writing this book I have spoken to many Reform supporters whose deeply held concerns about the future of Canada I share. I sympathize with the yearning for something new, for a leader untainted by the failings of the present system. But I felt that if people were going to vote for Reform, it was important for them to consider what effect that decision might have beyond merely replacing Brian Mulroney and the Conservative government. This book attempts to do this and provides a voter's guide to Reform Party policies and its leader.

Out of the Wilderness

I t is unusual in Canada for a political figure or a political party to arrive quickly and decisively on the national stage. It is especially rare for a man who is unknown to the public and who for years deliberately avoided the political spotlight to have the impact that Preston Manning has had on Canadian politics. Manning's success is only partly due to the extraordinary political circumstances that Canada faces in the early 1990s. Just as important are the history and personal development of the man whom those circumstances have brought to prominence. Preston Manning is a politician, but he is no ordinary politician.

The influences that have been brought to bear on Preston Manning could only have been created in Alberta. His father, Ernest Manning, was not just premier for twenty-five years but premier of what was often called a one-party state. Revered almost as a saint by many, he dominated Alberta political life during the years he was in power. Through Ernest Manning and his predecessor and mentor, William Aberhart, evangelical Christianity played a role in Alberta politics for which the only Canadian parallel is Catholicism in Quebec. Ernest Manning was both spiritual and political leader of Alberta. Preston Manning grew up under the tutelage and the shadow of his larger-than-life father.

The United States — its culture, political institutions, and doctrine of individualism — also had an enormous impact on political life and attitudes in Alberta. That influence is strongly demonstrated in the history and development of the Social Credit Party, which Ernest Manning ran for so many years: a free-enterprise party extolling the virtues of individual liberty, the traditional family, and the supremacy of God.

These influences, which were expressed in Ernest Manning as well as in the life and culture of Alberta during Preston Manning's formative years, played an important role in the development of the man who wants to be prime minister of Canada. To these influences, of course, Preston Manning added his own interests — most particularly, an attraction to the physical sciences, whose models had a profound impact on his approach to social and political questions.

Family Life

The rapid success of the Reform Party, especially in 1990 and following its 1991 Assembly in Saskatoon, has resulted in dozens if not hundreds of stories about Preston Manning — his style, personality, and manner of speech have now become public property. Those descriptions vary only slightly: Preston Manning is earnest, sincere, "preacherish," has no political "aura," is non-charismatic. He is dapper, pious, button-down, staid, pragmatic, low key. Whatever else these terms might otherwise imply, they are seen by observers as either part of his appeal or at least not distractions from it. In the words of John Howse of *Maclean's*, Manning's "mix of self-deprecating rectitude and apparent lack of charisma [is] appealing."

Almost every observer who knows both Ernest and Preston Manning comments on their remarkable similarity. For example, in Saturday Night, Alberta Liberal Leader, Laurence Decore, remarked:

> Preston's got a similar quality to his father — that evangelical mystique. There's something captivating about a preacher and the way a preacher can get his message across. His father had it and it's all wound up in a western twang. It's wound up in biblical images. It's very populist. And Preston's got it down to the kind of perfection that his father had. It makes him very appealing, and makes him sound very honest and forthright. I think it's easy to like what he says.

The fact that he seems to be a contradiction in terms — a grassroots prairie politician and an intensely private man — finds some explanation in his early home life. Ernest Manning was also intensely private — and very formal. John Barr writes in *The Dynasty*, his book on the Social Credit Party: "Everyone knew that Mr. Manning (as he was almost universally known; probably no more than half a dozen people ever called him 'Ernest') was Premier and that he was 'there' somehow, but his public appearances were sufficiently rare that he was never over-exposed. Manning did not invite familiarity."

All political leaders who survive long enough become the subject of jokes as well as editorial cartoons. Ernest Manning was no exception. According to Barr, two of the popular jokes of the time help reveal Manning's public image: "St. Peter searching through new arrivals for a psychiatrist, then asking him: 'Come in and help us out with the Supreme Being; he thinks he's Manning.' Another, Manning looking for a burial plot. He finds a nice one but protests its high cost. The owner says, 'But sir, it has a lovely view ...' Manning replies, 'You don't seem to understand. I'll only be needing it for three days.' "

Preston Manning was born in 1942 in Edmonton, just a year before his father took over the reins of the Social Credit leadership and became premier of Alberta. Ernest Manning kept his political life very separate from his personal life. After living in Edmonton until 1954, the Manning family moved to a dairy farm northeast of the city. Ernest hired a man to run the operation, but he worked on the farm himself when he could.

Preston Manning recalled: "My father was thought of in the community as Mr. Manning who kept a dairy farm in the valley and went into town during the week to run the government. The only impact on me was when the legislature opened. They used to have a tea party where they made all these fancy little sandwiches. I could usually get a bunch of these ... and take them to school. They were always objects of wonderment as to why people would make sandwiches so small."

Despite his privileged life, Preston was expected to carry out responsibilities. He worked on the farm, helping milk the family's seventy Holstein cows morning and evening. "My first job," says Manning, "was driving a 'honey wagon' at a nickel a load."

While Preston Manning's mother, Muriel, had no public role, she was known as a strong-minded person in her own right. This did not mean she was a counterweight to Ernest. Rather, this tall, striking woman provided the family's patriarch with a needed domestic support. As devoted to evangelical Christianity as her husband, Muriel Manning also provided musical leadership for Ernest Manning's weekly "Back to the Bible" radio broadcasts, which he had taken over from his Socred predecessor, William Aberhart.

Preston's only sibling, his older brother Keith, suffered from cerebral palsy and was away from home at special schools for much of Preston's childhood. Keith returned to the family home in his late teens. He died in 1987.

The Mannings were a very closely knit family with a small circle of friends. Beyond socializing within this group, Ernest and Muriel Manning entertained very rarely. "Cabinet wives were invited out once a year for tea; there were no social functions sponsored by the Mannings other than that," writes Barr, who worked closely with Preston Manning in the late sixties.

Church more than government probably dominated the Manning household. After spending ten to eleven hour days at the legislature, Ernest would add another ten to twenty hours a week preparing speeches and religious talks for "Back to the Bible," a program heard not only across Alberta, where its audience was well over 100,000, but across the prairies. Ernest Manning dominated family life just as he dominated the public life of Alberta: the spiritual leader and inspiration to tens of thousands of people, he was also the quintessential patriarch. And Preston Manning was, for most intents and purposes, his only son.

Preston evidently took this daunting responsibility seriously. He won the Governor General's award for high scholastic performance in grade nine and graduated from Horse Hill High School with a 93 per cent average. He was offered three scholarships to university upon graduation and enrolled in physics at the University of Alberta.

The impact of Ernest Manning on his son was enormous: it could scarcely have been anything else given his stature and his evangelical charisma. The particulars of that impact, however, are most important. While many children of political parents grow up developing their own political beliefs and views of the world as a way of coping with a dominant father, Preston Manning was moulded in his father's image. As he developed into adulthood, Preston drew comments about the similarities between his and his father's speech patterns, mannerisms, and even body language and posture. He was every inch Ernest Manning's son.

While he has said that his father did not bring politics into the home, Preston Manning acknowledges that the political influence was nonetheless felt early on: "The family itself did not play that great a role in politics in those days. But at a very early age, I began looking at things from a governing point of view because my father was the leader of the government."

At university in the early sixties he gave the impression of a rural kid completely isolated from the ways of urban society. He presented an odd image. "He was part of the Youth Parliament's Social Credit caucus at the same time Joe Clark, Grant Notley (the late, former leader of the New Democratic Party in Alberta), Jim Coutts (who became prominent in the Liberal Party under Pierre Trudeau), and others were representing their respective parties. He was a good speaker, but you never saw him on campus. People knew who he was, and the rumour was that his father didn't want him to hang around the university too much because it would be a bad moral influence on him," recalls Fred Walker, a student at that time. "He looked very out of place — odd enough in his mannerisms and physical appearance and dress to be the occasional subject of ridicule. He gave the impression of being a very serious and committed young man — but more an apologist for his father's party and policies. He didn't play a very prominent role."

When Preston first left the tightly-knit world of the Manning household for the larger world outside, the period was the early sixties. Later, when he took up the study of economics, he began to appear more comfortable. But he seems to have emerged slowly, almost as if from a cocoon of his father's making or from an isolation that came from living in his father's shadow.

In 1967, Preston Manning married a University of Alberta nursing student, Sandra Beavis. The religious home life he had experienced was repeated in his own family — as was the desire for privacy and separation of public from family life. He refuses permission to reporters to visit his home or to photograph his family. The Mannings' two sons, Nathan, fourteen, and Daniel, eleven, attend the Glenmore Christian Academy run by the First Alliance Church in Calgary. Manning's three daughters, Andria, twenty-two, Avryll, twenty, and Mary Joy, sixteen, all attended similar religious schools. Andria is studying pre-law and Avryll, science, at the University of Calgary.

Attending a service at the First Alliance Church in Calgary, where the family moved from Edmonton in 1990, provides a glimpse of the religious and social life which has helped mould Preston Manning. Manning would have attended churches like this one as a child and adolescent. The First Alliance Church is located in south Calgary in a middle to upper-middle class neighbourhood. Arriving at the church, one of the first things one notices is the evidence of a very well-to-do congregation: the parking lot is full of expensive, late-model cars. It is all very orderly and a bit more formal than one might find at more established churches. For example, there is a section of the parking lot designated for "First Time Visitors Only."

The nave of the church is done in wall-to-wall carpeting, and the pews are upholstered in dusty rose tweed. The congregation seems well-to-do; people are very formally dressed, and the atmosphere is suggestive of the 1950s. A group of teenage girls sits together, as does a group of elderly women. The rest of the congregation is dominated by middle-aged people. The women are dressed in suits and jackets and one is struck by the number who are wearing strings of white pearls. The men present repeated lines of grey and dark blue suits.

The main floor of the church is full, despite it being a warm and sunny long weekend. The congregation is all white except for two black men standing at information booths in the lobby, providing literature on the church.

Before the service begins, people congregate in the large lobby: there is animated conversation about summer holidays, rented trailers, and the like. This is a community; clearly people know each other well and there is a noisy friendliness. The socializing continues in the aisles until the service begins.

Over the din of conversation comes an announcement over the loudspeaker: "The service will begin in three minutes." It is more reminiscent of a play than a church service. After the congregation is seated, about a dozen distinguished-looking, white, middle-class men — the church elders — march down the aisle and take their privileged place in the front pew. The only woman at the front of the church is the soloist.

First-time visitors to the church are asked to identify themselves. As the service begins, registration forms are passed down the pews. They ask for information that you might normally find on a demographic survey, including age group. The form also asks that the person describe what it is that he or she wants to get from the church. This is not for first-time visitors: everyone fills out the forms.

The sermon, given by a pastor from Ohio while the regular minister is on sabbatical, is a warning about "unmarked spiritual danger" — that Christians are in danger of pursuing the wrong kind of pleasure and avoiding the right kind of pain. "Satan's goal," says the pastor, "is to keep you from the highest pleasure." It is given with more colour and force than in a United or Catholic service: peppered with references to personal experience. He is a good speaker.

As the sermon proceeds, many people take notes, writing them on the blank back page of this Sunday's hand-out. Virtually everyone has brought his or her own Bible and they follow the reading of Scripture by the pastor. A glance at the Bibles shows that they are well-used — extensively marked with underlining and notes in the margins.

When the service ends, people do not leave quickly. The same socializing that began with their arrival continues in the lobby. Simultaneously, a group of Filipinos arrive and file into another room in the church for a separate service.

The First Alliance Church is representative of many evangelical congregations: they tend to be close, if not closed, communities. While the evangelical church in St. Albert attended by the Manning family would not have been identical to the First Alliance in Calgary, it would have been very similar, reinforcing values much more widely accepted then than they are now. Given the private nature of the Manning family and its lack of socializing, its main "community" was very likely a religious one, similar in makeup to that found today at the First Alliance Church. This group would have been culturally conservative, dominated by wealthy families and, more particularly, the wealthy patriarchs of those families. If Ernest Manning's family was isolated from the changing world around it, as it seems to have been, that isolation would not have been challenged by the evangelical community — a community whose beliefs and moral imperatives commanded its members to avoid a culture which was becoming, by the late fifties and early sixties, increasingly liberal and, from the church's point of view, immoral.

The Influence of Evangelical Fundamentalism

Judging the weight of the various influences that have moulded a political figure can never be a precise exercise. But it is clear that both through the church which the family attended and through Ernest Manning, lay preacher and powerful personality, Preston Manning was deeply influenced by evangelical Christianity. He told *Maclean's* that his commitment had intensified over the years. "I have always been interested in relating religion to business, science, politics and conflict resolution." To understand what has influenced Preston Manning, then, one must understand his religious affiliations.

When William Aberhart, who was later the first leader of the Social Credit League, founded the Prophetic Bible Institute in Calgary in 1925, it was meant to rival other seminaries. Its board, led by Aberhart, said that they were convinced "… that many of the theological seminaries or colleges are disseminating Modernism and infidelity in all their various destructive forms … the time must come in the very near future when churches … will be calling for preachers who will be able to teach them the Word of God that liveth and abideth forever."

The Prophetic Bible Institute's first student was Ernest C. Manning. In 1927, at eighteen, he had heard Aberhart promoting the school on the Socred leader's weekly "Back to the Bible" broadcast. He quickly became Aberhart's protégé, helping him run the school as well as taking over the "Back to the Bible" broadcasts when his mentor died in 1943.

The right-wing evangelism preached by Aberhart and embraced by his student not only allowed for political activity "in the world," it demanded it. This idea was expressed by Ernest Manning in 1964: "There is no way in which a truly born-again Christian can divorce his own nature from any phase of his activities … it is completely contrary to the Scriptures that Christians … should avoid the sphere of public life …"

Aberhart's theology included a genuine compassion for the poor — and an understanding of class. "It was this brand of theology," says Reverend Ben Smillie, "which held out the greatest hope for the poor." It was a theology of transcendent hope: "A theology which preached the rescuing of the poor and dispossessed encouraged the suffering masses to expect the imminent return of Christ. It also promised judgement for the oppressors — the railways and the banks."

The specific Christianity of Ernest Manning was actually more closely attuned to fundamentalism than was Aberhart's. The latter had moved, says Social Credit scholar Alvin Finkel, "towards views that resembled the social gospel," a more liberal religious view of social action. Manning's gospel was the "gospel of individualism," says Finkel. "... he viewed humans as essentially alone in a struggle to achieve eternal salvation and believed that a collectivist state belittled that struggle and made individuals more vulnerable to behaviour that might lead to eternal damnation."

Throughout his political career, Ernest Manning was motivated by religion and, more specifically, by anti-socialism: "Socialism, to Manning, is a system which largely prevents the individual from attaining the state of grace and hence salvation ... Giving to the individual societal benefits such as free medical care ... breeds idleness ... causing a breakdown in his relationship with God." Manning argued that "where the state imposed a monopoly on a service ... the sinful philosophy of state collectivism scored a victory."

This evangelical view of humans as essentially alone in the struggle for salvation leads to a gospel of the individual and also, naturally enough, "in the world" to the gospel of free enterprise and capitalism. It compels many of its adherents to elevate capitalism to the level of Biblical command. Richard Neuhaus, an American evangelist, says it is "imperative for Christians to support capitalism. It is an amazing thing ... It comes from the grace of God."

This fundamentalist view commands its adherents to promote capitalism as the "best hope" of the poor. According to Reverend Ben Smillie, using Ernest Manning as an example, these evangelical sects "have religiously sanctified the privileges of the economically powerful." The multi-millionaire Ernest Manning could denounce the "Godless materialism" of the communist system, while materialism sanctioned by God allowed him to "equate [his] wealth with the blessing of God."

Fundamentalism may appear to be "traditional," but fundamentalists are as modern in their doctrine as the modernity they have organized to fight. They develop philosophies which contain the idea of "inerrancy" — the conviction that the Bible has to be literally correct in all details. It is evangelism's "most obsessive" doctrine and is used as a weapon in denominational struggles. Martin Marty, in *America*, compares "the mass of believers to the people who take security from the knowledge that Marxist theorists stand behind their revolution."

Of course, it was not just right-wing evangelists who felt obliged by the faith to enter the world of politics. The progressive version of religious involvement in social movements was called the social gospel, and it played a major role in the perspective and growth of the social democratic Co-operative Commonwealth Federation (the forerunner of the NDP). According to Ben Smillie, in his *Beyond the Social Gospel*: "The protest which developed out of the social gospel was motivated by the belief in the coming of God to a marginalized people. Central to Social Gospel belief is the conviction that it is impossible to love God and neighbour without developing a theology of hope ... it meant 'building the New Jerusalem' on the streets of every city and hamlet on the prairies." It was not a transcendent hope, but a hope for the here and now.

While William Aberhart had that theology of hope — though it was transcendent and not earthly — it was largely absent in Ernest Manning. The compassion of Aberhart was residual in Manning, who looked south of the border for his inspiration and found it in individualistic American fundamentalism.

In contrast to the glorification of free enterprise and the individual, which characterizes Ernest and Preston Manning's fundamentalism, the social gospel of the CCF — the most famous practitioner of which was Baptist minister T.C. "Tommy" Douglas — emphasized co-operation and social and economic justice accomplished through political action and government intervention. The result, in Saskatchewan, says Ben Smillie, was hospital insurance, medicare, rural electrification, dental plans, old age pensions and labour standards to protect workers.

Preston Manning's church, the First Alliance in Calgary, is a member church of the Christian and Missionary Alliance of Canada. The 1990 edition of its manual sets out its constitution, bylaws, policies, regulations, and statements on marriage and divorce, and the role of women. As an evangelical church, it adheres to the doctrine of "inerrancy" — that is, the Bible is correct in all details and cannot be deviated from.

Two other areas of church doctrine are worth noting. The role of women in the church is subordinate to men and is dictated by the Bible: "Christ is the head of every man and the man is the head of every woman and God is the head of Christ." In the church, as elsewhere, "It is recognized that equality and submission can be compatible as seen in Jesus Christ. There is no inferiority implied in submission ... in the man-woman relationship."

The attitude towards homosexuality is also set out in the manual in the section on marriage. "In no case ought any person to enter into any so-called 'marriage' with a person of the same sex. Homosexual unions are specifically forbidden and are described in Scripture as manifestations of the basest forms of sinful conduct since they ... desecrate God's creational design."

There are fourteen articles in the manual on remarriage after divorce — articles which describe in great detail the strict conditions under which remarriage will be allowed. Those who remarry after being divorced "on other than scriptural grounds are guilty before God of adultery."

These articles of Preston Manning's faith are not simply his personal, private beliefs. They impel his actions and command him to act in the world to change it. Preston Manning readily acknowledges the powerful influence of his faith on his thinking. The nature of that faith — its rejection of "collectivism," its glorification of individualism and free enterprise, its view of women as submissive to men and of homosexual men and women as the "basest of sinners" — must be reflected in "all spheres" of his life. This conviction is as much a part of his faith as the articles themselves.

The American Influence

The influences on Preston Manning come from several sources. One is simply the general political culture of Alberta, which has been characterized by a strong individualism, repeated upheavals of western alienation, and separatist movements. The political response to that alienation has, in Alberta, a peculiarly American flavour.

Many Albertans have periodically turned their gaze southward to American political practice for "institutional alternatives" when regional representation in the national government has proven ineffectual. According to Calgary political scientist, Roger Gibbons:

> The relevance of that practice came not only from the comparative success of the American system in handling the forms of territorial conflict that were plaguing Canada but also from an influx of American settlers into the Canadian West, similar agrarian experiences on the Canadian and American plains, and the influx of American ideas through agrarian organizations, publications, and leaders in the early decades of this century.

Preston Manning, in his speeches about the history of western reform movements and parties, most often refers to the Progressive Party. This party rose rapidly on its criticism of business profiteering and the tariff — winning sixty-five seats in Ottawa in 1921 when it was little more than a year old. Gibbons says it was one of the main sources of American political ideas in the West. While it did not adopt the many institutional mechanisms advocated by the Reform Party, and earlier by Social Credit, it "fastened upon non-partisanship which was not an aspect of mainstream political thought." The Progressives saw the party system, rather than the parliamentary system, as the "root cause of western political impotence." Similarly, in the 1960s, Preston Manning and his father attacked political partisanship in the Liberal and Conservative parties, arguing that their differences were superficial and their competition harmful to the cause of the social and economic policies of the right.

Alberta-based protest movements were attracted to those American political institutions which were effective in addressing the normal tensions between the "centre and periphery" of large federal systems. The elected senate, separation of powers, senate ratification of executive appointments, congressional oversight of the federal bureaucracy, and a committee system with real power all served the political aspirations of the western U.S. states well and were adopted by both western reformers and separatists (who had no faith that such institutions would ever be established in a Canada dominated by Ontario and Quebec).

The relatively large number of U.S. immigrants to Alberta added to the American influence in its political culture. Western separatists, while they focused primarily on "political impotence and economic exploitation," also brought to their politics an ideological attack on Ottawa which borrowed a great deal from the American right. In Alberta, both reform and separatism tended to be right-wing. According to Gibbons, "Ottawa is charged with socialistic ... Marxist leanings, with being soft on communism abroad, excessive centralization, explosive bureaucratic growth and anti-Americanism." Elmer Knutson, head of the West-Fed movement, claimed Trudeau was a Marxist and was creating a "United Canadian socialist republic which is just one letter from the U.S.S.R."

Other issues driving western separatists include gun control, excessive immigration, abortion, the abolition of the death penalty, metrification, equalization payments, the welfare state, and high taxes — as well as bilingualism. Some of these parallel American right-wing issues and the American preoccupation with the rights of the individual.

The western separatists' ideological revolt has other common features with the "American conservative revival" says Gibbons. "The American tax revolt, intensified nationalism ... the reaction to a perceived decline in moral standards, continued distrust of elected politicians, the reaction to successive liberal administrations in Washington, plans to deregulate the oil and gas industries, and the revival of communist conspiracy theories all find reflection in western Canadian separatism."

This separatist sentiment has not always had an active voice in Alberta, yet it is never far from the surface. And while wheat farmers in the thirties identified strongly with their American counterparts on the issue of tariffs (which American farmers didn't pay), that identification was supplanted by those in the oil business in the fifties and sixties. Oil company owners, many of them American themselves, identified strongly with their U.S. cousins, and Alberta was often described as a sort of second-string Texas.

The American free-enterprise spirit and the cult of the individual is strongly embodied in the oil-patch culture. The Reform Party owes a great deal to the marriage of American conservative thought and the money of the oil patch.

American individualism and conservative thought are by no means the only dimension of Alberta or western political culture. Yet, it is clear from an examination of the Reform Party's policies, its proposed democratic reforms, and the issues which most excite its members, that these ideas form the core of its thinking. Preston Manning grew up immersed in Alberta political culture, and the evidence suggests he took much of the American conservative dream to heart.

Yet, the issues which drove western separatism did not lead Preston Manning's father to any thought of separatism. Ernest C. Manning rarely if ever used the spectre of "western alienation" in his political strategy. He was a federalist and, though he ran an increasingly right-wing regime as the fifties wore on, he did not express that ideology in anti-eastern or anti-Quebec terms.

The Influence of Social Credit

The Social Credit League began in 1932 when its most famous leader, William Aberhart, became attracted to the ideas of English engineer, Major C.H. Douglas. Douglas's frustration with industrial society's failure to deliver prosperity to the common people led him to develop a theory of simple monetary reform aimed at increasing consumer buying power through the universal distribution of unearned income — called social credit. While it was a radical, urban-oriented doctrine which also attacked the concentration of wealth, it easily gained popularity in rural Alberta whose population was already engaged in a struggle against wealth concentrated in eastern Canada.

Its rise to power in Alberta was attributed by Canadian political scientist C.B. Macpherson to three main factors: its similarity to evangelical religious doctrine; the sudden poverty and insecurity of Alberta's middle class; and Aberhart's particular ability to blend these factors in the building of his party.

The influence of the Social Credit Party — or League as it called itself — on Preston Manning was principally the influence of Ernest Manning. But Preston Manning is also an acknowledged student of all western protest movements and particularly of Social Credit. Many of the techniques used by the Reform Party are similar and sometimes identical to those used by Social Credit in its earliest days, under its founder William Aberhart.

By the late 1960s the Social Credit government was a party of big business. But it did not start out that way. It reached that point largely under the stewardship of Ernest Manning. In its earlier form as a populist party, it was much more eclectic, containing both left- and right-wing tendencies and sentiments, including a strong appeal to urban workers. Its explicit appeal to urban workers was successful enough, according to political scientist Alvin Finkel, to attract thousands of working-class activists to the party and working-class votes in the early years of the party. It eventually lost that urban base of workers through its mean-spirited treatment of the unemployed in the Depression and the narrow-mindedness of the Socred cabinet, including Aberhart.

Even in its origins, the Social Credit League's claim to being grassroots is disputed. Political scientist C.B. Macpherson described the party as "authoritarian": "Aberhart's organization was strongly centralized ... His headquarters, not a delegate convention, decided and announced that candidates would be run in every constituency, issued a draft platform and instructions to the constituencies, limited the agenda of constituency conventions, and laid down the procedures for nominations." The structure of the Social Credit League was only superficially democratic: it was based on local study groups, zone assemblies, constituency and divisional conventions. The delegates from these conventions attended annual provincial conventions.

Even this superficial democratic structure broke down in the choosing of candidates for provincial elections. Warning about the possibility of opportunists — he called them disguised old-line party candidates — seeking nominations, Aberhart stated that in order to serve the best interests of the party, each proposed candidate had to be interviewed by him and his advisors.

The role of the constituencies was limited to putting forward a list of three or four acceptable nominees. Aberhart and his hand-picked board would then choose the person who would run. Aberhart consistently chose conservatives whose only deviation from conservative orthodoxy was in the area of monetary reform — excluding many in the rank-and-file who favoured more progressive reforms.

Much of Aberhart's approach and many of his techniques were undemocratic in the extreme, yet were often presented and used to create the illusion of democracy. According to author David Laycock "Intense participation was crucial to Social Credit movement building and electoral success. However, it was a limited participation ... compared to [the CCF] ... the role of 'the people' in democratic action is simply that of 'demanding results.' ... popular-democratic traditions were compressed into a psychologically unassailable and ideologically exclusionist vision."

Both Aberhart and Manning believed that the ordinary citizen was incapable of actually making policy: participatory opportunities lay strictly in the areas related to winning elections, spreading propaganda, and building the party organization. Once the general will of the people had been expressed, experts chosen by the party and leader would be used to determine how that would be achieved.

The illusion of democracy was created by a number of political techniques, including "straw votes" and "voice votes." At his huge rallies, Aberhart would call for voice votes on the general results desired by the people — usually very broad universal goals such as "prosperity" or the end to insecurity. Thousands of people, already mesmerized by Aberhart's oratory, shouting out their desire for particular goals, created the feeling of participation — even if the goal was predetermined by Aberhart.

Within the party, the straw vote was used extensively at the constituency level and was presented as a test of their support for Social Credit candidates. But it was also a subtle way of making supporters feel that they were genuinely involved in movement building — as well as a method of repeatedly endorsing Aberhart as the leader. The straw votes never failed to achieve the desired objectives. Aberhart would also ask his constituency organizations, by radio broadcast, to direct him to carry out a certain course of action, convincing them that he wanted to know their feelings on an issue when he was simply orchestrating support for his own plan.

Laycock describes two other important aspects of Aberhart's leadership: his authoritarian style and the control exerted by his party organization and "... the portrayal of [his own] leadership and organizational activity as transcending the sordid world of 'politics.' "

By the time Ernest Manning took over the Social Credit League in 1943, it had already been transformed from a mass-based, populist party and movement to a party electoral machine dominated by an increasingly autocratic leader and premier. Ernest Manning perpetuated that autocratic leadership and also moved the party further to the right. Realizing that the party was widely ridiculed as the "funny money" party because of its preoccupation with monetary policy, he replaced it with what J.S. and J.T Osborne, in their guide to Social Credit, describe as "the paranoid rhetoric of 'free enterprise and anti-socialism.' The old enemies — banks and financiers — were displaced by the threat of 'bureaucracy, regimentation and totalitarianism.' Social Credit became overnight the friend of individualism and 'sound business practice.' "

Manning exerted his control over the party to mould it in his image but also to ensure its continued dominance in the province. In 1948, he purged the party of its openly anti-Semitic elements, which had allowed critics to attack the league as a Nazi party in disguise. This faction included not only neo-Nazis, but a group called the Douglasites, who were named for the intellectual hero of the League and the advocate of wealth redistribution. The Douglasites denied being anti-Semites, claiming only to be against "a cutthroat gang of thugs known as the International and Political Zionists."

Manning moved decisively to block the Douglasites at the 1948 convention and most of them left the party. "The departure of the Douglasites left Manning in complete control of the party and government ... he had used their views to push out the socialist-leaning elements of the party ... Now ... that the Douglasites' public views had become too extreme, he used them as the lever to push them out of the league."

Yet, while Manning publicly rejected any notion of a Jewish conspiracy, he continued to view the world in conspiratorial terms and to govern accordingly. He held to the world-wide communist conspiracy theory right until he retired in 1968 and beyond, describing it in 1969 as follows:

There is no doubt in my mind at all, that world communism operates a very definite program designed to extend communist philosophy and the communist concept into every nation of the world and particularly to undermine the democratic nations by communist propaganda ... Socialism and communism ... really largely a matter of degree, has a vested interest in social unrest because they always exploit the hardships, the poverty of unemployment, and adverse social conditions, to the attainment of their political objectives ... This same effort, along different lines, is evident, in my view, in news media which are very ... favourably slanted, to socialistic philosophy ... You even have the same thing, to varying degrees, in the field of education. It isn't by chance that you find these [sic] agitation of Marxism and so forth in many of our universities. It isn't by chance.

Just as Ernest Manning's evangelical Christianity had moved to the right of William Aberhart's, so had his political ideology. Whether one prompted the other is unclear, but certainly they would have reinforced each other. His ready equation of socialism (by which he meant the fairly mild social democracy of the Cooperative Commonwealth Federation) and communism would certainly find confirmation in his fundamentalism. With the Douglasites and the left-wing elements purged, the party came increasingly under the influence of evangelical Christians who had been attracted to the party because of Aberhart's and Manning's leadership. In 1950, one headline in the national Socred paper read: "Godless Materialism Condemned: Convention Speakers Urge Return to God as Necessary to Salvation."

The Socred government demonstrated a steady antagonism towards Ottawa since the 1930s starting with the federal government's disallowance of its monetary proposals. But by the sixties, the focus of that antagonism had changed from being primarily regional to being driven by ideology. In Manning's view "... the federal government had now become the dangerous experimenter." There were still regional grievances but "... neither the Saskatchewan nor Manitoba governments of this period were particularly out of harmony with federal thinking ... The Alberta government ... was not so much interested in building up the power of the provincial state ... as it was in downgrading in general the role of government in society," argues Finkel.

As a result of Manning's move away from the old Socred "funny money" policies and his embrace of a wide-open free enterprise philosophy, big business, in turn, quickly embraced the party. During the war, Edmonton and Calgary newspapers — the party's sworn enemies due to Aberhart's attempt to pass laws controlling them — printed favourable editorials. The Conservative-Liberal alliance, which had been eroding Socred support, faded away.

Ernest Manning's abandonment of any pretense at maintaining a coalition of popular classes and Socred's open alliance with big business might have severely damaged the government's popular base if it had not been for a stroke of incredible luck: on February 13, 1947 Imperial Oil hit its first well at Leduc and changed the history of Alberta.

The wealth provided by the province's oil allowed the government to spend huge sums of money which benefited much of the population. In addition, the industry drew hundreds of thousands of new immigrants as well as the wealth and power of the U.S. oil giants into the province. By 1961, half the Alberta work force would be employed directly and indirectly in the oil and gas industry. By 1966, royalties and taxes on oil and gas — even at rates generously low to the companies — accounted for one-third of government revenues.

While it had its roots in "populism" and started out as ideologically eclectic, Social Credit ended up on the right, in contrast to the populism of the CCF government next door in Saskatchewan. Manning's Social Credit government attempted to halt the growth of trade unionism in Alberta while T. C. Douglas's government, in 1944, passed the most progressive labour legislation in North America and gave civil servants the right to unionize. While actual social programs were relatively generous, Manning never let up in his rhetorical attack on the welfare state. He was opposed to the universality of medicare — which the CCF pioneered. The CCF called for economic planning and moved to some extent to take public control of natural resources. Manning's Socred government held to the "trickle down" theory of wealth creation promoted by the Alberta business community — and because of the extraordinary wealth created by oil was able, to some extent, to make it work.

While the CCF responded to the social and economic crisis of the thirties by drawing its core of leaders from existing class-based farmers and workers' organizations, explains Finkel, "Social Credit leaders were mainly lower-middle-class professionals with no clear links to either the movements of the oppressed or to the ruling class." Social Credit, increasingly as its years as a government passed, took on the characteristics of American populist parties of the right, seeing and appealing to the population as a homogenous and undifferentiated mass of people without specific interests based on social class.

By the time Preston Manning had taken an active interest in politics, at age eighteen, it was 1960. Social Credit had long since lost any claim to being populist or grassroots, and no longer drew its support from discontent or hard times. Instead, it built its success on its record of providing relatively stable, predictable, and competent public administration and — equally important, given the power of the oil industry — on its pro-business policies and low taxes and royalties on oil and gas. Its steadily declining membership and membership dues were offset by generous corporate donations.

Ernest Manning was, like his predecessor, revered by his caucus and party members and held in similar regard by much of the population. Alf Hooke, his long-time cabinet colleague, in his biography of Manning described him as "the man I worshipped almost as a saint." Manning managed to maintain this hold on his followers right to the end even though he had effectively abandoned much of what the old-timers in the party had held dear.

Just months after he resigned as leader in November, 1968, Manning shocked Hooke and almost everyone else by accepting an appointment to the Board of Directors of the Canadian Imperial Bank of Commerce, one of the bastions of "financial orthodoxy" that Social Credit had attacked for much of its history. William Aberhart had made that attack famous by personalizing the attack on the elite whom he blamed for "poverty in the midst of plenty": "At the present time, this great wealth is being selfishly manipulated and controlled by one or more men known as the 'Fifty Big Shots' of Canada."

The Social Credit Party which influenced Preston Manning, then, was a party moulded by his father, a man who commanded a religious devotion from his party and supporters and exerted virtually total control over that party and its government. The party Preston Manning experienced as the son of its leader and as a member in its final years in power was a party that was neither populist nor grassroots. It was openly a party of big business and largely an extension of the personality and beliefs of Ernest Manning.

Conclusion

The early influences on Preston Manning — the evangelical fundamentalism, the radical free-enterprise conservatism and anti-socialism of his father, and the powerful attraction of political ideas and institutions from the United States — can certainly be said to have created a politician-in-waiting. But he would have been a politician oddly out of place in 1960s Alberta. What these powerful influences had moulded in Preston Manning was a politician of the past: a politician for the 1940s or 1950s, a politician who was in many ways a carbon copy of his father. And Ernest Manning, so long accustomed to running Alberta more as a father figure than an active politician, had changed little if at all, in the twenty-five years he had been in office. Both men were socially and politically isolated from the changing mainstream of Canadian society.

Tremendous changes were taking place in Canada in the 1960s, and Alberta did not escape them. Waves of immigration brought new colour and new cultures to the streets of Canadian cities while social movements of women, native people, the poor, students, and peace advocates swept across the country creating the most serious challenges to the political, cultural, and social status quo in thirty years.

These movements had great impact on the main political parties, which reflected them in their policies and the leaders they elected. It was not a coincidence that Pierre Trudeau was swept to power, in part, by young people, nor that the Conservative Party chose the progressive "Red Tory," Robert Stanfield, as its leader. Yet these changes were not the things which would influence Preston Manning — except, as we will see in the next chapter, in reaction to them.

Indeed, as Preston Manning has said on many occasions, Ernest Manning continued to have a great influence on him long after he retired as premier — and still does. Growing up in the shadow of his larger-than-life father, adopting not only his beliefs and political style but his physical mannerisms, speech, and body language, Preston Manning was prepared for a world that no longer existed.

Preston Manning Charts
His Father's Course

Like any other young person, Preston Manning began to feel his own way in the outside world when he left high school. He did so very much as his father's son, but he nevertheless began to identify his own personal preferences as he participated in the outside world from which he had been so isolated. In 1960, Manning enrolled in physics at the University of Alberta in Edmonton. A few years later, this attraction to pure science would have a profound effect on how he would approach social problems and political questions. Indeed, it was not long before he was scientifically studying the prairie populist movements to determine how they succeeded and where they failed: lessons he would put to good use twenty-five years later.

At university Preston Manning rejected the social life of the campus and restricted his political activity to the young Socreds and the Youth Parliament. While he shared his father's famous name, he was not the leader of the campus Socreds.

But as he spent more time on campus, received his B.Sc. in physics, and enrolled in economics, his confidence apparently grew and he began to choose as his associates those young men with whom he felt the most political and religious affinity. The most influential was probably Erick Schmidt, a graduate student in sociology and a former theology student, who had been a candidate for the Baptist ministry. Another was Don Hamilton, a United Church minister who became, like Schmidt, a businessman. Owen Anderson, a political science student and head of the campus Social Credit, remembers meeting Preston and being introduced to Schmidt by him. These four formed the core of a group of so-called "young turks" who would have a major influence on the Social Credit party and government.

That influence would be expressed through the relationship between Preston and his father. Ernest Manning had become extremely isolated from the changing world of Albertan society. Regular party democracy in Alberta had been in suspension for almost twenty years, and Ernest Manning gave every indication, by the infrequency of his public appearances and his political philosophy, that he was living very much in the past.

Preston Manning, as he escaped that same isolation, began to act as his father's eyes and ears on a changing world. The constant challenges to Social Credit policy and philosophy from the other young parliamentarians — like Joe Clark, Grant Notley, and Jim Coutts — forced the young Preston Manning to consider political questions that he had never considered before. And that process, says Don Hamilton, had an impact on Ernest Manning:

> Manning was a great leader of the government ... but he didn't have any executive assistants or anyone to tell him what was going on out there. When Preston was at university, he ran up against criticism of the government — especially on social policy — and he in turn talked to his dad about some of these things ... which had not been addressed.

While there is no clear record of exactly what these challenges to Social Credit policy were, we do know the issues that were being raised across the country, not just on campuses but within a whole range of institutions, including churches, trade unions, and traditional women's organizations. Issues of poverty, racism, war, and women's inequality were beginning to be raised: the harbingers of the more militant movements, which would sweep the country just a few years later.

Preston Manning took these issues — and their implied criticisms of Social Credit policy — back to his father. His exposure to these issues, which thousands of other young people would come to see as a collective condemnation of "the system," did not challenge Preston Manning's acceptance of conservative ideology. Rather, it challenged him to consider ways in which that ideology — and his father's government — could adapt to meet the criticisms and thus remain a viable force in this new context.

It was not simply that Social Credit was found by Preston Manning to be wanting in areas of social policy — though this was how the problem would be posed — it was more that conservative ideas and conservative government were being challenged by socialism. Left-wing thinking was influencing events and people, not just through the obvious vehicle of the New Democratic Party (formerly the CCF), but within the Progressive Conservative and Liberal Parties as well. Indeed, there were no better expressions of this trend than the three eventually prominent challengers Manning faced on campus: Joe Clark, Jim Coutts, and Grant Notley.

Manning fought the trend with enthusiasm — and paid for it with ridicule in the campus press. In a profile of the four political parties running for seats in the model Parliament, the February 7, 1964 edition of the *Gateway* ran the headline: "Socreds Erupt in Campus Politics." Preston Manning told the paper that free enterprise had to reform to continue its existence. The social reforms were to be "... [the] individual responsibility ... of every Canadian citizen" while economic reforms had to deal with the "defects ... in our economic system which are bringing free enterprise into disrepute."

In a more detailed review of the party's platform, Manning raised the spectre of socialism: "We believe that Canada is drifting towards socialism even though the majority of Canadians are opposed to collectivism and the welfare state." He also hinted at a theme which would dominate his political thinking for twenty-five years. Declaring that the traditional parties could not reverse the trend to socialism, Manning stated, "We believe that Canadian citizens [from all parties] who believe in ... free enterprise must band together."

Preston Manning was out of sync with student opinion. While all other parties were calling for a reduction in student residence fees, Manning called for an increase. When students planned a demonstration over the issue, Ernest Manning called the university president and warned that such a demonstration would hurt students' chances of future cooperation. The demonstration was cancelled. The Socreds finished last in the election with eight seats out of sixty-five, fewer than in 1963.

The growing threat of socialism was taken very seriously by Ernest Manning. His long-held conviction that a communist/

socialist conspiracy threatened the world could only have been reinforced by his son's experience on campus. Preston Manning's eagerness to meet this challenge was received with enthusiasm and encouragement from his father. The changing politics of Canada in the 1960s were destined to forge, between Preston and Ernest Manning, a political partnership and a political project aimed at renewing and consolidating conservatism in Canada. The first hints of that project would be seen in Preston Manning's initial foray into the world of "real" politics.

That initiation came in the 1965 federal election when Manning ran against Tory incumbent Bill Skoreyko and NDPer Robert Douglas in Edmonton East. Unopposed for the Social Credit nomination in this riding, he was just twenty-three years old. He had already appeared on political platforms with his father on several occasions, but this was the first time he actually had to campaign and face the media during a contest — and it was one he was very likely to lose.

The young man who campaigned in that election was not today's polished leader of the Reform Party. In the words of *Saturday Night* writer, Ian Pearson: "... the candidate with the thick black-rimmed glasses stared broodily into the distance, like Buddy Holly's lugubrious twin brother."

The inevitable comparison with his father appeared in the pages of the *Edmonton Journal* of November 5, 1965. The headline proclaimed "Second Manning Voice Evokes Some Misty Eyes." Covering a party rally, the reporter waxed nostalgic: "If you weren't looking at the speaker you would swear, when he said certain words and phrases, that it was the father speaking."

Manning generally stuck to the right-wing platform of Socred national party leader, Robert Thompson. Thompson had declared that the issue in the election "would be whether we are going to preserve the freedoms that let Canadians express their initiatives. There are people today who are willing to sell the souls of their children to socialistic welfare principles rather than stand on the principles that got them where they are today."

But there were also the beginnings of Preston Manning's own commitment to an ideologically pure political movement and hints at the political project he and his father were already planning. There was a hint of criticism of party politics. He was committed, he said, to acting on principle: "This means putting politics behind and voting on an issue no matter who introduces it." He advocated "crossing party lines for the sake of Canada."

One of his motivations in running federally, said Manning, was his concern that politicians tend "to put political considerations ahead of the country. Instead of weighing what is right or wrong, their chief concern is whether their stand on an issue will gain or lose votes." He attacked traditional politicians then, just as he does now: "Canadians must realize that there is absolutely no point in returning ... the same set of characters that were sent to Ottawa before ... [Canadians] are sick and tired of political wrangling, propaganda and promises." Twenty-five years later, Manning would tell Canadians: "[People] want to do more than change around the players who are already there."

Preston Manning placed third in the 1965 election, and it would be twenty-three years before he tried again. But he was not through with politics and in the next few years began to develop and apply his own brand of conservatism. Its free-market, technocratic principles would first have great influence on his father.

Social Conservatism

While Preston acknowledged his father's great influence on him, Don Hamilton, a United Church minister and a close friend of Preston Manning's, claims that influence went both ways: "His impact on his father was remarkable. He had enormous influence." Hamilton, a young Socred himself, was in a position to know. He, Preston Manning, and three or four others worked hard in the late sixties to influence the party in the direction of what Ernest Manning referred to as "social conservatism."

This was the name that Ernest and Preston Manning gave to the conservative philosophy which would employ the tenets of free enterprise and the energy of entrepreneurs to solve the social problems to which socialists normally turned their efforts — and, to Preston Manning's mind, turned to the disadvantage of conservatives and Social Credit. In a speech to Reform Party supporters twenty-five years later, Preston Manning characterized this socially conscious free enterprise as a "combination of Rambo and Mother Teresa."

Ernest Manning's convictions had long ago taken him in the direction of a more orthodox, right-wing conservative party. While Preston influenced him on social policy, Ernest Manning's commitment to a "pure" conservative party was taken up by his son. This was almost certainly the source of Preston's 1965 election statement that MPs should cross party lines on matters of principle. The elder Manning believed, and had argued since 1963, that there needed to be a "realignment of political thinking in order that the Canadian people may have a clear-cut alternative in the exercise of their freedom."

According to Alvin Finkel, Ernest Manning believed that two factors reduced the chances of Social Credit leading that realignment: the domination of the eastern wing of the party by extremists and the inability of the party to shake its image as the "funny money" party. Instead, Manning saw a reconstructed Progressive Conservative Party as the national vehicle for "real" conservatism.

But in Alberta he believed that the Socreds already stood for that genuine free-enterprise conservatism and that the party could renew itself and continue to rule Alberta even after he retired. He set out to accomplish both these goals and in both he would be ably assisted by his son, Preston.

Alf Hooke, one of the original Social Credit cabinet ministers in 1935, remembers Manning's plan and the fact that there were powerful people who supported it:

> On at least two occasions Mr. Manning told me in his office that he had been approached by several very influential and wealthy Canadians and that they wanted him to head up a party of the right with a view to preventing the onslaught of socialism these men could see developing in Canada. They had apparently indicated to him that money was no object and they were prepared to spend any amount of money to stop the socialistic tide ...
>
> Mr. Manning indicated to me also that he was working on a book which he would hope to publish ... in which he would endeavour to outline the views these men represented and recommendations he would make in keeping with their views.

Today, Mr. Hooke recalls asking Ernest Manning if these men were Social Crediters, "... because this is what I and others were promoting. 'Oh, no!' he said, 'These are wealthy and influential men,' " implying that they were beyond Social Crediters in importance. "I asked Mr. Manning who they were, but he declined to tell me. But he did indicate that they were mostly from down east. The only one from here was R. A. Brown, Jr."

Manning believed that a new party was not feasible. Instead, he supported a coalescing of right-wing forces into the Progressive Conservative Party. He would use his influence to spread that idea across the country. Confident of his personal power and the obvious need for such a movement, apparently he did not intend to take an active organizing role. He would provide the idea; others would have to respond to it.

Preston's influence in his father's endeavour was his addition of the technocratic principles to the notion of "social" conservatism. It was, Preston Manning believed, a way of taking away some of the appeal of the socialists and left-wing liberals whose attention to social issues had, in part, brought them to power. At the same time, it was to provide business with huge new opportunities for profitable investment in sectors traditionally left to government.

Such a political project, encompassing both a national movement and a rejuvenation of a provincial government and party was no small task. Furthermore, old-line Social Creditors could not be expected to carry it out because it violated a key element of Socred theology: it rejected monetary reform as irrelevant. According to Finkel: "Hooke, although as anti-socialist as Manning, was aghast that among the backers of this new political project ... were financiers — apostles of financial orthodoxy."

The task of formulating the new conservative philosophy fell to Preston Manning and the group of young Socreds around him. The cost of this project was borne by the "influential and powerful Canadians" who had approached Manning. They, under the leadership of R. A. Brown, Jr., president of Home Oil, established the National Public Affairs Research Foundation (NPARF) in 1965.

The NPARF was an extremely secretive organization, but it was known at the time that it included on its board of directors some very orthodox people: Cyrus McLean, chairman of the B.C. Telephone Co.; Renault St. Laurent, a lawyer and son of the former Prime Minister; R. J. Burns, a prominent Calgary lawyer; and A. M. Shoults, president of James Lovick Ltd. of Toronto. Most of the board members were friends of Brown's and were not involved in the foundation at all. Two of the men, R. J. Burns and A. M. 'Scotty' Shoults, barely remember the foundation. Burns recalled, "I may have just been a front man, doing Bobbie Brown a favour. These other fellows were in the same situation as me, just called upon to sit on a board. They were never active participants."

The first major product of the NPARF was produced by Preston and several of the other young Socreds around him. It was called "The White Paper on Human Resources Development." Considered left-wing by many of the Social Credit faithful, it was intended to present a moderate image of the Social Credit to the public. But according to Finkel, it was vintage Ernest Manning.

"Manning's anti-collectivist orientation was now inelegantly phrased to be a commitment to integrating physical and 'human resource' development: 'to facilitate the harnessing of the economy based on the principles of freedom of economic activity … achieving objectives stemming from humanitarian values … based on the concept that the individual … is the supremely important unit of consideration." Accompanying this technocratic language, says Finkel, was a restated commitment to the government's long-standing opposition to universal social programs. It also quite likely reflected Preston Manning's background in physics and economics: "Human social problems were to be seen as akin to problems involving the physical world. The government wanted to 'apply new and advanced techniques, initially conceived for industrial application, to the analysis of social problems …' "

The white paper, says Don Hamilton, "… was a result of the influence of Preston." It had a major impact on the government of Ernest Manning, much of it positive. The preoccupation with a scientific approach to government led to a major financial commitment to broad-based research. A "Manpower for Human Resources Development" program was slated for $175 million to fund capital projects for existing and new universities, and new medical science centres were planned. Community development programs (rooted in free enterprise) and expanded agricultural research also resulted. Conditions would improve in mental hospitals and prisons. An Alberta Service Corps, modelled after the American Peace Corps, was established.

The white paper demonstrated the flexibility that a right-wing government could have in a wealthy province. It could maintain its ideological purity by rejecting direct wealth redistribution while spending large enough sums of money that employment was created. But it also revealed the absolute commitment Ernest Manning had to ideology. Alberta's wealth did not cloud the premier's mind or soften his approach: following the correct approach to solving a problem was as important as the problem itself.

This attention to ideological consistency was a legacy which Preston Manning took closely to heart. As we will see in the chapters on the party and on policy, the younger Manning would demonstrate a commitment to ideological purity that repeatedly put his whole political enterprise at great risk — a risk he was nonetheless willing to take.

The likely source of Preston Manning's expressions of non-partisanship in the '65 election — and his future attacks on all "traditional politicians" — were also revealed in his father's view of the white paper: "This paper is non-partisan ... If the time and energy, presently spent in political manoeuvring for partisan advantage, were instead channeled into a supreme constructive effort to solve the problems and meet the challenges confronting our nation, Canadians would not only be happier but infinitely further ahead."

This position seems to suggest a world where there is consensus; a world without competing ideologies that dispute how a "happier" society is to be built. While such a position reflected political realities in Alberta, where one-party rule was the norm, the national picture was quite different. The problem in Canada was the threat of socialism — a problem that Ernest Manning and his associates had already identified. The solution here was not an appeal for a kind of benign non-partisanship but a concerted effort to move Canadian politics to the right by consolidating all right-wing forces into a single political party: the Conservative Party. Ernest Manning's planned book, the inspiration that he hoped would drive this effort, was Preston Manning's next research assignment.

The Mannings' Master Plan

Ernest Manning's book, *Political Realignment: A Challenge to Thoughtful Canadians*, revealed a man of deeply and rigidly held values — right-wing, evangelical, libertarian values — frustrated by his inability to stop the trend towards "collectivism" and "socialism" in Canadian life. He was frustrated even more by the failure of like-minded people to recognize the great threat this trend posed and to come together to stop it.

Throughout the book, Manning despairs that "like-minded" free enterprisers are divided into two camps with irrelevant partisan differences. He calls for an American-style two-party system in which forces of the right would be in one party and all forces of the left — presumably made up of NDPers and left-Liberals — in the other.

The need for strict adherence to ideological principles is repeated and emphasized throughout the book: "There ought to exist ... for every public administration a clearly defined framework of values and principles upon which governmental activity and programs will be based." And later in the book: "Governmental actions and decisions should always reflect the pursuit of essential values and goals rather than uncoordinated, spontaneous, administrative reactions to political pressures and vague symptoms of public unrest."

The Mannings' preoccupation with clear "principles" and their irritation with "vague symptoms of public unrest" was reinforced by a yearning for stability "which was formerly provided by the large rural agricultural sector." Decrying the changes affecting "home and family life," Manning says "It is imperative that [other institutions] preserve those [family] principles and values essential to political and economic stability ..."

Another theme which is repeated throughout the ninety-four page book is the need for the "development of comprehensive policy." Such policy would have to be "scientifically" determined and, like other aspects of government, would be accomplished by an elite: "hundreds of like-minded individuals in parliament, the civil service, in the party organization and in the country at large."

Manning agonizes in the book over the "inconsistency" and "contradictions" that the current political system has created, and he suggests that these anomalies occur because the current system is not based on principle and scientific policy-making. The solution to this problem and to political instability is a party and government strictly guided by ideology and functioning with the application of science — in an economy demonstrating the "Free Enterprise Way of Life."

Manning ends the book with a call for the political realignment he had spoken of for almost five years. It would create a "polarization": two competing parties, committed to well-defined ideologies would offer people a clear choice.

And what if this appeal for a realignment — a national merging of Social Credit and Conservative forces with those of right-wing Liberals — should fail? There was one last alternative: if the artificial divisions among true conservatives continues, "a wholly new political party committed to the social conservative position will find an ever-increasing number of advocates ... among an aroused Canadian public." Another set of circumstances might create the conditions necessary for a new, principled politics: "Historically it can be shown that the development of a 'great crisis' ... 'great issue' ... or 'great personality' on the national scene, or some combination of these, may prove sufficient to force both people and politicians back to fundamentals and political realities ..."

It can be easily argued that these statements — which were Ernest Manning's and not Preston's — were prophetic, except for the fact that it took another twenty-five years for a "great crisis" to produce the conditions necessary for a "wholly new political party." That it would take another generation and be accomplished by another man does not diminish the fact that the prescription for this new politics and new party remained almost thought for thought, goal for goal, unchanged. Preston Manning tried several times to seize the right moment to bring about his father's prophecy before succeeding. But he did not tamper with the prophecy itself.

All the elements emphasized by Ernest Manning would eventually be included in his son's plans: a pure, consistent right-wing ideology, a consistent set of policies reflecting that ideology, the new practice of politics which identified and filled the need for an elite of "like-minded" men (or mostly men) to run the party and to be candidates for Parliament. In addition, there would be the same non-partisan theme: Preston, like his father before him, would present himself and his political project as fundamentally different from "normal" politics. He would suggest that he was not primarily a politician. He, like his father before him, would encourage Conservatives in Alberta to adopt more truly conservative principles so as to make a new Alberta party unnecessary.

Preston Manning continued to work for the National Public Affairs Research Foundation until the end of 1968. This position was the first of many research jobs that he would have over the years that were characterized by two things: unusual secrecy and employers who were almost always conservative governments or corporations in the oil and gas industry.

Don Sellar, then a reporter for the *Calgary Herald*, first revealed the existence of the NPARF in the summer of 1966. Almost a year later, on July 1, 1967, he wrote again on the organization: "The NPARF ... has kept details of its studies under wraps while offering its services to any political organization that wants them." Sellar pointed out that Preston Manning and Owen Anderson, one of the young Socreds advising Manning on the white paper, were working full time for the organization, "operating out of a downtown Edmonton office building."

The article continues:

> The NPARF name is not even painted on their door and their office secretary contributes to the secrecy of their operation by answering the telephone ... 'Preston Manning's office ...' Few of its employees know about all the research documents being prepared in such places as Ottawa, Montreal, Toronto and Edmonton because the work is being done in separate sections and assembled in Edmonton.
>
> Mr. Anderson (working on a comprehensive national public policy for Canada) has been permitted to hire any number of people to carry out his work and now has about 19 researchers under him. Preston Manning, in writing his book, has travelled all over North America gathering information on technological change.

Owen Anderson today laughs at the notion that he "had nineteen men under him" but acknowledges that he may have had that many researchers working on papers for him, as de facto director of the NPARF.

According to Sellar, now a senior editor with the *Toronto Star*, and who knew many of the people involved through his father, the secretiveness of the NPARF was simply a reflection of the fact that its backers and founders were men who shunned publicity. "They didn't want people knowing that they were involved in this sort of thing." The "sort of thing" they were involved in was for the most part a right-wing think tank. While the institute did some policy papers for government it had a broader mandate as well, according to Owen Anderson:

> This was our contribution to the debate of the day. We were saying that there was a need for more fundamental debate in this country. 'Here's some ideas — what do you think of this?' We were trying to get people to come out and take a stand and discuss some of these issues ... We even contributed to the public debate. [We would hold public meetings] and people would come out talk and debate. We would circulate these papers — we'd give them to political leaders, people on the campus ... and to any business people we knew.

In November, 1967, just a new months after the publication of *Political Realignment*, Preston Manning embarked on one of his more mysterious assignments: a five-month contract to be carried out at the high-tech research and production "campus" of one of the largest military firms in the United States, TRW Systems Inc. The campus, a sprawling complex of many buildings housing various laboratories, was located in Redondo Beach, California. While Manning spent from October, 1967 to March, 1968 at the complex, neither Manning's friends nor TRW's company archivist is certain just what he did or whom he did it for.

Frank Booth of TRW did find Preston Manning's "card," but said it was incomplete. With no copy of Manning's work on file, "It seems likely," said Booth, "that Mr. Manning worked for one of the government agencies" which regularly used the research facilities, rather than directly for TRW.

Manning's closest associates seem equally in the dark about why he would have gone to TRW in particular (he did study systems analysis there, but he could have studied that in many places not connected with the military) and how he made his initial contacts with the corporation. Owen Anderson and Erick Schmidt visited TRW, but neither were forthcoming about Manning's work. John Barr, another Manning associate, recalls: "It was very much a sidelight of what was going on in Alberta. It was very much a personal thing with Preston. It was kind of obscure at the time as to what the heck it meant." Barr assumes initial contact was made through corporate connections of some kind.

In his own references to his work at TRW, Preston Manning describes the company as a high-tech corporation. That is accurate as far as it goes. TRW, which now ranks fifteenth in worldwide defence firms, was a major defence contractor in 1967–68. It was responsible for the "basic system design" of the Minuteman Missile and the technical direction of all the contractors engaged in its construction. It also worked on most of the Pentagon's other missiles: Pershing, Polaris, and Bomarc, as well as on rockets and satellites for NASA.

TRW stands for Thompson Ramo Wooldridge and was the result of a 1958 marriage between the high-tech Ramo-Wooldridge firm of California — an electronic brain factory — and a Cleveland auto and aircraft parts company, Thompson Products. By the late seventies, it had $870 million in sales.

Perhaps its most famous moment came in the late seventies when two TRW employees were arrested for espionage. They had passed on fatally damaging information about the new CIA spy satellite which TRW had built. The centre for deciphering the satellite's data was at the Redondo Beach campus of TRW — the same complex at which Preston Manning had worked ten years earlier. The story of the spy scandal was chronicled in the book and later the movie, *The Falcon and the Snowman*.

According to John Barr, Manning's time at TRW was spent producing a "thick study on the applicability of general systems theory to socio-economic development models." This "exotic training" was instrumental in forming Manning's ability to come up with "a host of ideas on how modern systems analysis and management theory could be applied to overhaul politics and government."

The application of general systems theory to a host of problems was one of TRW's major areas of expertise. Manning studied its application to the building of ballistic missiles, according to his own references in later studies. But TRW was also pondering their applicability to social problems. According to Lenny Segal, of the California-based Pacific Studies Center, Simon Ramo, a company founder and formerly with Howard Hughes aircraft, was already applying the theory to social problems.

While it was not until 1970 that the aerospace industry experienced a decline, Ramo was anticipating it — and perhaps the end of the Vietnam War as well — and began talking about the social-industrial complex replacing the military-industrial complex. He was advocating conversion: applying and adapting the analytical and management techniques of aerospace — and by implication, private capital — to the problems of drug abuse, education, and transportation.

The other application of such theory was in Southeast Asia. The American belief in the "domino theory" — the conviction that a communist victory in one country in the region would lead to victories in all of them — led to the development of a number of projects aimed at what became known as "rural pacification."

In Vietnam, where an anti-communist project already raged as warfare, that pacification was sinister and included the Phoenix Project. Supervised by William Colby, the future head of the CIA, it was established to "neutralize" the guerrilla's clandestine government in the countryside. For the most part, it turned out to be an assassination program: Colby later reported to congress that 20,000 Viet Cong rural political leaders had been killed.

In the rest of Southeast Asia, the pacification took a different form. In Thailand it took place under the project Agile, organized by the Advanced Research Projects Agency, an arm of the U.S. military. It involved providing enough social, economic, and infrastructure assistance to peasants that liberation movements — or insurgents, depending on the point of view — would have less political appeal. According to Segal, it was designed to "give them some hope, provide them with services."

There were many institutions and universities working on rural pacification in the late sixties, including the Rand Corporation, Stanford, and Michigan universities and others. TRW Systems was not noted for this type of work, but it was certainly capable of carrying it out. Segal notes: "The title of Manning's paper certainly fits within the general description of what pacification was all about. But of course there were people who may have had altruistic points of view as well as those people who were very cynical and just saw it as a way of fighting communism."

The same year that Preston Manning produced his paper at TRW Systems, he and his wife made what Manning has described as a "fact-finding trip" to South-East Asia to assess the American role in Vietnam. "I wanted to check out whether the theory that if Vietnam went communist, all the region would go communist meant anything. Over there, people certainly believed in the domino theory," Manning told *Maclean's* magazine.

Just how a civilian, the equivalent of a tourist, goes on a fact-finding trip is not clear. Nor is it clear which people Manning spoke to in coming to his conclusion or if he had contacts arranged for him through his employer or others in the U.S. It is difficult to know if his work at TRW was related to any agency's work in Southeast Asia. Ron Wood, the Reform Party's public relations officer, responded to a request for a copy of Manning's study with the statement that it "might be confidential" and later said it would "be impossible to get a copy." Questions about his TRW work and the connection, if any, to his Southeast Asian trip were among those Preston Manning declined to answer for this book.

In September, 1968, Ernest Manning announced that he was going to retire as leader of the Social Credit League and as premier of the province. There were many, especially the young men like Anderson and Schmidt, who had fond hopes that the heir apparent, Preston Manning, would take up where his father left off, rejuvenate the party and lead it to victory in the election slated for 1971. They were disappointed. When Anderson and others approached Ernest Manning with the suggestion that Preston run for the leadership, he discouraged it, if not ruling it out altogether. He was not fond of the idea of a "dynasty" and he felt that Preston, at twenty-six years old, was simply too young and inexperienced to control a cabinet of older politicians.

Preston Manning apparently agreed. His role would not be a public one. Instead he would work behind the scenes to promote the cause of the new social conservative philosophy and the idea of political realignment. He and the young Socreds close to him formed the Social Conservative Society. Preston, Owen Anderson, Erick Schmidt, who worked on the white paper with Manning, Don Hamilton, Bill Johnson, Ralph Thrall, and Gordon Rasmussen formed the group, which met about once a month for two years up until Ernest Manning's retirement.

"We were seeking out ways to implement social conservatism in Alberta," says Don Hamilton, now a Calgary consultant and active member of the Reform Party. "We were trying to create something new in a milieu of a very old party. But it was not something that ever really got off the ground. We were talking about reform — but from within [the Socred party]. But it was too late ... We are given a lot more credit than we probably deserve. We were only a handful of people."

When Ernest Manning retired and it was clear that Preston would not seek to take his place, the search was on for a suitable successor. There were some younger Socreds in the caucus but Ernest Manning (according to long time cabinet colleague Alf Hooke) and the members of the Social Conservative Society preferred the fifty-five-year-old Harry Strom. Strom had indicated an open mind regarding the dropping of monetary reform from the Socred platform and was interested in the "human resources" thrust developed by Preston and his friends.

When Ernest Manning resigned, the Social Conservative Society ended its periodic deliberations. Instead, its key members, though not Preston, worked on Strom's leadership campaign which incorporated some of their free-enterprise solutions to social problems: rather than government intervention in the economy and income redistribution, Strom promised to increase funding to education. Strom won the leadership.

Soon after his retirement, Ernest Manning established M and M Systems Research Limited and hired Preston as the firm's main researcher. Here Preston Manning would remain until after his election as leader of the Reform Party. The atmosphere of secrecy continued to surround the work of this organization as it had the NPARF, though in the beginning it is likely that both Mannings did work for the provincial government on policy development — broadening out later to do more and more work for resource and energy companies in Alberta.

Other members of the Social Conservative Society continued their efforts to implement the philosophy by going to work for the Strom government. Owen Anderson became executive assistant to Strom and later co-ordinator of federal-provincial research and policy development. Don Hamilton headed up the Alberta "peace corps" and worked as Strom's executive at the time of the 1971 provincial election. They added to their numbers by hiring John Barr, who became the executive assistant to the minister of education, Bob Clark.

The efforts to revive the fortunes of a moribund Social Credit government were doomed. As Finkel argues, "Reorganization of government departments ... may lay the basis for better planning, but it has little immediate impact on voters." Despite the major changes, the Socreds, focusing their campaign on the "socialist" threat from the NDP rather than on the resurgent Tories of Peter Lougheed, lost the 1971 election.

While Preston Manning did not work directly with his young compatriots in the Socred government of Harry Strom, they continued, according to Don Hamilton, to consult regularly on an informal basis. The political approach of Harry Strom's young lieutenants bears a striking resemblance to much of Preston Manning's strategy for the Reform Party. To what extent Manning helped develop these political ideas is not clear but they bear examination.

Echoes of Reform

While the Strom government continued to press the right-wing attack on federal programs targeted by Ernest Manning — "bilingualism and biculturalism, tax reform, medicare, regional development programs" — it shifted its attack from the ideological to the regional. "The young men behind Strom, aware of the power of Quebec's appeal as a separate culture and region requiring special treatment ... wished to cast western Canada in the same light," says Finkel.

A book of essays published by Anderson and Barr, entitled *The Unfinished Revolt: Some Views on Western Independence*, seemed deliberately to exploit the emergence of separatism as a national issue following the breakthrough of the Parti Québecois in the 1970 Quebec election.

While right-wing politicians and business groups were attacking Liberal finance minister Edgar Benson's tax reforms in 1969, Barr chose to make his attack a western one: "The thought that

Mr. Benson was prepared to sabotage United States investment in Western Canada as a part of a federal tax-reform scenario outraged Westerners ..." At the time of this and other such attacks, there was no western independence movement, but Barr and Anderson did their best to foment one, suggests Finkel.

They attacked bilingualism not from the old Manning perspective promoting a single Canadian culture, but from a regional perspective, pointing out that there were more Ukrainians and Germans in Alberta than French residents. And in an echo of Preston Manning today, they invoked the name of Louis Riel as one of their regional and spiritual forbears.

According to Finkel: "Anderson, the major figure in Alberta's new federal-provincial relations bureaucracy, seemed, like Barr, to slip invariably into Quebec-bashing in his comments on federal policy towards Alberta."

Throughout this period, Preston Manning stayed out of the political limelight. Don Hamilton, one of his closest friends then and now, suggests today that Manning stayed out of politics "in order to get ready. He wanted to make his own mark. He was living under the very large shadow of his father. He was preparing himself. The time was not ripe [then] but when it was, he was ready."

Part of that preparation was his continued close relationship with his friends in the defunct Social Conservative Society. In addition to their exploitation of the regional issue, Strom's advisors promoted other policies which now form key planks in the Reform Party's platform twenty years later: an elected Senate and a guaranteed income plan which would replace all other social programs and regional development programs.

The appeal to western alienation, together with the new social conservative policies, was not enough to save Social Credit, but it was a clear attempt to awaken a sleeping but always present populism. The technique was tried and tested but the sentiment wasn't strong enough nor the party as a whole dynamic enough for it to work. Preston Manning decided to stay out of electoral politics, very likely as a result of the failure of this populist appeal. As he said to Ian Pearson in 1990, and repeated to many interviewers: "My interest in western populist movements gave me the sense that these things are produced every so often. After the Social Credit thing was over, I had a feeling that I would prefer to wait until another populist movement came along than to get in on the tail end of the last one."

It wasn't long before Manning realized that it might be a long wait. Not only had the revival of Social Credit failed, the effort to merge Social Credit and the Conservative Party also got nowhere. There was a Conservative Party "Thinkers' Conference" planned for August, 1967, just as *Political Realignment* was coming out. Press reports at the time suggested a distinct lack of interest: "The news that Mr. Manning's pamphlet ... was about to hit the book-stores was greeted with a dull thud at Conservative convention headquarters and short, sharp denials that the Alberta premier is being invited to the Tories' pre-convention policy conference ... 'There is no chance of his being invited,' said Gene Rheaume, executive secretary of the convention planning group ... Manning's appearance ... would apparently be 'over many peoples' dead bodies,' said Mr. Rheaume."

Ernest Manning, accustomed to being treated as though he were part saint, part monarch, evidently over-estimated his influence at the national level. To be sure, there were those in the Conservative Party who would have welcomed him and wanted him to run for the leadership. Ernest Manning, however, showed no interest in the position. The political thrust of the party was in the opposite direction to that advocated by the Premier of Alberta. At the August convention, the Conservatives elected Robert Stanfield as their leader, perhaps the most progressive — virtually socialist in Ernest Manning's eyes — Progressive Conservative the party had ever chosen.

Five years later, Preston Manning and his father met with Joe Clark. Preston recalled his father lecturing Clark, saying that there was one thing worse than not getting elected: "... that's to get elected and not have the faintest idea of what it is you want to do." Preston explained, "Joe ... [was] really interested in getting power ... but ... really thin on what ... to do with it ... Joe would argue that I was totally interested in ideology and policy and new ideas and that I was as far on the other side as he was on his. And there's probably some truth on both sides."

Why did Preston Manning not simply join the political fray to press his beliefs and principles within the Conservative Party, the chosen vehicle for social conservatism? "Preston just didn't believe that he could accomplish what he wanted to accomplish at that time," said Hamilton. Manning himself confirmed that assessment: "I never felt that the two national parties were vehicles for the type of changes we wanted to see."

Preston Manning's first foray into politics — from his candidacy in the 1965 federal election, his efforts to rejuvenate Social Credit in Alberta, and his attempts to modernize right-wing conservative thought — ended with the defeat of the Social Credit government in Alberta in 1971. But Preston Manning would never be far from politics. He remained very close to his father and committed to his father's dream of political realignment. His work with Ernest Manning in their small consulting firm not only kept that relationship strong, but the work they did for the energy and resource companies in the next fifteen years kept him close to those elements in Alberta society most likely to reinforce his political views. The oil companies and their representatives were among the strongest advocates of unfettered free-market economic policies, were pro-American in their views, and looked longingly south of the border for their political inspiration.

They also had the financial resources to put behind their political objectives if the opportunity arose. If Preston Manning was obliged to wait for the right moment to pursue his political agenda, he could scarcely have chosen a better place.

3

Serving the World of Private Enterprise

Much of Preston Manning's political work from 1965 until the fall of the Socred government in 1971 had focused on rejuvenating and modernizing what he and his father recognized as a discredited conservative philosophy. The radical sixties presented conservatism and capitalism with a major problem: the focus of all the new social movements, and the rejuvenated older ones, was the failure of the "capitalist system" to respond to the needs — economic, social, and cultural — of the young, women, native and poor people, and the otherwise marginalized.

The efforts of Preston Manning and his young associates had been primarily aimed at saving Social Credit — the provincial bastion of social conservatism — in Alberta. Ernest Manning's efforts had been focused equally at the national level. While on the surface both efforts seemed to have failed, Ernest Manning did not see events in this light. Very soon after Lougheed's victory, Ernest Manning privately endorsed him as the defender of the faith in Alberta. (Lougheed had stated prior to the election that he wished the Socreds would fight him instead of trying to seduce him.) Allan Hustak described the change in his biography of Lougheed:

> Thirty-six years of 'God's government' had come to an end ... but in terms of Alberta's history it was a triumph of style rather than substance — the secular equivalent of a revival meeting — a new minister had been selected to do a better job than the old one but the faith remained the same. There was no substantive change in political philosophy.

It was not long after the election of Peter Lougheed that he and Ernest Manning became close associates. They have reportedly remained so until this day.

This may explain in part why Preston Manning declined to get involved in politics. The federal scene was distinctly hostile to his right-wing conservatism and more specifically to his father's efforts at "realignment." Provincially, Preston Manning could certainly have considered working towards the leadership of the Social Credit. It still held a third of the legislative seats and remained a viable party. But the goal of political realignment in Alberta had already been accomplished. Social Credit, spent force or not, was now considered irrelevant by the man who had led it for a quarter of a century.

At nearly thirty years old, Preston Manning had emerged from his six years of political experience with a political ideology, a political objective, and an approach to politics firmly worked out. These elements of Preston Manning's thinking did not change much, if at all, in the proceeding fifteen years before he founded the Reform Party.

For a man immersed in the political world and one who took politics so seriously, Preston Manning had a peculiarly dispassionate view of his subject. He was not a glad-handing kind of politician. He was, says John Barr, a "problem solver." This was the only thing, according to his associates at the time, which got Preston Manning excited. Referring to Manning's time at TRW Systems in California, John Barr recalls: "He was very excited about the systems analysis approach to problem solving." Barr further describes Manning, then and now, as "the most logical and analytical politician in the country. If you present Preston with a problem, Preston will approach the problem not from a moral point of view but from a systems analysis point of view ... He's a great enemy of irrationality and emotions and that sort of thing."

The problem to be solved — a lack of a political vehicle for a national, anti-socialist, conservative party — could not be solved in the early 1970s. The elements were not there. But it was in these terms that Preston Manning saw the problem. Socialism was gaining ground because issues such as poverty and the treatment of women and aboriginal people were now prominently on the public agenda. While other politicians — from all the parties — were approaching the problem of how capitalism could be a means to the end of solving these problems, Preston Manning and his father saw capitalism as the end — and the means of saving it was to find a way to neutralize the socialist appeal.

While Preston Manning was obliged by conditions to put his and his father's political project on hold, the broad objective of defending capitalism from the socialist threat would still be pursued. It was to this broad objective — though not to it exclusively — that M and M Systems Research, the Manning firm, would turn its attention. Social conservatism was by no means exclusively a philosophy of government. In fact, it could be seen as just the opposite: a philosophy of anti-government. The supplanting of government by private enterprise in as many areas of social life as possible was the key objective of social conservatism. M and M Systems Research would pursue that objective, for the time being, from outside government and primarily with private enterprise.

Advancing the Role of Private Enterprise

In January, 1970, M and M Systems Research produced a paper entitled "Requests for Proposals and Social Contracts." It was likely their first major piece of work that was not actually commissioned. It was a think-tank piece which was, to private enterprise, what "The White Paper on Human Resources" was to the Social Credit government: a statement of how social conservatism would actually work. In its detailed proposals it was a plan for the privatization of social housing, regional development, health care, education, day care, and research and development.

The preface to the paper, which had both Manning names on the title page, read: "This document proposes a strategy for establishing a new set of relations between governments and private enterprise in Canada. Pursuit of this strategy would vastly expand the responsibilities and opportunities of Canadian business and industry, and enable Canada to attain important national goals."

The paper was sent to "several thousand key persons in the private sector ... [and] several thousand Canadian legislators ... including the Prime Minister ... Premiers, Mayors ... federal and provincial cabinet members, Senators and M.P.s and municipal councilmen" for "consideration and appraisal. Comments, criticism, recommendations and inquiries would be most welcome ..."

Two versions of the paper were produced: one for business and one for government. The subtitle on the business edition read: "A Strategy to Advance the Role of Private Enterprise in Canada" while the government version described the proposal as "A Strategy for Organizing Resources to Achieve Social Goals." While the business version of the preamble referred to the attainment of "national goals," the proposal which was sent to governments expressed "the hope that its implementation may contribute to social and economic progress in Canada."

Whether promoting vague "national" goals to business or "social and economic progress" to governments, the proposals were the same. The paper detailed a plan for reassessing many if not all of the current social, educational, and economic programs of governments with a view to shifting those services and programs to the private sector.

The plan was modelled after a number of American initiatives, including the War on Poverty which attempted to harness free enterprise to solve ghetto poverty. But principally, the theory was inspired by Manning's work and observations at TRW Systems in California. He refers to the success of systems approaches in the U.S. military and space programs, including "building a missile to carry an H bomb." TRW helped produce the Minuteman missile. A "Requests for Proposals" system was also used "for the purpose of developing sophisticated weapons systems and accomplishing the exploration of space."

The title of the paper, "Requests for Proposals and Social Contracts," was a modification, for social purposes, of the military's systems analysis approach: "Requests for proposals and government contracts." Combined with this system for achieving goals was the "contracting out" of services which the U.S. War on Poverty program gradually adapted after starting out as a government-run project. The paper describes a massive contracting out of services across the board and re-defines and limits the role of government to "management."

> Governments as a matter of policy should ... concentrate on the work of 'governing' — that is, on the 'management of public affairs'; the carrying out of

managerial functions such as defining goals, evaluating capabilities ... assigning responsibilities, allocating resources ... monitoring results. An increasing proportion of the operational aspects of policy implementation should be assigned, again as a matter of policy, to the ... non-government sector ...

The paper defines the "private sector" to include business and non-profit organizations. Recognizing that the latter would have difficulty competing with "aggressive" businesses for "social contracts," the Mannings nonetheless see a role for them: "In situations where idealism and voluntary help can be effectively harnessed, and the main financial concern ... is to simply cover expenses, the non-profit groups should be able to underbid their profit-oriented competitors."

The paper does not get into the detail of how these new service contracts would be cheaper than the services being provided by government agencies. But the preceding description of the non-profit group gives a hint: cheap labour. Reducing labour costs, of course, is the main method of reducing the costs of social services, which are labour-intensive.

The paper goes on to look at the various areas described earlier and applies the "RFP–SC" model (Requests for Proposals–Social Contract) to them. While it is expressed in systems language it is essentially a contracting-out model. Vocational education would be handled by industry, at their facilities; sections of the health care system would be handled through the "establishment and operation of medical clinics for employees and their dependents" at places of employment.

The primary guideline for this new system would be "productivity (or functionality) of the social services sector. Productivity in the fields of health care and education is reflected by the results obtained for each dollar spent in these areas."

The paper ends with a description of the positive contributions the RFP–SC strategy could make — contributions that echo the approach to social policy advocated today by Preston Manning and the Reform Party. The advantages of the system are: "Controlling government bureaucracy and taxation; Obtaining greater results per dollar spent on human needs; Advancing the role of private enterprise in Canada; Developing more creative and lasting solutions to some of the greatest problems and challenges of our times."

Preston Manning's views on the need for an ideologically pure political party and for government to play a minimal role have not changed since he helped his father write his book. The Manning proposal demonstrates the most detailed description of his approach to social policy that he has likely ever produced.

While Reform Party policy will be examined in a later chapter, it is instructive to take a brief look at the party's social policy as it compares to Preston Manning's 1970 proposal. Under "Alternatives to the Welfare State," the Reform Party would "encourage families, communities, non-governmental organizations and the private sector to reassume their responsibilities in the social service areas." Then, as now, Preston Manning would reform society by handing over social problems to charity and private enterprise.

The Private World of Private Enterprise

The short biography of Preston Manning provided by the Reform Party in 1989 says very little about his work history. In most of his interviews, he refers vaguely to "long range planning studies" done for a group of blue chip oil and resource companies. They include Syncrude, Nova Corporation, and Trans Alta Pipelines.

An earlier biography released by the party in 1987 is more detailed. Its style is Preston Manning's. "Manning Consultants Limited (MCL) is a private company specializing in the acquisition and development of professional expertise, and its application to the planning, research and communication needs of its clients. The principal clients of MCL have been private sector decision makers, particularly in the resource development and utility sectors ... and governments."

MCL never developed into a large firm, although Ernest Manning's great wealth could easily have financed the expansion of the firm. Perhaps Manning simply preferred a small-scale operation. It could also have been a reflection of the fact that the Manning father and son team was still very much committed to pursuing their social conservative project, a project better entrusted to them alone. Preston Manning's own comments reinforce that notion: "I can keep close to the campaigns and to the mechanisms of the political system. We also use the firm to do work on the issues."

The work done for the energy companies and utilities was largely political consulting; that is, consulting on political questions of government intervention, taxation, royalties, and regulation. From 1973 to 1975, Preston Manning served as project manager for a research study done for "a consortium of Canadian energy utilities which involved an examination of the energy rate regulation practices of the Federal, Ontario and Alberta jurisdictions."

Manning and his father did a significant amount of high profile work for the Peter Lougheed government, including representing it on a study team developing a proposed Western Electric Power Grid and a study of the future role and structure of the province's Electric Utility Planning Council, a joint body of government and private utility representatives.

Besides his work for the large energy and utility companies, Preston Manning apparently also worked for individual politicians. Rob Fricker, who was an associate of Manning's in the late seventies, stated that he "worked with various politicians, helping them get elected and stay elected."

Preston Manning also worked for two of Canada's most influential business-sponsored think-tank lobby groups: the Canada West Foundation and the Business Council on National Issues (BCNI). The latter organization is widely recognized as the most influential big business lobby group in Canada and represents the largest corporations in the country. The paper prepared by Preston Manning in 1978 for the BCNI is no longer available but is described by Manning as "background research with respect to the entrenchment of basic economic rights in the Canadian Constitution." "Basic economic rights" is another phrase for "property rights." Big business pressed hard for the entrenchment of these rights in the constitution leading up to the negotiations over the Charter of Rights established in 1982. Property rights were not included in the Charter, but are a major plank in the Reform Party's constitutional platform.

In 1975 Preston Manning was commissioned to do a major study on Confederation by the Canada West Foundation, a Calgary-based think tank. The foundation was established in the early 1970s by Calgary millionaire developer and coal magnate F. C.

Mannix, and headed by A.J.E. Child, the president of Burns Meats. Some of the key people in the foundation would play a major role in the formation of the Reform Party, including Stan Waters, the future Reform senator, and Stan Roberts, the co-founder of the Reform Party.

Preston Manning's study of Confederation, which was not completed until 1977, was a classic example of his interest in systems analysis and problem solving. It also revealed his studied lack of concern for the subtleties of culture, heritage, political history, and governance which come into play in any constitution or constitutional reform process. Preston Manning approached the problems of Confederation in exactly the same way that he would have approached a problem in physics. It is, from this perspective, a remarkable document.

The title of the study is "A Realistic Perspective on Canadian Confederation" and it is based on the principal, almost exclusive, assumption that Confederation is a simple "deal." He proceeds from that assumption to create a "deal model" of Confederation for the purposes of considering how constitutional reform might proceed.

The 125-page study presents as its key working concept a "National Unity Matrix" in which the country is divided into "geopolitical regions." In order to resolve the problems and tensions of the country, the model, with appropriate columns for each input, identified "Aspirations and Concerns (in order of priority)" for each region and for the country as a whole.

Along one axis are the regions and the country, and along the other axis are the aspirations, concerns, and the various elements of the solutions under the general heading "Proposals for Satisfying Identified Aspirations and Concerns: Federal Actions, Provincial Actions, Constitutional Reforms, Private Sector Actions."

The study lists half a dozen appendices at the end, one for each region of the country. These detail regional aspirations and concerns as well as the proposals for satisfying them. However, only the appendix for "The Western Provinces" has been completed. The remaining regions and the country as a whole were scheduled "To be completed at a later date, provided suitable sponsorship can be secured."

The paper reveals some of Preston Manning's thinking on constitutional matters today and suggests that the deal model is still his preferred approach. It is a model that is neat and simple, largely because it leaves out many of the factors on which constitutional reform and negotiations have historically foundered.

> ... it should be accepted that the price of getting the concerns of one region dealt with satisfactorily, must include cooperation of that region in meeting the aspirations and concerns of other regions. Moreover, in putting forward proposals ... region 'X' must do more than simply make demands of others.
>   ... there will be a number of unique aspirations ... and demands for remedial action. Operation of the deal model then requires that these items be satisfied in whole or in part through trade-offs.

The federal government would play two roles: representing the national "aspirations and concerns" and "facilitating" the bargaining process. In a veiled reference to his, and his sponsor's, perception that Ottawa was dominated by the aspirations and concerns of Quebec, Manning states: "If the attempt [by Ottawa] to play this dual role led to irreconcilable conflicts of interest, and threatened to undermine confidence in the integrity of the bargaining process, then consideration would have to be given to other institutional arrangements ..."

Manning does not describe or give any hint as to what those other "institutional arrangements" might be. But the assumption of even the possibility of a "conflict of interest" reveals Manning's suspicion of Quebec and Ottawa's potential complicity in giving Quebec too good a deal.

The structuring of the constitutional reform process to include a potential "conflict of interest" shows up dramatically in Manning's current views on the matter. On February 1, 1991, Manning said in Montreal, referring to the capacity of Canadian national leaders to negotiate for Canada: "Either you represent the rest of Canada in this or you represent Quebec. But you can't represent both ... As long as you're playing both sides ... you can't be trusted by the rest of Canada to articulate its interests."

In other words, anyone speaking for both Canada and Quebec is in a "conflict of interest."

The deal model of Confederation as proposed by Manning dismisses or ignores some of the most important factors which make changing the terms of Confederation so difficult. There is no place in the model for differences in ideology or political situation among the partners at any given time of negotiations — a key ingredient for determining "aspirations and concerns." More important is the fact that the regions are made up of provinces which have separate governments and unique histories. The West is a good example. Despite many similarities in their early histories, Alberta and Saskatchewan have historically defined their "aspirations" very differently.

Free Enterprise and Grassroots Democracy

The Reform Party's 1987 biography of Preston Manning states that "Over the past fifteen years Mr. Manning has been involved in community development work, primarily in the Lesser Slave Lake region of Alberta. He is currently President of Slave Lake Developments Ltd., a community development company which had its origins in a joint venture between community residents and energy companies ..." Manning resigned the position in 1988.

For those who have worked in the field of community development, the description of Slave Lake Developments Ltd. as a "community development" company might sound contradictory. Community development has meant, in aboriginal communities in particular, that the community takes control of its social, economic, and cultural development. Where it has succeeded, it has often meant wresting control away from traditional power-holders — which almost always include private business.

Slave Lake Developments (SLD) is clearly not community development in this collective, community-controlled sense, but simply entrepreneurial capitalism. It was exclusively a real estate development company, building apartment buildings and office space. The company was formed in 1969 by a group of local businessmen — including the now very wealthy Walter Twinn of the Sawridge Indian band, a Conservative appointed to the Senate by Brian Mulroney in a last-ditch effort to get the GST passed.

A full-colour supplement in the *Western Report* magazine in 1989 celebrated the SLD's twentieth anniversary. It claims that local businessmen started the project and then approached Preston

Manning for "some outside expertise." But the project has been marked by controversy from its start. The local newspaper, run by Bruce Thomas, exposed a major conflict of interest involving the principals of the company. Four of the main shareholders were members of town council, and it was discovered that they had sold themselves town land for their first project.

According to Thomas, it was naïveté on the part of the local investors, but he questioned Preston Manning's role from the beginning. "Manning was calling the shots. It was his baby all along. The questions were, number one, why was Manning involved and number two, [why did he allow these kinds] of people to become involved?" Thomas criticized the project in his paper as doing little for economic development. "It was still only a certain class of people involved and if this was local ownership, why was it that Preston Manning was president and every time we tried to do a news story, we'd have to call Edmonton or St. Albert [where Manning lived]? We'd have to track down Manning."

Leo Boisvert, Slave Lake's first mayor, was chairman of the board of SLD and is still a close friend of Manning's. He was involved in another conflict of interest in 1973 and was forced to resign as mayor over it.

Another director of the company was also an employee of the Social Credit government's Human Resources Development Authority — the product of Preston Manning's research paper — and was involved in negotiating a grant for SLD from Canadian Mortgage and Housing. Thomas recalls that it was this individual who issued the news release on the grant, urging Thomas "Now don't you tell anyone you got this press release from me." This same original board member caused more controversy in the late seventies when Preston Manning unsuccessfully attempted to bail out his former associate's failing car dealership using SLD.

Manning's public statements suggested that he did not take this conflict of interest particularly seriously. Thomas recalls that when the issue broke, the local Chamber of Commerce invited Manning to speak at a public meeting to "calm things down. He said 'Well you only have so many people in small communities — these [SLD directors] are leadership people, so naturally they're involved in SLD — they just happen to be involved in town council.' "

Manning became publicly involved again in Slave Lake when two Lougheed government ministers were forced to apologize for secretly ordering an RCMP investigation of Thomas and two other men in an attempt to put a halt to bad publicity regarding local economic development. Thomas had pointed out that most of the government's economic development money was going into the town of Slave Lake. Manning publicly criticized the media and the politicians for making an unnecessary fuss, saying of the RCMP issue, "... both press and politicians have waxed eloquently about the alleged injustice of this foolish action."

While SLD certainly does not qualify as community development based on the standard definition, it did fit exactly the kind of community development which resulted from the white paper produced by Preston Manning in 1967. It was, according to Manning, an "experiment to show what free enterprise can do." The experiment also involved a holding company in which Mobil Oil and Imperial Oil bought shares. It was community development only in the narrow sense that 70 per cent of the 309 shareholders came from the community of Slave Lake.

In the mid-1970s, aboriginal people of Alberta were struggling to get access to the hundreds of millions of dollars of construction and other contracts being let to small companies in the development of the heavy oil in the tar sands of northern Alberta. Aboriginal people of the north were among the poorest in Canada, suffering unemployment in the 85–95 per cent range and living in communities deprived of even the most basic amenities and services. Their organizations had had little success in forcing the companies and the government to share some of the tremendous wealth being generated by the development.

The people involved were represented by three aboriginal organizations: the Indian Association of Alberta (IAA), the Métis Association of Alberta (MAA), and the Federation of Métis Settlements — representing those Métis living on a half-dozen "settlement areas" established in the late 1930s. The main oil sands development at the time was the giant Syncrude project being developed by a consortium of the large private oil companies.

Trouble was brewing for the oil companies early on: aboriginal groups were engaged in land claims, court actions, and an attempt, by the IAA, to file a caveat on land which included all oil sands land. Various threats, court actions, and retroactive legislation by the Lougheed government to protect itself, was putting the oil sands development at risk.

The threat to the multi-billion dollar development resulted in a series of meetings between Syncrude's Frank Spraggins and the two levels of government. The result was the establishment of two agencies designed to help aboriginal communities and individuals get access to the millions of dollars in sub-contracts in the Syncrude project. One, called the Indian Equity Foundation (IEF), was to provide start-up capital; the other, the Indian Oil Sands Economic Development Corporation (IOSEDC), was to provide technical advice and assistance to aboriginal entrepreneurs so that they would be able to bid competitively with more established firms.

But according to Fred Lennarson, a consultant with the IAA in the late seventies and early eighties, Syncrude was simply not complying: two years into the project and with millions already spent, aboriginal contractors were still on the outside. Syncrude was not providing the information it was obliged to provide. Lennarson met with Syncrude in Edmonton to try to straighten things out.

> When I met with Syncrude, they made all sorts of excuses saying they didn't know from one day to the next what their needs were going to be. I just said that I had managed large projects myself and that I knew they simply weren't telling the truth. I told them they were in default of the agreement and that if they did not start providing the required information within two weeks I would be advising my clients to sue for breach of contract.

It was this imminent threat of court action which prompted the Syncrude Consortium to bring Preston Manning into the picture. Rob Fricker, in charge of Socio-Economic Affairs for Esso Resources at the time, still recalls the situation vividly:

> [Lennarson] had been working for [the IAA] and came to Calgary and Syncrude and made very threaten-

ing noises about what the Indians were going to do with respect to the oil sands and other developments. As a result of that — or stimulated by it — a number of people got together. Frank Spraggins [head of Syncrude] talked to a few people early on, of which Preston Manning was one. We met a couple of times and then decided we should meet on a more regular basis — to keep our information base up.

For the first meetings of this group, which would soon include Esso, Gulf, Shell, Alberta Gas Trunkline (NOVA), Calgary Power, and Canadian Utilities as well as Syncrude (and later the Bank of Nova Scotia), Preston Manning worked for free. "After we'd gone on for some time, it was clear that someone had to do the coordinating and because Preston had been doing some of it we asked him. Then he asked for some payment to defer his costs," said Fricker. "Because of his contacts he was a natural to be invited at the very beginning. He was the only one who was not an oil company or a utility." Fricker did not elaborate about Manning's contacts, but it was well-known in political and oil circles that Ernest Manning, the head of Manning Consultants, was very close to Conservative Premier Peter Lougheed.

The group referred to itself internally as the Economic Development Discussion Group (EDDG), but it never became public — for good reason, says Lennarson:

> The reason they didn't want people to know about them is that it smacks of a kind of collusion. They would always refer to themselves as 'a bunch of guys got together' or 'a bunch of companies' but it was a lot more than that. They had a structure, a budget, did research and analytical work and were proceeding with projects.

One of the solutions to the threat of aboriginal action was devised within the EDDG but was actually announced as a government project. Two development organizations, BANAC (Business Assistance for Native Albertans Corporation) and Venture Capital Corporation (VCC) were developed in the group before they became public. These two organizations were almost identical in stated purpose to two existing corporations — IOSEDC and IEF.

The crucial difference was that the existing organizations were native controlled: BANAC and VCC would be business-controlled and, more specifically, according to the EDDG proposal to the Lougheed government, "… independent of the MAA (Métis Association of Alberta) or any other native organizations …" BANAC's nine-member board would have five members from the private sector, three from the aboriginal community (preferably businessmen), and one who was the chief executive officer. Rob Fricker was to get that position — with the authority to appoint all the other board members. The BANAC proposal explicitly stated that participation by native groups, non-governmental organizations, and all levels of government would be limited "to a total of 25 per cent." The venture capital agency — VCC — effectively eliminated native organizations by establishing a minimum price for voting shares of $100,000.

The Métis Association went along with the proposals, but the Indian Association of Alberta and the Federation of Métis Settlements rejected it. Elmer Ghostkeeper, President of the Federation, said publicly that "the scheme would be putty in the hands of the oil companies. We won't have anything to do with it." The IAA also rejected it, saying BANAC and VCC would be used to "buy off" native opposition. IAA President Eugene Steinhauer said the plan " … will be a direct violation of Indian self-determination in this province." Even Sam Sinclair, President of the Métis Association, became disillusioned. "As soon as there was a majority of white businessmen on the board, the thing never worked. They never listened to native people after that," says Sinclair.

Preston Manning played a key role on the EDDG, according to Fricker. "Preston was the instigator of much of this. Though the committee paid him … he took a very proactive role. Largely on the initiative of Preston, we put together a pretty sizable conference on native economic development."

The conference was designed to overcome the difficulties created by aboriginal opposition to the BANAC and VCC proposals. If the IAA and Métis Federation would not support the proposals, the oil companies and Manning hoped to circumvent them by bringing aboriginal entrepreneurs and oil company executives together themselves. Manning was put in charge of organizing the conference, and he produced a discussion paper for participants.

Part of the paper analyzed past failures in native economic development: "Government sponsored approaches to economic development have tended to give highest priority to the support of group enterprise with employment as the greatest goal, rather than assisting the individual native entrepreneur and emphasizing the importance of wealth creation and return on investment."

Manning's efforts to promote the conference, and indirectly BANAC and VCC, created concern within the Indian Association of Alberta. An IAA report documented a number of occasions on which Manning's statements and assurances were at odds with the IAA knowledge of the facts. An internal IAA report on a meeting with Manning stated, "Manning's remarks are at variance with reports from other sources," in several areas. The first was Manning's claim that the conference was getting a "very positive" response — a claim unsupported by IAA's contacts. More importantly, Manning took pains to distance himself and the conference from BANAC and VCC though the IAA was aware of his intimate involvement in creating the two company-dominated agencies. Manning's earlier claim to be working for Sam Sinclair of the Métis Association and that the MAA was "promoting" BANAC were denied by Sinclair.

Manning had claimed in his meeting with the IAA that the VCC proposal was prepared by the government's Native Secretariat and only then discussed by the industry. Fricker contradicts this: "BANAC and VCC were discussed in our group before they were drawn up. They were proposals from me." The Native Secretariat did play a major role eventually.

Manning also told the IAA that the conference was first proposed by Sam Sinclair — a claim he denies: "I went along with it but it wasn't my idea. It came from the oil companies."

Manning had assured the IAA that BANAC and VCC were not on the convention agenda while at the same time his colleague Rob Fricker had stated in writing that the convention " 'should result in commitment to action by the participants ... to support a coherent economic development strategy for native people.' (By which he means BANAC and VCC.)"

In more general terms, Manning had presented himself to native groups as a secretary to a group of "industry representatives" whose purpose was to "discuss the role of industry in Native economic development." Yet in the written terms of reference for EDDG, their concerns are clearly stated: "government rules, regulations ... requirements, and hearings related to native jobs, training ... and rights; proliferating Native proposals, hearing interventions and legal actions."

Fred Lennarson saw the proposal as simply a crude divide-and-rule tactic:

> They were concerned ... about the assertion of aboriginal rights in areas where they sought to exploit resources. If they had an aboriginal community with a leadership which was causing them problems the oil companies (through BANAC and VCC) would make available to dissidents in that community, resources to engage in economic development and take the community apart.
>
> They weren't just looking for people who were 'simpatico' — they were worried about native leaders who were going to cause them problems and they were trying to devise a strategy for undercutting them.

Elmer Ghostkeeper, the Métis Federation president, agrees with this assessment. "Anyone wanting to help on land claims, they bought off with business development grants. After that they seemed to lose interest in fighting for land claims. If they [BANAC] sensed that you had figured them out they would turn against you and just ignore you. We had our own little developments up in Paddle Prairie. It was clear we weren't getting support for them because we didn't support BANAC. I told Rob Fricker that one ingredient for making 'bannock' is baking powder — and that was the native people."

Ghostkeeper recalls getting to know Preston Manning during that time and had lunch with him on more than one occasion. "He asked a lot of questions but didn't say what he was doing. He would ask where I thought the Federation was going. But he never revealed his own political ambitions — never really committed himself."

Despite the public rejection by two of three aboriginal groups in the province and the refusal of Ottawa to accept joint funding, the Lougheed government went ahead with the BANAC/VCC proposal on its own. The decision, according to information obtained by the IAA, was made personally by Peter Lougheed. There is little doubt that Ernest Manning's direct access to the premier of Alberta played a key role in the decision, a role hinted at by Fricker: "Preston's father and Lougheed spoke to each other on a regular basis and respected each other." Preston Manning's "contacts" had paid off. And when BANAC was established, it was housed for its first two months in the offices of Manning Consultants.

Manning, by his own account, continued to work for the EDDG until at least 1986. Fred Lennarson believes the group had many other issues on its agenda: government legislation, taxes and royalties, the environmental movement, labour issues. "In our discussions with the EDDG, there'd be references to different kinds of concerns. Implicit in these discussions was [the suggestion] that they were working on other stuff. I felt I was only getting a peek at the overall structure."

Conclusion

Preston Manning's fifteen-year career as a consultant reveals a great deal about him. First, it demonstrates an unchanging commitment to free-market economic and political principles. From his and his father's paper on privatization in 1970, and their experiment in free enterprise in Slave Lake, through his study on property rights for the BCNI in 1978 and his promotion of "wealth creation" as the solution to aboriginal poverty in northern Alberta, Preston Manning's belief in free enterprise as the guiding principle for public policy and general prosperity did not waver.

That belief was often inspired by American initiatives such as the War on Poverty — a program that in the end failed to accomplish its stated goal of bringing decent living standards to the ghettos of America's large cities. Failure there — the only place where this theory of social conservatism was actually applied with any degree of commitment — seems to have had little impact on Manning's conviction that it was the only way forward.

Perhaps this is not so unusual in a man who was so powerfully attracted to systems theory and the notion that such systems models could be applied to complex social and cultural problems. The combination of religious and political commitment to free-market philosophy and attraction to a systems approach created a conviction which was not easily breached by social and political reality.

There is a disturbing aspect to Preston Manning's steadfast commitment to free-market principles and strategies: it seemed to permit him to separate his personal morality and conduct from his public actions. Every individual who knows Preston Manning well testifies to his great honesty and his personal integrity. Yet in his dealings with aboriginal people and their democratic organizations, he proved willing to use deception and back-room manoeuvring in the interests of the oil companies he worked for.

His work for the oil companies in the late seventies through the mid-eighties revealed another pattern in Preston Manning's behaviour, a pattern rooted in his and his father's anti-socialism. That anti-socialism was the flip-side of their free-market philosophy and at times was an even stronger motivation in their actions. It resulted in a clandestine mentality on the part of both men: a way of thinking about politics which grew out of the convictions that there was a communist/socialist conspiracy which threatened the foundations of the country.

Another revealing and consistent pattern in Preston Manning's fifteen years in the political wilderness reinforces the sense that conspiracy played an important role in his political thinking. A highly political individual, indeed a man preoccupied with political questions, and a student of Canadian politics and history, Preston Manning nevertheless declined to take part in any form of public politics at any level. Aside from his 1965 foray into electoral politics, Preston Manning never ran for any office: not at the provincial level, the municipal level, nor even for the school board.

It is very unusual for a person with such strongly held convictions to stay completely out of the democratic process in his broader community. Yet at no time did Preston Manning attempt to engage in the normal, day-to-day political life of his community. He believed that the country was moving dangerously in the direction of socialism, yet he did nothing in any democratic forum to try to stop it — despite the fact that his name alone would have given him an instant entry into the process.

Not only did he not enter the normal political process, he avoided the kind of community service work often done by businessmen, who are moved to give something back to the community in which they have become successful. There was no involvement in the United Appeal, Kinsmen, or on the boards of cultural, sports, or recreational bodies.

Fred Lennarson, a man who has observed Preston Manning for many years, suggests an explanation: "He doesn't look at politics in the same way as other politicians. He looks at history dispassionately and says, 'What has happened before ... what is happening now, how will things work themselves out down the road — and how can I position myself to be there at the right moment?' "

Preston Manning's lack of any experience in the day-to-day world of democratic politics and his long isolation within the confining relationship with his father produced two other patterns in his life deserving of attention. First, the only part of the broad and varied Alberta community with which Preston Manning had any contact at all was the business community and to some extent the world of government. The quintessential "problem solver" dealt exclusively with the problems of the most powerful corporations in Alberta. His clients were not drawn from a broad spectrum of Alberta society — indeed not even from small business. His personal familiarity with the problems of the disadvantaged — or even of other sectors of the economy such as agriculture — is extremely limited.

The other effect that this narrow focus and political isolation have likely had on Preston Manning is that they have denied him the opportunity to work with a wide variety of people and to learn to make judgements about their character — the normal sorts of judgements people engaged in their various communities make every day. It is this kind of experience that gives people seeking to lead others, the ability to assign responsibilities and delegate authority. In the closed and exclusive world of M and M Systems Research, in the 1950s cocoon of his father's influence, Preston

Manning would have learned few of the skills needed to engage in the modern world of the 1980s and 1990s. That isolation was to have a great impact on Preston Manning's politics.

Waiting for the Moment

Preston Manning and his father had postponed only part of their political project in 1967. The negative response to Ernest Manning's book *Political Realignment* had convinced them that their goal of an anti-socialist, social conservative party at the national level would have to wait until conditions were more favourable.

But the broad objectives of social conservatism could still be pursued through M and M Systems. Its primary work for the oil and utility companies was explicitly political work and consistent with the objective of an unfettered free-market economy. Most of the contracts that are public and acknowledged by Preston Manning were aimed at assisting private, mostly very large, companies in their efforts to push back government regulations, taxes, and royalties. While access to most of the work done is not available, M and M Systems was involved in communications advice as well as "information gathering" and analysis. Explicitly political advice was provided to some of Canada's largest corporations in their efforts to avoid contractual agreements to assist in genuine native community development.

The other work done by Preston Manning involved think-tank projects — promoting privatization and property rights — or work for the Conservative government of Peter Lougheed. All of this work reflected, to a greater or lesser extent, the philosophy and objectives of social conservatism.

But while the goal of a reformed Conservative party seemed to be on the back burner publicly, the conditions for such a party were constantly being tested. Don Wanagas, a reporter in Edmonton since the early seventies, recalls Preston Manning's name "popping up" repeatedly throughout the mid-seventies. "My boss would come in, all excited, talking about some guy who was ready to start another political party in Canada, or someone across the table at lunch would have the same story in a totally different context. The guy always turned out to be Preston Manning."

The sheer determination of the Mannings, both Ernest and Preston, and the unchanging nature of their goal characterized them as almost marginal to the Canadian political process. The only parallel throughout the mid- to late seventies was the sectarian groups of the far left. Both seemed unaffected by the dynamic and changing world around them; neither seemed to respond to any reading of what the Canadian public was actually thinking or wanted in the way of government policies. Preoccupied with ideology, the far right and the far left were both driven by "visions" which seemed divorced from the world around them.

And both operated with a similar clandestine mentality which assumed that the only way to achieve power was to meet secretly and plan to move at just the right moment — when the conditions were exactly right.

The Mannings' free-market ideology was not rooted in any expressed community sentiment or shared vision: it was inspired by an imagined threat of a left-wing conspiracy and supported almost exclusively by corporate interests whose principal goal was less government interference. Their aspiration to govern was not driven by new ideas about how government could be more responsive to its citizens but by a negative view of government: a vision of dismantling government, not reforming it.

The Movement for National Political Change

In 1978, Ernest and Preston Manning again felt that the time was ripe to press forward with their agenda to reform national politics. Ernest Manning was in the Senate and Preston was spending a good deal of time in Ottawa. Together they began a process much like the one Ernest Manning tried to initiate in 1967 with his book, *Political Realignment*. It was a non-partisan effort to draw together like-minded people from both the Conservative and Liberal parties. Brian Hay, now a Toronto business executive, has been a close associate of Preston Manning's since the mid-seventies and was a key figure in the Reform Party in Ontario through much of 1990. He recalled the 1978 initiative:

When Ernest was very involved in the Senate and playing a full role there, he and Preston were instrumental
in bringing together about a dozen western MPs from
across party lines ... they had a sort of Thursday morning coffee club at the Chateau Laurier. The idea was to
— on a non-partisan basis — discuss regional issues,
with everything from transportation, to fiscal policy to
regional economic expansion. I believe it happened
over a period of months if not years. But according to
Preston and others, participation in it was actively discouraged by the party whips, largely because it was
perceived to be a dilution of the party way of doing
things.

The Ottawa meetings apparently developed into something
more formal — and something much broader than just the parliamentarians. The formation of the Movement for National Political
Change (MNPC) first came to the attention of the media in September, 1978, when the organization produced a statement on its
objectives. Like the Social Conservative Society and the National
Public Affairs Research Foundation, it was a very private, if not
secretive, organization. Dan Powers described the movement in
the *Edmonton Journal* as "an organization which has kept a rather
low profile."

According to Preston Manning, who was executive director of
the MNPC, the organization had a mailing list of "a core of
between 250 and 300 people across the country. Some of these
people," said Manning without elaborating, "are plugged into
different groups."

The MNPC was hoping to build a membership of 1,000 people
in western Canada with a view to having a large enough base to
assemble a "national program." It was described in the same rather
vague manner as previous efforts: it was a "political education
movement," and it was founded because "Canada's traditional
federal parties are not up to the task of solving the country's
problems." The immediate goal was to invite "Canadians
from all walks of life interested in studying national issues
in the hope of bringing about," in Manning's words "change

or reform in the policies and performances of existing parties."

If the educational program was successful, the movement planned to hold regional conventions in various parts of the country, leading, it was hoped, to a "national get-together." The movement was very reminiscent of the Mannings' efforts in 1967-68 and of Preston's efforts in founding the Reform Party almost ten years later.

The September statement was called "Something New Is Being Born" — the same slogan used by Preston Manning in the speeches he now makes on the Reform Party. The "Something New" included:

• A restructured economy based on the principles of a New National Policy
• A renegotiated Confederation which, while respecting the past, would embrace a broader definition of Canada and new arrangements for recognizing and balancing national interests
• A new Movement for National Political Change which would either radically transform one of the existing federal political parties or produce a viable new political party capable of displacing one of the existing entities.

The goals, and the language they were expressed in, were almost identical to the goals and language of the political realignment movement which had foundered in 1968. While the language seemed vague, it was vague in 1967 as well. Then, as in 1978, the phrases had clear meaning to the Mannings. The "principles of a New National Policy" were simply free-market principles of less government intervention; a "broader definition" of Canada was one which would not recognize special status for Quebec; and a "viable new political party" referred to a new conservative party of the right.

Preston Manning described those attracted to the movement as dissident Liberals and Tories and "those who are repulsed by the present operation of the federal political process."

The claim that the movement wished to attract people from all walks of life may well have been a hope of the Mannings and those close to them. But the people who were close to them were from a much narrower walk of life. According to Brian Hay, they were from:

Everything from the Edmonton and Calgary Chambers of Commerce, to some of the organizations that were springing up around [the notion of] "Alberta first" if not "Alberta separate." There was a noisy if not highly visible group of Albertans who wanted to separate. Doug Christie was around then — he wasn't involved but he was the most radical exponent of it at the time. The people Preston was dealing with were pragmatists and federalists. There are people around Alberta who have a fair amount of clout who wanted to get a feel for what was going on ... who were wanting to see change and were in a position to effect change but who didn't necessarily hold public office.

The Movement for National Political Change did not meet its objectives of 1,000 western members and there is no record of any regional conventions taking place. It may be that the election of Joe Clark and the Conservatives in 1979 had some impact on the group, but according to Hay, it had more to do with the worsening economic situation facing the oil patch:

The western separatism of the late 1970s was not built on alienation as much as it was "It's our turn." It was built on the swell of success rather than the depth of failure. [The feeling] was "We finally have the capacity to do what we want to. We have the economic power..." But ... that got completely beat down by the double whammy combination of the recession and the NEP (National Energy Program). People in the oil industry became focussed on survival rather than freedom. They didn't have any money ... It [the MNPC] probably died just about the time the NEP came into place.

Hay's description of the demise of the movement suggests that its principal figures and financial backers were people in the oil companies. It had been the oil companies who, ever since the early 1950s, had replaced farmers as the "base" for Alberta-style western alienation. Canadian oil companies, no matter how low their

taxes and royalties, had always felt hard done by when compared
to their counterparts south of the border.

And it had been Canadian oil men — like Home Oil's R. A.
Brown who set up the National Public Affairs Research Foundation — whom the Mannings had identified with in their
political objectives. In addition, it was these same companies
for whom the Mannings had done the bulk of their consulting
work. When the oil men dropped out, Ernest and Preston Manning did as well.

The Early Eighties: An Explosion of Prairie Populism

It is ironic that the efforts of the Movement for National Political
Change collapsed in 1980 with the advent of the National Energy
Program because it was this program that was by far the greatest
threat to the oil industry. It took billions of dollars out of the oil
companies' revenues and indirectly out of Alberta government
coffers. The Lougheed government felt obliged to reduce royalty
rates and tax revenues at the same time in order to assist the oil
industry.

But while the fight was apparently taken out of the industry by
the recession and the NEP, it was just beginning at the grassroots.
In 1980, Alberta witnessed the birth of more parties and groups
expressing western alienation than the province had seen for decades — possibly in its history. The separatist Western Canada
Concept Party, the Christian Heritage Party, the Confederation of
Regions (CoR), and the Representative Party all organized around
the growing discontent among the political right in Alberta. Even
the small group keeping the Social Credit faith alive attempted to
rebuild on the strength of "western alienation."

While there were differences in these parties, they all shared a
common package of issues, the same issues that would later attract
thousands of people to the Reform Party: bilingualism/bicultural-
ism; abortion and the death penalty; privatization; the call for
unfettered free enterprise; the question of the debt and annual
deficits; attacks on the Conservative party for being too left-wing;
and calls for U.S.-style political reforms such as elected judges
and referenda on moral issues.

Here were precisely the conditions that Preston Manning had
been hoping for: the next populist wave. Yet, just as these

genuinely grassroots movements were being formed, Preston Manning's movement was winding down.

There is little doubt that Preston Manning could have provided this group of parties with the leadership they desperately needed to solve their main problem: credibility. Hal Shultz, director of a lobby group, Albertans for Less Government, put the matter succinctly: "Until a credible leader shows up who is philosophically conservative the political parties on the right won't have any success."

But according to Don Hamilton, Preston's old friend and political associate from the Social Conservative Society, Manning was not interested: "Most of us chose to wait and let that phase pass because otherwise we'd have just fallen into the trap of being another one of the fringe parties."

By 1985, despite vigorous organizing efforts, the protest parties had accomplished little. The Western Canada Concept had managed the best showing, capturing 12 per cent of the vote in the 1982 provincial election. But with the election of the Mulroney government in 1984, the fortunes of these parties dwindled even further. In 1985 several of them, recognizing that their sheer proliferation made them appear marginal, came together to form the Alberta Political Alliance. But none could provide the new amalgamated protest party with anything resembling an acceptable leadership figure. And Preston Manning was still not interested.

"And Along Comes Preston Manning and He Puts It All Together"

At about the same time, however, there was the beginning of serious talk of a new political party of the right among the kind of people Brian Hay referred to as "pragmatists." Among them was Ted Byfield, owner and publisher of the popular magazine *Alberta Report*. According to Byfield:

> A lot of meetings occurred before the Reform Party got going. There was a meeting in the basement of a building in Edmonton — I can't remember the name of it. This was about three or four years before [the party was

founded]. People were calling for a new party and saying "What could we do about it?" It was called by a
guy named Bob Chapman who ran Chapman Webber
Motors. Ron Southern [owner of ATCO Industries] was
there, Gordon Gibson from B.C., and Jim Grey from
Canadian Hunter Oil. We met for the whole evening
and came to two conclusions: one was that there had to
be another party, and the other was that such a party
would have little chance of success.

The extent to which issues in the oil patch drive Alberta politics
can scarcely be overestimated, and the meeting attended by Ted
Byfield and his associates provides a good example. While there
were clearly other issues which concerned this group of wealthy
men — and they had interests other than oil — Byfield explains
the gut issue which was the engine of Alberta politics in the first
half of the eighties. It had, says Byfield, to do with the "deal of
Confederation" which was:

> ... We gave the provinces control over resources. In the
> American system the federal government retained con-
> trol of resources and the land but ... compensated the
> regional interests by means of the elected senate. That's
> how they paid off, if you like, the smaller states. We
> did it on the basis of resources. But for 100 years,
> control of resources was not sufficient ... to outweigh
> the enormous weight of central Canada. Then, in the
> seventies, when this OPEC thing came along, oil and
> gas were worth an enormous amount of money. So
> finally the rules began to work for the other side — the
> smaller provinces. And what the hell do they do? They
> come along and change the rules just when they began
> to work for the smaller provinces! These guys aren't
> running a country, [we said] they're running an empire.
> You got to the point where you saw the word Canada
> printed on a truck and you'd think, "Those interloping
> bastards, get them out of here!" Then you'd say "I can't
> be thinking this way, what am I saying?" It tore the guts

out of a lot of people. They couldn't do anything about it.

Byfield and others were ready to act, but it seemed to him that others were always taking the initiative — others he wouldn't have anything to do with. "The issue would always get linked to crazies like [Doug] Christie and those guys and you'd think, 'Oh, great, what the hell's the use?' Then, all of a sudden, along comes Preston Manning and he puts it all together, and we think, 'This is the guy we've been waiting for.' "

It was sometime in 1986 that Preston Manning assessed the political situation and decided — once again — that the time might be ripe for a new political party. And this time he got it right. He began to talk privately with selected people about the creation of a new party.

One of the informal meetings was with Ted Byfield and six to eight of the editorial staff at a restaurant in Edmonton. "He outlined at the time his concept of what could be done. It was more a question of him fulfilling a need that we kept portraying. We didn't seek him out — and he always had a wider view than western alienation. He emphasized the western point of view because he knew it had to start there."

In the two years following the election of Brian Mulroney's Conservatives, conditions in Alberta had become even more promising for the formation of a new political party of the right. In fact, the election of the Conservatives was perhaps the key catalyst for such a project. Allan Tupper, a political scientist from the University of Alberta, explained to *Saturday Night* that Albertans had very high expectations of the Mulroney government: "People really thought that the election of a national conservative government with a strong Alberta representation would fundamentally alter Canadian politics."

It did not take long for the disillusionment to set in. And the first to be angered were, once again, the oil companies. They had fully expected the Conservatives to reverse one of their biggest irritants and annoying reminders of the Trudeau era: the petroleum gas revenue tax. The government finally removed it in 1987 but not before it had created real hostility in the oil industry which had helped get the Conservatives elected.

Corporate interests were also dismayed at the perceived inability of the new government in Ottawa to meet its own commitments of reducing the debt and getting the annual budget deficit in line. Those who believed that they had, in Brian Mulroney, a genuine advocate of minimal government found that the universal social programs, subsidies to farmers, interprovincial trade barriers, and a web of other government regulations remained virtually untouched.

But there were other issues which angered a much broader public than just the oil industry. The Mulroney government's repeated and highly publicized use of patronage rankled Albertans who had identified such practice with the hated Trudeau era. It rankled even more when that use of patronage and advantage led to criminal charges and cabinet resignations, especially when these embarrassments to the Conservative government seemed to occur mostly in Quebec.

The simmering resentment created by these issues broke into the open when Ottawa decided to grant a large CF-18 jet maintenance contract to a Quebec company, when a Manitoba company had submitted a lower bid and had greater expertise. This signalled to many westerners that Quebec interests would override those of the West. Added to the emotional and political mix was the long and nasty fight in Manitoba over the issue of official bilingualism in that province. French rights in Manitoba, established in 1870, had been revoked by a later government. History notwithstanding, the perceived imposition of French language rights so close to home seemed to contribute to Albertans' sense of powerlessness.

The disappointing performance of a Conservative government was crucial for Preston Manning's project to proceed. He had told Ted Byfield that no matter which party formed a government, that party would eventually come to represent the views of the provinces which ensured its election — in other words Ontario and Quebec.

So long as the Conservative Party was in opposition, Preston Manning knew that there would be little chance for a new party. The Conservative Party has historically been the party of opposition, especially in the West. People angry at Liberal government policy, from the right, gravitate to the Conservative Party regardless of who the leader is. Preston Manning was waiting for the

Conservatives to come to power, knowing full well that governments can never behave like oppositions. His party could only take root in an atmosphere of dissatisfaction with a Conservative government.

Preston Manning has always been clear about both his political agenda and his preferred political vehicle for achieving it: it is a radical free-market agenda and it would be brought to fruition on a wave of popular anger. Harnessing these two forces together — the mass power of broad-based discontent and the financial power of those supporting an unfettered free-market philosophy — was Preston Manning's party-building task. These were two quite different constituencies motivated by overlapping objectives.

The half-dozen protest parties of the early eighties had tried unsuccessfully to take advantage of the mass discontent: anger at Quebec, western powerlessness, the death penalty, metrification, and calls for conservative economic policies. They had failed in part because their political style and imagery repulsed the other crucial Alberta constituency: the powerful oil industry whose interests were almost exclusively tied up in free-market economic policies. Preston Manning, who had worked on behalf of those interests for twenty years, was the man who would bridge the gap.

After two years of disappointing Conservative rule in Ottawa, Preston Manning had once again floated the idea of a new political party, promoting himself as the man to initiate it. What he did not know at the time was that there were other people, powerful people, talking about the same thing. According to Ian Pearson writing in *Saturday Night*, while Preston Manning was discussing this idea in Edmonton: "... in Calgary, a group of lawyers and oil men disenchanted with the Tories had decided that a new party was the only alternative. The moving forces were lawyers Bob Muir, Doug Hilliard and the late Marvin Dill, who had organized the Canada 1 and Canada 2 yachting challenge for the America's Cup and now drew together some of the same backers to talk about a new political party."

One of these was oil man Jack MacKenzie. Another was Cliff Fryers, who would become the Reform Party's chief fundraiser. "We were talking about doing something and someone mentioned that there was this guy, Ernest Manning's son in Edmonton," said Fryers. "They found out he was saying, 'Now is the time for a populist party.' But he hadn't made any moves. They called him down to Calgary and after they met with him, they said, 'Yeah, we're impressed. We can start something.' "

According to Pearson, Manning had attracted increasing attention in Edmonton, from a similar group of wealthy businessmen. Multi-millionaire developer Jack Poole, the retired founder of Daon Developments "organized a series of informal lunches to introduce Manning to the upper echelons of business and law." Here, too, the principal players were disenchanted long-time Conservative supporters. They were also impressed with the seriousness of Preston Manning and his plans for a populist party.

Preston Manning's long wait was over. The same class of powerful men, who had gone to his father in 1967 asking him to head up a new conservative party of the right, were now prepared to endorse his son as their man to head up an identical project. The previously missing ingredient, a broad base of disenchanted voters, was now present. Canadian politics was about to change.

Through his new connections in Calgary, Preston Manning linked up with another like-minded businessman in Vancouver, the late Stan Roberts. Roberts was a marketing consultant, former president of the Canadian Chamber of Commerce and head of the Canada West Foundation for which Manning had done research work in the mid-seventies. Roberts had also been floating the idea of a new political movement of the right, and together he and Preston Manning formed the Reform Association of Canada. The movement of wealthy westerners for a new political party now had core groups in Edmonton, Calgary, and Vancouver. Roberts and Manning were known in this small but significant group as the "twin pillars" of the new movement.

The Roberts connection brought into the movement a man who was prepared more than anyone else to give the new party idea a major push: Francis Winspear. Formerly of Edmonton, Winspear was a Victoria accountant and millionaire who had approached Roberts and told him, "If you feel as I do and want to change the political system, I'll give you the money to form a party." With the $100,000 start-up cheque from the eighty-four-year-old Winspear, Roberts and Manning planned the founding "assembly" of the Reform Association for Vancouver in May, 1987.

The first organizing efforts of Manning were crucial to maintaining the momentum of the new party project — and particularly its credibility. The recent proliferation of marginal protest parties were still fresh in the minds of Albertans, and any hint that this effort was just another in a series would have been its death knell. This was particularly true of big business, the most critical constituency of all. Referring to them, Manning said "They're waiting until we can prove we have a party that's here to stay. This founding convention is the key."

The organizers ensured that the founding convention created a strong public impression. Manning took as few chances as possible regarding who would show up. Though Ted Byfield donated an ad for the gathering, billed as "A Conference on the Economic and Political Future of Canada," (it was later changed to an "assembly") in his *Alberta Report* magazine, attendance at the founding meeting was by invitation only.

It was decided in advance that the attendance would be limited to 300 people. Each of the four western provinces had Delegate Selection Committees appointed by Manning and his organizers. These committees were authorized to choose sixty delegates from their province. The Conference Steering Committee would choose another sixty, including "delegates at large whose presence would assist the Conference to achieve its purposes, and observers from national organizations and other parts of Canada who might share the Conference's objectives."

With a hint of things to come regarding Reform Party candidates for federal elections, the delegates to the conference had to meet certain criteria. In general, they were to be "the very best representatives and spokespersons from every federal constituency and economic sector across the West ... " More specifically, according to the pre-conference document produced in January, delegate selection was to be based on a number of criteria, including: "Delegates should be sane and responsible citizens, capable of mature and balanced judgments on important issues and capable of accurately representing the concerns and aspirations of their fellow citizens."

In addition to having "interest and experience" pertaining to at least one of the topic areas being dealt with by the conference, "Delegates should be committed to seeking fundamental reforms in the position of Western Canada within confederation and open-minded (not narrowly partisan) with respect to the choice of political vehicles."

An additional check on the suitability of those attending was the nomination procedure. Delegates had to be nominated, though how the nominators were chosen wasn't revealed. The nominators were reminded to "carefully review the delegate criteria" before making nominations and instructed that "The more information you can provide to the Committee concerning your nominee, the better." Delegate registration forms would be provided to the "Selected nominees."

The political vehicles open to discussion at the conference were reforming an existing political party (all but the Conservatives were ruled out later in the document), organizing a new Western-based Reform Party; and investigating the separatist option.

The Vancouver conference accomplished what Preston Manning had hoped it would: it set the stage for a national conservative party of the right. It was billed exclusively as a conference on the future of western Canada and referred repeatedly in the pre-conference literature to westerners' feelings of alienation: "Many Western Canadians are convinced that there is a structural and policy bias in Canada ... in favour of the heavily populated Golden Triangle ... "

But in his address — Ted Byfield made the key-note address on western alienation — Manning made it clear that what they were starting was a national party:

> A new federal party representing the West should have "room to grow" into a truly national party. A new federal party, created initially to represent the West, should aspire to become that truly national party, and nothing should be done in the early stages of its conception and birth to preclude it from eventually gaining support all across the country, particularly in those regions of Ontario, Quebec, Atlantic Canada and Northern Canada which share many of our concerns and aspirations.

While the publicity surrounding the conference reiterated the western Canadian theme and most of the talk at the conference was along these lines as well, the word *western* was never intended to be an official part of the new party's name. The pre-conference document sent to nominators had on its front page, "Co-ordinated by the Reform Association of Canada." While the conference did adopt the slogan, "The West Wants In," they also voted to form a "national" party.

For Preston Manning the start-up of his enterprise was an almost complete success. While the media response to the three-day event was generally a bit skeptical, there were no public relations disasters. Its low-key tone was just what Manning had intended and arranged through his careful screening of delegates. The launching of the party was smooth and trouble-free. He had successfully established a new party; it was geared to promote itself as a party responding to western alienation and could therefore legitimately take advantage of that sentiment; it was declared a national party, a status it could now pursue at its own speed, depending on conditions.

The next key stage in the Reform Party was its first convention as a full-fledged party and not just an association. Planned for the fall in Winnipeg, it would have delegates who were not hand-picked by Preston Manning's committees, and there would be a leadership vote. Both of these factors had the potential to cause trouble and both delivered on that potential.

By convention time, the party had 2,500 members. Three hundred and six delegates attended, and the provincial breakdown indicated the geographic appeal of "western protest" in the West: there were 140 delegates from Alberta, 91 from B.C., 65 from Manitoba, and just 10 from Saskatchewan.

The party chose Preston Manning as leader, but not without some blood being left on the floor. In a controversy which would dog Manning for a long time, Stan Roberts, the second "pillar" of the party, withdrew from the leadership race, charging registration irregularities, and claiming that there was party money unaccounted for. Declaring that the party had already compromised its "honesty and integrity," he denounced Manning and his executive supporters as "right-wing Christian fanatics" and stormed out of the convention. The fact that only twenty people followed him allowed Preston Manning, who demonstrated a detached calm about the events, to limit the damage.

The other bit of rough water the founding convention had to weather was exactly the kind of thing Manning dreaded most: the lunatic fringe which he knew would be attracted to his party. June Lenihan, a Vancouver delegate, stated, for the press to hear, "I'm one of the people in this room willing to admit that I am an evangelical, right-wing, anti-abortionist redneck, anti-socialist, ultra-conservative, fundamentalist Christian." That statement summed up Manning's dilemma: it was the June Lenihans of the world whom he depended upon to build the initial base for his party that at the same time could destroy its credibility if he could not control them.

Manning's speech and comments to reporters revealed the contradiction of his mission: the marriage of western discontent with a new conservative party of the right. His appeal was still to the West: "The core of this party's mission is achieving economic justice for the West, to rectify the historic exploitation of our resources and our people by Central Canada." But his historic mission of replacing the Conservative Party was there, too: "The Progressive Conservative Party at the federal level has a congenital inability to govern ... it cannot be considered an appropriate vehicle for the implementation of a reform program."

The success of the Reform Party depended in large part on the performance of the party it wanted to replace. Its growth was directly proportional to the decline of Brian Mulroney's government. And it was precisely because of the Conservative's successful fight for free trade that the Reform Party's growth reached a plateau in 1988. The next election had not been expected until the spring of 1989 when the Reformers hoped to be better prepared. Instead it was held in November, 1988, as Brian Mulroney decided to take a chance and call an election on the free trade agreement.

The Conservatives' hard-ball campaign in favour of free trade cut away a lot of the free-enterprise vote which might otherwise have gone to the Reform Party's candidates. It also confirmed the view of those who said Reform could only prosper at the Tories' expense. Yet Reform's showing, after organizing for only a year, was a respectable one. Running on a platform of a triple-E Senate, fiscal restraint, an end to official bilingualism, and support for the free trade agreement, the party made its presence felt, at least in Alberta and B.C. It fielded candidates in seventy-two of the West's eighty-six ridings and ran in all of B.C.'s thirty-one seats and Alberta's twenty-six.

The profile of the candidates in the Alberta ridings revealed that the party is almost exclusively urban and middle class. Of the twenty-six candidates, half were professionals (including two teachers) and ten were in business or management consulting. A tradesman, a farmer, and a rancher filled out the roster. Four of the Reform candidates were women, compared to two for the Conservatives, five for the Liberals, and seven for the NDP.

Overall, Reform received 275,767 votes or 7.3 per cent of the votes cast in the West. But in Alberta ridings they placed second in nine and third in seven constituencies and got 15 per cent of the vote, third after the Tories with 52 per cent and the NDP at 17 per cent. Preston Manning took on Joe Clark, the symbol for Manning of everything that was wrong with the Conservative governments of the past twenty years. He was soundly beaten but managed to improve his public profile in the province on which he would depend in the next two years for the bulk of his members and his financial support. Given Albertans' high expectations of Brian Mulroney, the Reform Party had reason to be pleased with its showing.

The party, saddled with the disadvantage of having no elected members in Parliament with which to maintain a national presence, focused in early 1989 on building its base in the West. Content for the moment to accept minimal national media attention, Manning kept up a dizzying organizing pace, making over 250 speeches in 1989, principally in western provinces.

The party was still identified with a few high-profile emotional issues and its policies reflected this. Many were a blend of policy and political rhetoric attacking either the Conservative Party by itself, the three major parties as a group, or wrong-headed policies of previous governments. The 1989 policy Blue Book coming out of the August, 1988 Assembly in Calgary is peppered with comments such as "we question the motives of the current Government and Minister underlying recent policy [on energy]" and, in relation to balancing federal budgets, "Perhaps the most stunning illustration of the failures of the Mulroney government ... " The policy titled "Opposition to Fraudulent Western Initiatives" described the Western Diversification Initiative as an "incredibly bloated bureaucracy" making "politically motivated decisions," and as "a bureaucratic slushfund reminiscent of previous Liberal schemes."

The strong rhetoric of the policy book revealed not just its members' embittered rejection of the Mulroney government. It reflected, as well, the historic position of right-wing western protest movements as perpetually in opposition to the federal government. Having lost so many past battles to influence national affairs, Reform Party members appeared to have difficulty crafting policies based on a belief that they might actually get implemented.

The Conservatives' free trade deal with the U.S. stole much of the attention away from the Reform Party in the 1988 election. But in 1989, Reform's fortunes improved dramatically. Ironically, given Preston Manning's stated coolness to provincial politics, substantial momentum was gained from widespread disaffection with Alberta's Tory government under Don Getty. Building on that disaffection and Preston Manning's popularity in the province, the party won a federal by-election in Calgary and a provincial Senate "election" called by Getty as a way of forcing the issue of an elected Senate.

Greg Mason, with the public opinion polling company Prairie Research Associates, has said of Stan Waters's massive win — 41.7 per cent of the vote — in the Senate election, "This was a profound anti-Conservative vote and a personal affront to Mr. Getty ... [People] are cynical about the relationship between the government and its supporters, especially with respect to the Gainers' plant." Gainers' owner, Peter Pocklington, had received many favours from Getty including a $67 million loan that he never repaid. According to Mason, "What this victory means is that people are really anti-Getty."

Despite a fourth-place finish in her Beaver River riding in 1988, Deborah Grey easily defeated the other candidates in a March, 1989 by-election in the riding. Grey, an evangelical Christian, had attended a B.C. Bible School for three years after high school and had taught there for a year. She is, in many ways, typical of Reform supporters, especially those of the evangelical right. Untypically for Reform, she is from a working-class background with a history of odd jobs until she obtained her Bachelor of Education and began teaching in 1978.

Barb Boneau, Grey's NDP opponent in the race, has criticized Grey for attempting to capitalize on the Quebec issue in her 1989 campaign. According to Boneau, "Grey would go to a Ukrainian community and attack bilingualism by saying 'Why not Ukrainian?' But she wouldn't mention her opposition to multiculturalism."

Strongly anti-abortion and anti-feminist, Grey has used her seat in the House of Commons to attack federal childcare spending, saying that it is "... probably a waste of money ... and may be discriminating against parents who choose to raise their children at home." As an MP she has presented petitions on the rights of the unborn and the RCMP dress code.

While Deborah Grey became a high profile Reformer by an accident of the by-election, Stan Waters was high profile within the party almost from the beginning. He had been Manning's key economic advisor before the 1988 election and had important connections in both the business community in Calgary and in the Canada West Foundation, the principal western-rights think-tank in the country. Waters's key role in the party and his important connections in other organizations will be examined in more detail in the next chapter.

Setting the Stage for Eastern Expansion

The elections of Waters and Grey not only helped cement the Reform Party's hold on Alberta, but they also provided Preston Manning with an unexpected presence on the national stage. While it was only a foothold, it was a stroke of good fortune which would assist him in his determination to transform Reform into the national party he had always intended it to be.

Manning and his closest advisors had already set the stage for that transformation at the 1989 Assembly. There were two key elements to the preparations to expand into Ontario and the Atlantic provinces: getting approval for a speaking tour in the east and reworking the policy book to give it appeal beyond Alberta.

There was little if any support for expansion at the assembly. After all, it was Manning who had repeatedly stated that western protest parties that strayed beyond their home territory inevitably betrayed their mandate by appealing to the provinces — Ontario and Quebec — that could put them in power. But such was

Manning's stature that the delegates gave their leader what he wanted: their blessing for an eastern tour.

In policy, too, the assembly accepted the party's revision of the rhetoric and western flourishes, which had characterized the previous Blue Book.

The actual policies were re-worked to make them more saleable to a national audience. One example was the policy on the banking system. The 1988 policy attacked the Conservative government's policy, which, it said, "... led to a more concentrated banking system and a renewal of monopolistic banking practices." It went on, in a tone reminiscent of the Social Credit Party, to denounce the centralized banking system. The 1989 Assembly produced a one-sentence policy: "The Reform Party supports a more competitive banking system, including the presence of regional banks."

Some of the 1988 policies were so western-oriented they would have puzzled, if not alarmed, eastern voters. Under "Reform the RCMP," the book stated "Westerners and Northerners are becoming increasingly disturbed by the central Canadian composition, bureaucratization and orientation of the RCMP ... it seems more and more unrepresentative and unresponsive to our needs." This language disappears in the 1990 version, and the policy simply calls for restoration of the RCMP "to its former stature" as a force "representative of the ... West and North and responsive to our needs."

Though the party remained constitutionally and politically a western party after the 1989 Assembly, the policy book based on that assembly was completely purged of any mention of "the West." Manning's foreword in the 1988 edition talks of the likelihood of a divided Parliament after the next election in which "Western Reformers would be in a powerful position to pursue our agenda." The booklet is peppered with phrases like, "A fair shake for the West," "Reform MPs will look out for Western interests," and numerous derogatory remarks about "Central Canada" and "Central Canadian interests," "Central Canadian terms" as well as "Quebec-centred" biases of Mulroney.

Virtually all of this western, anti-central Canada terminology was purged from the 1989 edition of the booklet. In Manning's two-and-a-half page foreword, entitled "The New Canada," there is not a single reference to the West or westerners. Gone, as well, was the "Declaration of Adoption" in the 1988 book, which recognized "the supremacy of God."

The sanitizing of the policy book was done by the Party Policy Committee (PPC), without any mandate from the assembly. It was a body which would play a major role as Manning guided the party away from its western orientation towards national party readiness. Appointed by the party's Executive Committee, and chaired by Preston Manning, its key members were Stan Waters and Stephen Harper. Harper was the Chief Policy Officer of the Party and the only other person, besides Grey and Waters, whom Manning trusted to speak for the party.

With a policy book completely cleansed of any reference to the West and most of its specifically western policies, plus the assembly's authority to take the Reform message to the East, the stage was set for the next phase in Preston Manning's plan to create a new conservative party.

From left to right: Premier E.C. Manning, Preston, Muriel Manning, and Keith in 1957. *Photo courtesy of the Provincial Archives of Alberta.*

Ernest Manning (foreground) and Preston Manning on election platform in 1963. *Photo courtesy of The Edmonton Journal.*

At university, Preston Manning often played apologist for Ernest Manning and the Social Credit. This cartoon appeared in *The Gateway* on October 25, 1963. *Photo courtesy of The Gateway.*

Preston Manning in 1964. *Photo courtesy of the University of Alberta Archives.*

Alberta needs strong representation in Ottawa

R. HERB JAMIESON   PRESTON MANNING   SIG SORENSON

"Canadians need economic freedom and security"

"The future belongs to those young enough and vigorous enough to shape it"

"Canada cannot afford the high cost of a welfare state"

This is the challenge before us, who say that we believe in personal freedom and private enterprise, to show, by our actions, that we can make it work. This will be done by the monetary plans incorporated in the Social Credit party's platform whereby government would provide enough money—at the right price—in the right place—for the encouragement of economic growth.

Over forty percent of the population of Canada is composed of persons under twenty-five years of age. This strong segment of our growing nation needs, and must have, a strong and active voice in federal Parliament. Enthusiastic youth must be willing to accept the responsibilities of government so that it may serve the interests of the nation, restoring the citizens' pride and faith in federal administration.

Welfare schemes, for all their good intentions, have to be paid for by someone. The necessary increased taxes shift the burden of paying for these schemes more and more onto the backs of the very people who are supposed to benefit from them "for free". The moment a man forfeits his right to choose what is beneficial for himself and those in his care, he forfeits his guarantee of security.

Give Alberta strong representation in Ottawa

ON NOVEMBER 8 VOTE SOCIAL CREDIT

| JAMIESON, R. Herb | X | MANNING, Ernest Preston | X | SORENSON, Sigurd | X |
| Edmonton-West | | Edmonton-East | | Edmonton-Strathcona | |

Inserted by The Alberta Social Credit League

Election poster from 1965 showing Preston Manning, R. Herb Jamieson, and Sig Sorenson.

Preston Manning and his wife Sandra at a Social Credit convention on December 5, 1968. *Photo courtesy of the Provincial Archives of Alberta.*

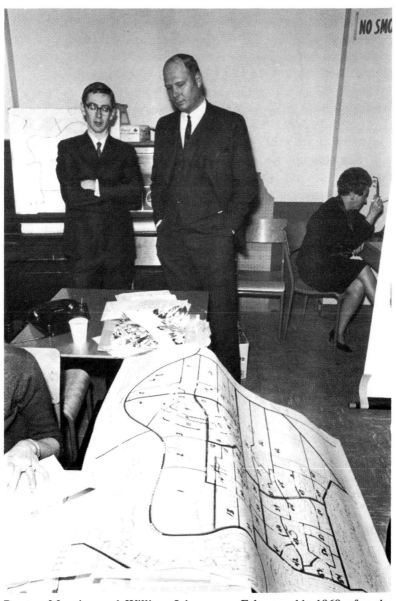

Preston Manning and William Johnson on February 11, 1969 after the by-election held in Strathcona East. *Photo courtesy of the Provincial Archives of Alberta.*

Connections

Political parties are known for and judged by, not just their leaders and their policies, but a host of other factors: their history and how they were founded; the social and political conditions that brought them to life; the social class of their members and supporters; the people and organizations that fund them; and organizations that share their political objectives or are attracted to them on the basis of a particular issue. All of these factors, in addition to the leader's style and substance, influence the overall assessment that people make of any party seeking public support.

This, of course, is as it should be. These factors are often unfavourably identified by a party's opponents — the NDP is criticized for its connections to labour, and the Conservative and Liberal parties for their connections to big business. Yet, whether the parties like it or not, these "connections" do reflect a party's priorities and, stated policies aside, whose interests it will serve — or serve first — if elected.

The Reform Party is no different in this respect than any other party. It, too, enjoys the support of several strong interest groups, the most obvious of which is probably the oil industry.

The Oil Companies

The Reform Party is very much an Alberta party. Not only has it grown and capitalized on the broad array of issues which make up "western protest," but it has, from its very beginnings, looked for its financial support and unofficial endorsement from the quintessential Alberta source of money and power: the oil companies.

It might be more accurate to say that Preston Manning was given the seal of approval by Alberta big business because the individuals who first sought him out or endorsed him were not all from the oil patch. But the oil patch so dominates Alberta business and is so powerful in determining its political agenda that knowing about oil becomes critical if we are to know about Preston Manning and the Reform Party.

Since the major discovery in the late forties, oil has played a dominating role in the life of Alberta. But that role has changed over the decades, particularly as it affected the politics of Alberta and Alberta's place in Canada.

The change in the impact of oil development parallels the change from the Social Credit government of Ernest Manning to the Progressive Conservative government of Peter Lougheed. Under Manning, oil development was almost exclusively in the hands of U.S. capital. Manning failed to persuade eastern Canadian capital to invest in Alberta (a fact still remembered with bitterness in Calgary), and his free-enterprise ideology prevented him from undertaking government development. As a result, say John Richards and Larry Pratt in their study, *Prairie Capitalism: Power and Influence in the New West*:

> Social Credit's development philosophy grew out of Manning's belief in the overriding necessity for an entente with American capital. Without such an entente, accompanied by highly favourable terms of development, Manning was convinced that Alberta would lack the capital, expertise, technology and markets to exploit its energy resource potential ... the accommodation negotiated ... [with] the major oil companies after Leduc was designed to provide [them] with a minimum of uncertainty over tenure, royalty charges, and property rights, and the assurance of long-term political stability.

This development strategy, pursued by Manning up until his retirement in 1968, created a stark contrast between Alberta and Texas, despite the frequent suggestions that Alberta was "Texas North." While the international giants like Imperial Oil dominated Alberta, the small independent producers in Texas successfully fought off eastern capital, such as Rockefeller's Standard Oil, by forming a populist alliance with farmers — who were fighting for mineral rights themselves.

The result in Alberta was very different. While small independents did battle with the likes of Imperial Oil and tried to pressure Manning and successive federal governments for changes, they never succeeded. While oil replaced agriculture as the driving force of the Alberta economy and the political focus of "western alienation," it was never populist.

Equally important until the 1970s was the fact that during the Manning era, Albertan entrepreneurs remained small scale and marginal. Richards and Pratt note: "Alberta's independents were too small to do much more than enter into unequal relationships with the integrated companies and thereby ensure themselves a stable share of the province's crude oil markets." This left the entrepreneurial function in the oil patch to foreign capital. It also ensured that the Alberta economy would remain undiversified and therefore vulnerable to over-dependence on oil revenue.

It was precisely this vulnerability which Peter Lougheed recognized and would play on to win the Conservative Party leadership — and the 1971 election. Lougheed had also recognized that the Socreds were getting old and, rather than enter that party, he would revive the long-dormant Conservatives. He formed the Lougheed Club, inviting his close oil friends in Calgary to join. They planned strategy at weekly meetings in the Palliser Hotel in Calgary. He won the leadership in 1965.

Arguing that Alberta needed a "third phase" in its economic development, after wheat and oil, in 1971 he persuaded the electorate — more specifically the urban electorate which now accounted for 80 per cent of the population — that industrialization was the key to Alberta's future economic stability and prosperity.

According to Richards and Pratt, Lougheed's government created the political conditions for "the growth among Alberta's business classes of what, borrowing from Max Weber, we might call 'the spirit of capitalism.' " Under his government throughout the 1970s, there developed a growing and powerful entrepreneurial class, which had a major impact on provincial politics and national finance.

No one was better placed, either in terms of pedigree or training, to lead the charge of independent Alberta capital than Peter Lougheed. The Lougheed family was an Alberta dynasty. Peter was the son of Edgar Donald Lougheed and the grandson of Senator Sir James A. Lougheed, "one of Alberta's pioneering capitalists and among its most powerful political spokesmen in the formative years of the modern prairie West." According to Richards and Pratt, "His life was devoted to the accumulation of property and capital and to the arts of political manipulation ... "

Peter Lougheed received his training at Harvard Business School and his experience at another Alberta business dynasty: the Mannix Group. This Calgary-based conglomerate was one of the handful of Alberta corporations that could compete success-fully at the international level. Founded at the turn of the century, it started out in construction and engineering, building most of the hydro dams for Calgary Power, and expanded into coal, oil, and gas in later years. Its partnership with a large American contractor allowed it into the international construction market.

Peter Lougheed joined the Mannix empire in 1956 and quickly became a "great success ... moving up the corporate escalator ... [to become] Vice-President and Director in five short years ... " of the Mannix company Loram (for Long Range Mannix). A "model of the new capitalist west," Loram was a perfect training ground — politically and corporatively — for a future Conserva-tive premier.

The Mannix family is described "as 'rich, private, dynastic and inaccessible' ... is staunchly right-wing and fiercely dedicated to western regionalism." Lougheed's subsequent recruiting of Man-nix executives into his government and his "quasi-corporatist style of government [and] penchant for strong executive government, were forged in the Mannix boardroom."

While Alberta capitalists had been obliged under Ernest Man-ning's pro-American development policies to play a subordinate role, under Lougheed they blossomed. By the late seventies, stimulated by government policies and fear of economic stagna-tion, they had transformed Calgary from a "hinterland service centre" to Canada's second largest financial centre and the world oil industry's third most important centre for oil finance.

In *Prairie Capitalism,* Richards and Pratt described Calgary's business elite in 1979 as aiming "at nothing less than a transfer of wealth, industries, and decision-making from central Canada to the western periphery — 'a fundamental change in the economy of Canada' as Premier Lougheed puts it." Powered by such cor-porate giants as the Mannix Group, Alberta Gas Trunkline, ATCO Industries (owned by Ron Southern) and Jack Gallagher's DOME

Petroleum, Calgary's business world — including real estate, construction, petrochemicals, ranching, and agribusiness — had already accomplished a major regional transfer of funds from the Canadian heartland to the West.

Alberta had finally become the Texas North that they had aspired to — except in one major respect. While they had their man Peter Lougheed at the helm at the provincial level, the wealthy business elite of Calgary had still not achieved the transfer of political power at the national level that primary producers in the U.S. had accomplished.

The so-called sun-belt states, including Texas and California, had led a successful attack on the political domination of the northeast states in 1980 — at the same time that Trudeau passed the National Energy Program in Canada. The elections of Ronald Reagan and George Bush — a Californian and Texan respectively — were dramatic examples of that power shift, and powerful reminders to the Calgary business elite that had yet to accomplish the same thing in Canada. Jack Gallagher, former head of DOME Petroleum, expressed the oil industry's desire for its own party: "Quebec has been represented by the Liberals, manufacturing interests by the Conservatives and labour by the New Democrats. But we have no party representing the primary producers of Canada — agriculture, forestry and fishing, mining and oil and gas."

If Peter Lougheed was the oil patch's man in Edmonton, then it was easy for their spokesmen to conclude that Preston Manning would be a good man to have in Ottawa. Frustrated, as Ted Byfield suggested, that so many political figures speaking for the West were from the fringe, the industry was relieved to find Preston Manning. They hope that he will end their frustration at being unable to translate their huge economic power into political influence in Ottawa.

According to Nick Taylor, former leader of the Liberal Party in Alberta (and still an MLA) and a former independent oil man in his own right, "Every oil man I speak to in Calgary is putting money into the Reform Party. I would estimate that just this group alone is putting in at least a half a million dollars a year."

Not all of that money shows up in official records, says Taylor, because not everyone wants it known and most don't need the tax deduction badly enough to register their donations. In addition, claims the Liberal MLA, Calgary oil money comes at a price. While Preston Manning says he and the party moved to Calgary so that he could be close to his daughters while they attended university, Taylor and others see it differently. "They [the oil men] would simply say, 'If you're our man, we want you close by where we can have access to you.' That's why he moved the Reform Party headquarters to Calgary and that's why he has decided to run in a Calgary constituency rather than take on Joe Clark again."

While Preston Manning may be close to the oil men in Calgary, he is still not one of them. However, it wasn't long after they had endorsed Manning as the leader of the new party that the Calgary business elite had one of their own as close to Preston Manning as anyone was likely to get. That man was Stanley Waters, and his Calgary credentials were impeccable.

Stan Waters

Stan Waters,who died in late 1991, personified the origins and the ideological thrust of the Reform Party. The son of middle-class English immigrants, he grew up in Alberta, joined the war effort in 1938, and developed a highly successful career in the Canadian Army. In the army, he was put in charge of the Mobile Command during the October Crisis in 1970 and appointed Army Commander in 1973. His Reform Party biography states, somewhat cryptically, "A series of larger appointments in Ottawa afforded Stan an opportunity to closely observe the operation of Canada's government and its departments."

Upon retirement in 1975, he joined the Mannix organization. According to the Reform Party biography, "His transition to the business world was both swift and successful." In six months, he was president of the Loram Group — outstripping even the rapid rise of Peter Lougheed in that same company — "engaged in national and international activities in construction, oil and gas, coal, engineering and manufacturing." He went on to other senior positions in venture capital and investment companies as well as real estate, including real estate in the U.S.

A military colleague described Waters as "dynamic, energetic. He immersed himself in Alberta political culture and took to it easily. He was always forthright and was attracted to simple, straightforward approaches to problems. He would be attracted by the Reform Party's approach."

Stan Waters's business connections with large oil and resource corporations paid off handsomely in the October, 1989 senate election. A story in the February 5, 1990 edition of the *Alberta Report* claimed the party had raised nearly $3 million, most of it from the grassroots. Mr. Waters's financial statement, however, reveals that of the $173,000 he raised (almost four times that raised by the Liberal runner-up), fewer than 5 per cent of the contributions came from people who contributed $40 or less. Most of the money came from corporations or corporate executives based in Calgary:

- $ 500 - Canadian Hunter Exploration, Calgary
- $ 500 - A. J. E. Child (Burns Meats)
- $ 1,500 - Ajex Enterprises, Calgary (President: A. J. E. Child)
- $ 500 - Robert C. Muir
- $ 500 - Ron Southern, Calgary (ATCO Enterprises)
- $ 500 - Colin Energy Resources
- $ 500 - Maraval Resources, Calgary
- $ 1,000 - Allaro Resources Ltd., Calgary
- $ 1,000 - Ranger Oil Ltd., Calgary
- $ 1,000 - Trans Alta Utilities Corp., Calgary
- $ 5,000 - Lincoln, McKay Development Co. Ltd., Calgary
- $ 10,000 - F. G. Winspear
- $ 10,000 - Exel Energy Inc., Calgary

According to the Reform Party background on Mr. Waters, he held a directorship in Exel Energy Inc. Francis G. Winspear is the millionaire who gave the party $100,000 in start up money.

In 1989, Waters joined Manning as one of the two key, articulate spokesmen for the Reform Party. The contrast in their styles and the content of their speeches suggests a "good cop, bad cop" strategy. Manning himself tried out a similar hockey analogy in a membership survey, suggesting that he was the centre while Stan Waters was the right wing. Party members rejected the idea because it required a left wing. As *Saturday Night*'s Ian Pearson put it, "If Manning was the centre and Waters is the right wing, then every pass Manning has to handle is a blistering slapshot."

Manning is clearly the party's most valuable asset, because he can, among other things, present the moderate, reasonable image that is crucial to the party's broad appeal. Manning gives Reformers ever-increasing party growth and credibility. Waters said what party members wanted to hear. At the Reform Party's 1989 Assembly, where, according to Ian Pearson "There was little evidence of any policies left of the National Citizens' Coalition," Waters hit many, if not all, the right buttons.

The Mulroney government, Waters said, "has spent $239 million in hand-outs to the so-called arts community through the Canada Council. And as you know, many of those hand-outs are to publish books that should never have been published, to mount paintings that should never have been painted, to compose music that should never be listened to." Says Pearson, "After thunderous applause, he attacked 'the 186 million dollars for scholarly research such as the social value of lawn ornaments.' And he decried the 5 billion dollars in hand-outs to foreign governments, most of them despotic, tyrannical, and undemocratic." Canada's actual overseas aid budget was $2.8 billion in 1990.

Waters's views and his frankness in expressing them covered a wide range of issues. On the topic of despotic governments, he referred primarily to black African governments. And his commitment to democracy was qualified:

> South Africa should think twice before allowing majority rule because most black-ruled African countries live under tyranny ... If history has any parallelism, you might find a very serious problem emerging in South Africa which may dwarf the objectionable features of the current administration ... it may be impossible to transport our version of democracy to South Africa.

Waters was the party's point man on many of the issues that get people signing membership cards. He called for an end to federal funding of advocacy groups and repeatedly singled out the National Action Committee on the Status of Women. He wanted to "axe" 75,000 (out of 540,000) federal public service employees and said that a Reform government would cut spending "across the board" by 15 per cent and "... put the federal government in voluntary receivership." Civil servants were one of his favourite targets. He attacked them for being lazy, like "those who lean over a desk trying to pick up some chick while you're waiting for service."

Waters often went beyond official policy statements to publicly promote other policies for the party. He denounced Alberta government policy forbidding the export of water. "We're quite prepared to send our renewable resources out of the country — coal, gas, and minerals ... Water is a renewable resource. If we have a great control of masses of water, we should consider very seriously using water as an export commodity."

Waters's involvement in at least four right-wing political groups pre-dated his key role in the Reform Party. He was a member of the elite Advisory Committee of the National Citizens' Coalition (NCC), a business lobby group, until 1989. In 1990, the NCC presented Waters with the $10,000 Colin Brown Award, named after the Coalition's founder and Waters's personal friend. Waters was also on the board of the Fraser Institute, the Canadian Institute of Strategic Studies, and the Centre for Conflict Studies.

The Fraser Institute has been described as the most right-wing think tank in the country. *City Magazine*, in a 1978 article by Donald Gutstein on "Corporate Advocacy," showed that "Canada's largest corporations supported the institute because it had the appearance of objectivity, spent most of its efforts propagandizing and attacked rent controls, taxes, regulating property, and supported unlimited profits through laissez-faire economics."

The Vancouver-based organization regularly calls for the privatization of education, lower tax rates for the rich, and the slashing of social programs. A recent study revealed the impact it has had on Social Credit policy in B.C. Their policies on cuts to social programs and education, government size, rent controls and restrictions on public sector unions revealed a "striking similarity" to the government's. Its trustees have represented Canada's largest corporations, whose total assets amounted to $248 billion with sales of $76 billion. Among the corporations with multiple representation are the Royal, Imperial, and TD banks; CP Enterprises; and Genstar. The Thompson and Southam newspaper chains, Maclean-Hunter, BCTV, and Premier Cablevision are all associated with and contribute to the Fraser Institute.

The Canadian Institute of Strategic Studies is a military think tank which operated for years as a lobby group for increased military spending and a hard line on the Soviet Union. Board members tend to be either academics or corporate executives. Some recent members include Brian Hay, until recently a key Reform Party organizer, and Conrad Black and Hal Jackman, two Bay street millionaires who hosted a black-tie dinner for Preston Manning in the fall of 1990.

The Centre for Conflict Studies is another right-wing military think tank specializing in "low intensity conflict" studies — in layman's terms, military intervention in Third World countries. It was founded by Maurice Tugwell, a former British Army major and expert in counter-insurgency.

But it is the National Citizens' Coalition that has the strongest ties to the Reform Party and most closely parallels its political objectives.

The National Citizens' Coalition

The connections between the National Citizens' Coalition and the Reform Party go back a long way. Their political agendas are virtually identical: deficit reduction, restriction of immigration, ending universal social programs, lowering taxes for corporations and high-income earners, and ending national medicare. Colin Brown, the founder of the NCC, began his conservative crusade in 1967 with a full-page ad in the *Globe and Mail* attacking the federal Liberal government's plans for a national medicare scheme.

At the same time, Ernest Manning and his son were launching Ernest's book, *Political Realignment*, calling for a social conservative party. According to Norm Ovenden of the *Edmonton Journal*, Ernest was one of the "moving forces behind the creation of the [NCC] and a founding member when the organization was incorporated in 1975." He remained on the Advisory Council for many years. He was joined on the founding board by his friend and former Socred national party leader, Robert Thompson and by Ontario Conservative premier, John Robarts.

As is the case with many of the organizations the two Mannings have been involved with, the NCC is extremely secretive. It refuses to reveal the sources of its funding — its 1991 budget is $2.4

million — or any of the names of its reported membership of 39,000. But a reading of its publications does occasionally list the names of its governing Advisory Council and reveals that it is supported by people drawn from the elite of Canadian business. An examination of council members over several years shows chairs and members of the boards of directors of the Canadian Imperial Bank of Commerce, the Bank of Montreal, Goodyear, Brascan, Canadian Pacific, Royal Trust, Bell Telephone, Stelco, Abitibi, Quebec's Power Corporation, and MacMillan Bloedel. In addition, the council has had board members from eight major insurance companies, seven advertising agencies, and fifty lesser corporations.

The National Citizens' Coalition seems to have almost un-limited funding for fighting campaigns in the interests of big business. It spent $200,000 in a key 1984 campaign fought against Bill C-169, a bill passed by all three political parties in 1983. Intended to prevent third parties from spending money in federal elections, it would have avoided the kind of spending done by business-funded political action committees in the U.S. The NCC won its court case. That victory allowed for millions to be spent by big business in support of the free trade deal during the last three weeks of the 1988 election.

It also mounted two successful campaigns against progressive tax reform: against Edgar Benson's proposed reforms in 1969-70 and again in 1980 against Allan MacEachen's. It spent $700,000 fighting the National Energy Program and Monique Bégin's Canada Health Act (still the basis for health care in Canada) in 1984. It took out full-page ads across the country asking Canadi-ans "So ... how would you like your open heart surgery done by a civil servant ... Or your gall bladder done by a bureaucrat." It went on to warn that "People would die ... " because of the new Act.

The campaign against the National Energy Program was so successful that Alberta became the most lucrative province for NCC fund-raising — an unnamed Calgary millionaire reportedly funded the opening of a Calgary office. The attack on health care failed, but another campaign — against the immigration of Viet-namese boat people — succeeded.

The attack on non-white immigration was typical of the NCC's tactics: choose a single-issue campaign, use full-page ads designed to fan public opinion, and wait for the letters to flow into Ottawa. In fact, the ads were inaccurate: the NCC claimed that each of the 50,000 Vietnamese would sponsor 15 of their relatives, leading to "at least 750,000 people in Canada in the not too distant future." The actual number of sponsored relatives was about 40,000.

Colin Brown's critique of the Conservative Party under Diefenbaker and Stanfield was similar to the Mannings': he considered the party socialist and left it in the early 1970s. In 1979, at the same time that Preston Manning was heading up his second ill-fated social conservative effort — the Movement for National Political Change — Brown and the NCC contributed to the demise of Joe Clark's government by mounting an aggressive ad campaign against Clark on a number of issues, including Vietnamese immigration.

And while the NCC spent $200,000 protecting the right of large corporations to intervene directly (with shareholders' money) in elections, it has spent over half a million dollars to prevent labour unions from spending members' dues for political purposes. In the Merv Levigne case, which they lost in the Supreme Court in June, 1991, they claimed such spending ($5.16 a year out of $338 in union dues) violated Levigne's rights under the Charter of Rights and Freedoms.

While Stan Waters was on the Advisory Council, the Coalition spent $840,000 in the 1988 election attacking Ed Broadbent as "Very, very scary." The campaign was a dismal failure, but demonstrated that wealthy Canadian interests were prepared to spend big money to influence election results.

There is no evidence that there are any direct ties between the Reform Party and the NCC. With virtually identical objectives and many personal ties overlapping the two organizations, formal ties would be redundant.

Stan Waters's son, Mark Waters, is also closely tied to the NCC and was recently hired to head up a front group, Albertans for Responsible Government. The ARG's sole purpose is to pressure the Alberta government to allow for "citizen-initiated referendums ... binding on the provincial government." Says Mark Waters, "Alberta is just the first step. If successful, the NCC will move the initiative into other provinces and hopefully onto the federal stage ... "

Besides the Waters's connection, there is also Eric Kipping, a former Conservative cabinet member in New Brunswick. He is a founding member of the NCC and a member of its Advisory Council. He is a key organizer for the Reform Party in the Atlantic provinces and attended the 1991 Assembly, pleading with the delegates to expand across the country.

Another NCC member prominently associated with the Reform Party, and a key-note speaker at the assembly, is Bill Gairdner, author of *The Trouble with Canada,* a book promoting many of Reform's policies and prominently reviewed in the NCC's news-letter, *Consensus.* Gairdner is one of the party's most frequent guest speakers at rallies and his views are examined in more detail later.

David Somerville, the NCC's current president and long its key organizer, has attended every major Reform meeting as an observer since the party was founded in 1987. Regarding the party, Somerville concedes, "We've obviously got a lot in common." In the April, 1991 issue of *Consensus,* Somerville is more open. In a front-page article, "A Prairie Fire Sweeps East," Somerville gives high praise to the party, stating that after hearing Preston Manning's assembly speech, "It was conceivable to think of him, for the first time, as Prime Minister Manning. I can predict with some confidence that the RPC will overtake the PCs ... " A Coalition poll in the summer of 1990 showed that 60 per cent of NCC members backed the Reform Party in English Canada.

As for the Reform Party's position on the connection with the NCC, Communications Director Ron Wood told the *Edmonton Journal* that the party welcomes a "tacit ally supporting the same issues. They've been expressing these concerns for a long time. It's only natural that people who have supported the NCC have since come over and are now actively supporting Reform."

Ted and Link Byfield and the *Report* Magazines

Ted Byfield, the original publisher of the *Alberta Report* magazine and the man who expanded it to include two other western magazines — *Western Report* and *British Columbia Report* — openly supports the Reform Party and Preston Manning. Long before Preston Manning presented himself to the *Alberta Report's* editorial board as the man to lead a new conservative party,

Byfield and his business associates had been looking and hoping for just such a party — and such a man.

The *Report* magazines can take a great deal of credit for the rapid rise in popularity of the Reform Party, particularly in Alberta and B.C. This is not to say all of the *Reports'* coverage is glowing — Ken Whyte and other reporters do cover the blemishes on occasion. But literally dozens of favourable articles as well as promotional editorials have been published in the three magazines since the party was founded in 1987. It was Ted Byfield who wrote and ran advertising supplements for the founding Vancouver meeting in several issues of the *Alberta Report* and gave the 1987 Assembly's key-note address.

In the spring of 1990, Byfield's media empire was on the brink of disappearing. Placed in receivership, the trio of magazines which had been so critical to Preston Manning's early success and his party's continued growth in Alberta were pulled out of the fire at the last minute by a wealthy oil man and one of his former executives. John Scrymgeour, the founder and former chairman of Westburne Oil, formerly one of the largest private oil companies in Alberta, put up "about a million and half," and his friend and former Westburne vice-president the same amount, according to Byfield. It still left the Byfields with about 30 per cent of the company and complete control over its editorial policies. Asked by Byfield what he wanted done with the magazines, Scrymgeour said, "Just keep doing what you're doing."

Rumours persist in Edmonton that Scrymgeour was asked by Manning supporters to save the magazines. Scrymgeour, who has lived in Bermuda for the past twenty years, denies supporting the Reform Party or being approached to save it. Byfield approached him but acknowledges the indirect role Scrymgeour played: "He's certainly supported us in what we're doing and we've been supporting it [the Reform Party]. So in that sense, he's given it support."

Link Byfield is Ted's son and publisher of the *Alberta* and *Western Reports*. While Link claims he is not a member of the party, he has written many editorials supporting it and Preston Manning. He is also the author of "Resolution One," a statement of the Reform Party's fiscal philosophy, which has become a kind of Reform commandment. (It states that all increases in federal revenue should be matched by reductions in spending until the budget is balanced.) The resolution was introduced to the party convention in 1989 with Link Byfield's name on it and backed by several constituency organizations.

Both Byfields have been criticized in the Alberta press for not making their political allegiances clear. Said Mark Lisac of the *Edmonton Journal*, "I kind of wish that Link and his dad would end their coy backroom associations and clarify ... " who they speak for.

No political party and no political leader can be held responsible for everyone who joins or identifies with his organization. But Ted and Link Byfield are not just members or supporters of the Reform Party — attracted off the street by the party's image or policies. They are key people in the history and ongoing growth of the party, had informal discussions with a number of millionaire Albertans about forming a party of the right, have easy access to the party's leader and central organization, and continue through their powerful media influence to promote the party in the West. They are, in short, among the few to whom Preston Manning listens and owes political debts. Their other associations and causes are therefore relevant to an examination of the Reform Party.

The Northern Foundation

The Northern Foundation was established in 1989, originally as a pro-South Africa group. One of its founding and current directors is Link Byfield. Since its establishment, however, the foundation has developed into a broad coalition of right-wing groups and individuals across the country. Howard Goldenthal, formerly a writer with Toronto's *Now* magazine, describes the foundation as a "clearing house" for right-wing groups and ideas, bringing together like-minded organizations in an attempt to consolidate and co-ordinate efforts at promoting conservatism.

The foundation's organizing pamphlet, "Standing up for Canada's Silent Majority" confirms that goal. It bemoans the fact that conservatives fought — "and mostly lost" — single issue battles in the 1970s and 80s and "laments ... what has become 'normal': ... turbans in the RCMP, destabilizing immigration policies, government funding to radical feminist and homosexual groups ... "

The foundation does not support any single political party; rather, it encourages "small-'c' conservatives ... to take control of the local riding associations of political parties" in order to revive small-'c' conservatism "as a moral and political force in Canada." It claims that "common-sense Canadians" are found in three groups: "economic conservatives, moral conservatives and social conservatives" who appreciate "Canada's British and Christian heritage and oppose forced bilingualism, destabilizing immigration policies and government-promoted official multiculturalism." It adopts the National Citizens' Coalition slogan: "More freedom through less government."

In most issues of its quarterly magazine, called *Northern Voice* (it was called *The Continuing Crisis*), the foundation donates a full page as a "free service" to conservative groups by advertising their policies and addresses. In the Fall, 1990 edition, it gave free space to the Reform Party, the Christian Anti-Communist Crusade, the Christian Heritage Party, the Confederation of Regions party, and the Mackenzie Institute for the Study of Terrorism, Revolution and Propaganda.

Other issues have featured REAL Women, the Freedom Party of Ontario, the National Action Committee on the Status of White Heterosexual Single Christian Men, the Alliance for the Preservation of English in Canada (APEC), and the Byfields' *British Columbia Report*.

The foundation's magazine carries a half-page ad in every issue for *The Phoenix*, a pro-white South Africa magazine, and regularly solicits support from members on special causes, from property rights to English language rights. Attacks on homosexuals and homosexual rights are frequent, including a call in the Winter, 1990 edition for "No Special Privileges for Homosexuals," which carried a special financial appeal for the fight against "tax dollars going to homosexual activists."

In its Spring, 1991 edition, it lists "thinkers and activists who are working for freedom." Among them are: David Somerville, of the NCC; Judy Anderson, of REAL Women; Ted Byfield; Link Byfield; Richard Pearman, who led the fight to have Sault Ste. Marie city council declare the city "English only"; Kenneth Hilborn of the NCC and pro-South Africa groups; columnist Barbara Amiel; and Michael Walker of the Fraser Institute.

It also had a special "salute" for seven political figures to whom they gave the special title "Northern" — three MPs, including Deborah Grey, and four party leaders: Elmer Knutson, Confederation of Regions; George Dance, Libertarian Party of Canada; Ed Vanwoudenberg, Christian Heritage Party; and Preston Manning, Reform Party of Canada.

The South Africa Connection

There is good reason to believe that groups sympathetic to South Africa have seen the party as an ally, especially in the days when trade sanctions, strongly supported by Canada, were proving damaging to the South African economy and its prestige.

That was in 1988-89. And it was during this period in particular that a number of pro-South African groups organized efforts to undermine Canadian policy and to spread pro-South African literature across the country. All of these groups had some degree of contact with the South African embassy in Ottawa: they ran the gamut from being set up by paid agents of the embassy to simply having long-term friendly relations with embassy staff, including ambassadors. Key individuals in those organizations have also played and continue to play important roles in the Reform party.

It is not surprising that these individuals and the South African embassy would see Reform as a friendly party. Stan Waters's frequent sympathetic references to South Africa and his warning that the country should be wary of one-man, one-vote democracy, identified the party in precisely this way. His attacks on Canada's policy of giving aid to black African countries and his labelling of them as despotic, corrupt dictatorships cast Waters as a hero for the extreme right.

William Gairdner, the man most often used as a key-note speaker by Preston Manning, is also an outspoken supporter of South Africa. In *The Trouble with Canada*, he repeatedly decries Canada's policy on South Africa and, like Waters, levels attacks on the "one-party dictatorships" of black African countries. He elevates South Africa to the unusual position of one of the "traditional" sources — along with Britain, Europe, the U.S., Australia, and New Zealand — of immigration to Canada.

Ted Byfield is also a prominent figure in the pro-South Africa community. He published a series of articles in his magazines

slamming Joe Clark for his pro-African National Congress policies. Byfield has also written for *International Conservative Insight*, a far-right foreign affairs magazine published by the
Canadian Conservative Centre and featuring articles by South
African ambassadors and many of Canada's right-wing journalists
— including Lubor Zink, Peter Brimelow, and Reform member
Doug Collins of Vancouver.

Preston Manning is not noted for commenting often on matters
relating to foreign relations. But he did tell his audience at the
Americas Society in New York that under a Reform government
Canada would be a better ally for the U.S. Closer ties with the
U.S. is enshrined as one of the party's "principles." By leaving
the area of foreign affairs policy out of his speeches, he effectively
assigned to Stan Waters, the only other major spokesman for the
party, the job of speaking for the party on this topic.

Waters's military background and his business connections got
the attention of pro-South Africa activists long before he became
the external affairs spokesman for the Reform Party. And that
attention paid off for both the party and Stan Waters. Arthur Child,
the president of Burns Meats, knew Waters probably since the
Reform senator arrived in Calgary in 1975. As head of the Canada
West Foundation (CWF), Child would have met Waters through
the Mannix family — Waters's employer and founder of the
CWF.

Child has openly supported South Africa "for twenty years"
and is the only Canadian to have been awarded the Order of Good
Hope, a medal that the South African government reserves for
those who do outstanding service for the country. Child donated
$2,000 to Waters's Senate campaign. He is also on the board of
the Canadian-South African Society (CSAS).

The CSAS was founded in 1979 and was involved, says Child,
in "trying to counteract the anti-South African sentiment in Ottawa — to put it simply, we were friends of South Africa." The
group met with representatives of the South African government
both in Ottawa and at the consulates in Toronto and Montreal. But
mostly the group was involved in propaganda work: "We distributed information on South Africa — mostly to MPs," said
Child. "Most of the literature was probably from South Africa."

The Canadian-South African Society was founded to bring
together Canadian and American subsidiary business interests in-

vesting in South Africa: about seventy-five percent of Canadian direct investment in South Africa is made by subsidiaries of U.S. companies. Their profit levels are high — often twice their returns from comparable ventures in Canada — due to their ability to pay extremely low wages and almost no benefits to black labour.

CSAS received almost all of its funding from the South African Foundation, a trade promotion group based in South Africa and funded by its corporate sector. The CSAS still exists; at least Arthur Child still pays the token membership fee of "ten or twenty dollars a year." But it ended its high-profile activity in 1985 when the media discovered that one of its members was H. E. Sauvé, husband of Jeanne Sauvé, who was then governor general.

The 300 members of the CSAS were mainly from large corporations, but there were also academics, churchmen, and a Quebec Superior Court judge. One of these is Professor K. H. W. Hillborn of the University of Western Ontario in London. He was on the board of directors and is a regular contributor to the right-wing foreign affairs magazine *International Conservative Insight*. He is one of the people honoured in the Northern Foundation's *Northerner* magazine, and is on the president's council of the National Citizens' Coalition. A recent member of the Reform Party, Hillborn hopes Reform foreign policy will be fleshed out "with all this orientation towards the likes of the ANC with its strong Communist component ... foreign aid should go only to countries not practising socialism."

Most of the thirty-member board are from Ontario and points east, but a few were from the West. One of these was Norman Wallace of Saskatoon. Wallace was a founding member of the Reform Party in Saskatoon's Clarke's Crossing constituency and has long had an interest in South Africa. He is a major contractor and is also on the board of the Potash Corporation of Saskatchewan, which sells to South Africa. He set up Eagle Staff Import Export Ltd. to further business ties with South Africa.

Wallace created considerable controversy in 1987 when he and others involved in a group called the Indian Business Development Association put up money for a South African tour for five Saskatchewan Indian leaders. While the trip was ostensibly to promote the sale of wheat to South Africa, it was also intended to give the Pretoria regime a public relations weapon. In the end, only one of the five made the trip, though his presence alone was used as a state show piece — using aboriginal conditions in Canada to demonstrate the Canadian government's hypocrisy.

Wallace cultivated a friendship with South African ambassador Glenn Babb and was instrumental in introducing him to other Saskatoon businessmen during a Babb tour to Saskatchewan in March, 1987. But as active as he was, Wallace was not the most prominent South Africa supporter to join the Reform Party early on. That title belongs to Donovan Carter, a former television broadcaster in Calgary, who now lives in Parksville on Vancouver Island.

Carter was identified as a paid agent of the South African embassy by the program "The Fifth Estate" in November, 1989. He was a member of a Calgary group called the Western Canadian Society of South Africa. He was also the host of a TV show called "South Africa Report," which used promotional tapes shipped from South Africa, when he was hired by the embassy in Ottawa. Carter discussed his work with Patrick Evans, the embassy's First Secretary, and they decided that the most effective way to undermine Canadian policy was to set up "friends of South Africa" front groups across the country. Carter eventually set up a network of nine such organizations. One was the Winnipeg South African Society.

His operation fell apart when two of his recruits from Winnipeg, Geoff Shaw and Ihor Wichacz, got increasingly worried about the tasks they were assigned and went public. At first they were simply engaged in letter-writing campaigns. They used their own and other peoples' names in letters sent to the editors of prairie newspapers and to the government in Ottawa. Then they were asked to infiltrate anti-apartheid groups in Winnipeg. Worried about the legality of such activity, they spoke to contacts in CSIS (the Canadian Security Intelligence Service), who told them to go ahead. They carried out their task, gathering information (with Wichacz stealing some), from the Manitoba Coalition of Organizations Against Apartheid.

Aside from setting up the front groups and forwarding bills for their activities to the embassy in Ottawa, Carter also placed a full-page advertisement in Calgary newspapers just before the 1988 Winter Olympics, calling for fairness towards South African athletes. These ads, too, were paid for by the embassy.

Carter did not restrict himself to promoting South Africa in his work with the front groups. Through him, Shaw and Wichacz regularly received materials from a whole range of right-wing groups, particularly from the U.S. Wichacz told "The Fifth Estate": "I started getting a lot of this right-wing revisionist literature, stuff concerning Lyndon Larouche [the founder of the right-wing U.S. Labour Party], the Jewish conspiracies ... literature concerning the Holocaust that never happened. Literature, let's say, from Posse Comitatas [a violent right-wing group founded in California in 1969] and the KKK."

Carter's contract with the embassy ended in September, 1989, in part because Carter was too eager, even for the South African embassy. But he remains an enthusiastic supporter. Events in South Africa please him: "I think that South Africa is going to be a marvelous place to invest in. I think the answer to it will be an Afrikaner-Zulu government. The ANC are not representative ... Mandela is nothing more than a thug-terrorist."

Carter's views about Canadian policy "stupid ... it's just sickening" — are as extreme as ever and his views on the Commonwealth even more so: "[It] is the most revolting organization I've ever come across ... so hypocritical it's unbelievable."

Carter worked closely with Stan Waters after joining the party soon after its founding. "I've been sending him certain intelligence reports that we get from England. I happen to be associated with a group that is the best intelligence group in the world."

Carter confirms that it was Stan Waters who wrote the rather cryptic foreign policy, which appeared in the 1989 Blue Book, and also confirms that it was inspired by Canada's policy towards black African states and south Africa: "It most definitely was. I had letters from him saying that's what he thought."

Carter is prominent in his Comox/Alberni constituency association and chairs its committee on foreign affairs. He spent an hour talking with Preston Manning and was responsible for touring him around the constituency during Manning's September, 1991 visit to the island.

There is little doubt that many pro-South Africa activists have found their way into the Reform Party. Some have gained prominence. Maurice Tugwell, a friend of Stan Waters, is former head of the Center for Conflict Studies, whose board Waters sat on, and is currently head of the Mackenzie Institute for the Study of Terrorism, Revolution and Propaganda. An expert in counter-insurgency, he is also on the board of the Canadian-South African Society, and an active member of the Reform Party.

Angus Gunn, a Reform member in Vancouver, is president of the Canadian Buthelezi Educational Foundation, which has sent $100,000 to Buthelezi. Buthelezi is the Zulu chieftain whose organization, Inkatha, is a rival of Nelson Mandela's African National Congress. Inkatha is suspected of working closely with South African security forces and was exposed in 1991 as having received funding from the South African government. Gunn, a University of British Columbia professor, has written several sympathetic books about South Africa. He says he hopes the Reform Party will take a "pro-business" policy on South Africa. Gunn, like Stan Waters, has warned against South Africa adopting a one-man, one-vote democracy.

Doug Collins, the B.C. Reform candidate Preston Manning prevented from running in 1988, is a member of the Canadian Friends of South Africa Society in Vancouver and has written numerous sympathetic articles on South Africa. The *North Shore News* for which Collins is a columnist, was among the most compliant community papers targeted by Don Carter's South African network. Collins is also a member of CFAR, the Citizens for Foreign Aid Review, an extremist right-wing group founded by Paul Fromm, the same man who founded the violently right-wing Edmund Burke Society in the late sixties. While Manning felt obliged to stop the candidacy of the outspoken Doug Collins, he seems less concerned about Donovan Carter, a man whose activities — including organized spying for a foreign power — have been mostly clandestine and therefore not an embarrassment to the party.

Single Issue Organizations

The Reform Party acknowledges policies and objectives in common with the National Citizens' Coalition and willingly accepts free ads in *The Northern Voice,* alongside extremist groups. But it is uncomfortable with the attention it is getting from some political groups, particularly in Ontario where its membership base is still relatively narrow.

Ontario has always been home to a wide range of extreme right organizations, and a recently compiled list shows over ninety such organizations. Many of these are small political parties, some of which have a history of violence. Many others are single-issue groups, and it is some of these which have identified the Reform Party as their best hope of advancing their cause.

While Preston Manning and party officials in every province where Reform is active have persistently denied that the Reform Party is right-wing, these groups have just as persistently declared the party the best hope for the right-wing by encouraging their members to join the party and work at the constituency level to get their issues on the Reform agenda.

The National Firearms Association

David Tomlinson, of the Alberta-based National Firearms Association, the principal anti-gun control lobby in Canada, has placed repeated ads in the organization's magazines urging its members to join the Reform Party and get anti-gun control resolutions passed at the constituency level. It has provided a draft resolution for its members to place on Reform Party local meetings. The resolution promotes the notion of gun control by an advisory committee of gun owners and firearms dealers. While it is Alberta-based, the party's large membership in that province lessens the threat. The NFA's large Ontario membership could have an impact on newly organized chapters of the party.

The Heritage Front

This Ontario group is led by Wolfgang Droege, a forty-one-year-old naturalized Canadian from Germany who recently served two years in jail for plotting to overthrow the government of Dominica. His Front claims a membership of 300 people. It has distributed its literature, calling for an all-white Canada, in various Toronto locations, including public school grounds. The Canadian Jewish Congress has lodged hate literature charges against the Front.

Droege denies being racist, but does see Canada's immigration policy as a threat to whites, "the most precious force on this planet ... We believe that eventually white people will become a minority in this country because of our immigration policies ... We are racial nationalists working for the interests of whites everywhere."

Droege has given the Reform Party his seal of approval. "They have given us some hope," says the Heritage Front's leader.

The Alliance for the Preservation of English in Canada (APEC)

Of all the Ontario organizations labelled "extremist," the Alliance for the Preservation of English in Canada (APEC) figures most prominently in the fortunes of the Reform Party. The evidence suggests a kind of love-hate relationship between the party and the virulently anti-French, anti-Quebec organization. While many in the upper echelons of Reform fear being associated with APEC and vigorously deny any such connection, there is a compelling attraction between the two. APEC realizes that it cannot achieve its objectives on its own and recognizes in the Reform Party a political vehicle for those objectives. And the party must look at the 41,000 members of APEC (38,000 in Ontario; the rest in British Columbia and Alberta) with envy. The prominent role of a "tough stand on Quebec" in Reform's policy makes these two organizations natural allies.

The Reform Party's stance on negotiations with Quebec is ambiguous when it comes to detail: it simply emphasizes that it will not tolerate special status and that it would be a very tough bargainer if it were in government. Reading between the lines, however, suggests that such a tough stance would necessarily look very much like APEC's.

Where the Reform Party is ambiguous, APEC is not: its conditions for the separation of Quebec are very explicit. If Quebec were to separate, it would be very much reduced from its current territory. APEC's separate Quebec would be deprived of the huge northern area that was once part of Rupert's Land; would be obliged to provide a "corridor of sovereignty" between Ontario and the Atlantic provinces; and would be obliged to allow "regional referenda" on separation in eastern and western Quebec and other smaller areas. APEC quotes Section 42(1) of the Constitution Act (1982) to back its claim that Canada has the right to partition Quebec. It promotes and distributes a book entitled *Partition: The Price of Quebec's Independence*.

Behind APEC's negotiating position is a much tougher stance — spoken but not always written down as policy. That is, that Canada has the right to "self-defence" in keeping Canada together. According to James A. Morrison, chairman of APEC, "Quebec belongs to Canada; it's not just Quebec's. It should not be allowed to separate ... The use of force in the defence of the Constitution is legitimate self-defence."

APEC's position on the language issue is virtually identical to the Reform Party's policy, although it is expressed in stronger terms. Both would have one official language — English — for the country as a whole with French being permitted in Parliament, the Supreme Court and the legislature and courts of Quebec. Both call for a language policy based on freedom of speech and reject any comprehensive language policy; both call for an end to bilingual criteria in the federal civil service.

Where there are no formal connections between the Reform Party and APEC there is, says Morrison, " ... a tacit agreement between us that we not interfere with each other." Yet Reform Party headquarters, and more specifically Preston Manning, were willing to allow APEC people to occupy key posts in its Ontario organization at its most sensitive, early stages. At least two of the people on the original five-person organizing committee, Michael Dean and Ernst Neisel, were members, and a third, Ron Peterson, supports them. "From what I've seen of APEC and from my experience, I see nothing wrong with what they're saying."

Anti-Abortion Groups

The Reform Party's policy of promising referenda on moral issues such as abortion, and Preston Manning's stated preference for a constitutional amendment to protect the rights of the fetus have caught the eye of all the anti-abortion groups in the country — and Ontario is no exception. While there has been no public call for members to join Reform, at least some party members have expressed concern that many have done so.

Confederation of Regions, Christian Heritage Party, Western Canada Concept

While these political parties are still active in various parts of the country, there is evidence that they are not averse to having dual memberships in the Reform Party. The Reform constituency organization in Peterborough, taken over by a group of CoR members is a recent example and is described in more detail in the next chapter.

William Gairdner

William Gairdner is a former professor of philosophy and literature, essayist and businessman. He is a member of the National Citizens' Coalition and one of the people praised in the Northern Foundation's publication as a leading activist for freedom. He is also a member of the Reform Party, was one of the key-note speakers at the Reform Party's 1991 Assembly, and has been featured at many of the party's rallies in Ontario.

Bill Gairdner's book is described by the Fraser Institute's Michael Walker as "a caring and comprehensive assault" on Canada's social welfare mentality. It has become, in the words of Southam News's Mike Trickey, "the de facto manifesto for Preston Manning's Reform Party." It has sold out several times, and at the party's 1991 Assembly in Saskatoon, hundreds of members lined up to buy it and have it autographed.

It speaks to Reformers in a way that Reform Party policy no longer does. One of the chapters is called "The Silent Destruction of English Canada: Multiculturalism, Bilingualism and Immigration." On immigration, Gairdner speaks of "invading cultures" and of implementing quotas on "non-traditional" immigrants. He describes traditional immigrants as those from "the U.K., the U.S.A., New Zealand, Australia and South Africa" and discounts non-whites from the United States and South America. In his book, Gairdner created a chart allegedly showing that the percentage of Canadians claiming they are of British extraction will decline to zero by the year 2051 unless "this alarming trend is reversed. In two hundred and fifty years Canada could be a Chinese nation." Gairdner also writes: "Surely any nation has the right to defend itself against demographic capture, or, if you prefer, against passive racial or cultural takeover."

"Immigrants to Canada," says Gairdner in his book, "should be instructed in the core heritage and culture of this nation, which is Judeo-Christian, Greco-Roman and Anglo-European. And they should be expected to assimilate to that culture." He speaks at length, as well, on the conspiracy against English Canada in a section entitled "Master Plan for the Francization of Canada."

While William Gairdner's book is not official party policy, according to Norm Ovenden, of the *Edmonton Journal*, Manning "turned down several invitations to dissociate himself from the author" by reporters and open-line callers who denounced Gairdner's views during Manning's visit to Toronto in June, 1991.

Sir Roger Douglas

Sir Roger Douglas was the New Zealand Labour government's finance minister who, in 1984, implemented the kind of radical "restructuring" that the Reform Party policy recommends for Canada. Together with Gairdner, he was one of the key-note speakers at the Reform Party's annual assembly in Saskatoon in April, 1991. He described to the assembly his ten principles for implementing structural reform. The key principles:

> 1 The conventional view is that consensus support must exist for reform before you start ... Consensus for "quality decisions," therefore, does not arise before they are made and implemented. It develops progressively after they are taken.
> 2 The second principle ... is to implement reform in quantum leaps using large packages. Do not try to advance a step at a time. You have to define your objectives clearly and move towards them by quantum leaps otherwise the interest groups will drag you down.
> 3 The third principle is that speed is essential ... the bureaucratic system will hold you back anyways. Even at maximum speed the program will take you some years to implement.

4 The fourth principle is once you start the momentum, never let it stop rolling ... until you've completed the total program. The fire of your opponent is much less accurate if they have to shoot at a rapidly moving target.

5 The fifth principle is consistency. Take the first step early and make it a big one ... to convince the community that this time somebody really does mean business. When you lack credibility, people will refuse to change.

None of these principles is written down anywhere in Reform Party policy and just because an invited speaker makes suggestions for effecting structural change does not necessarily mean his host will take the advice or even agree with it.

Yet, Douglas was introduced by Preston Manning, the only assembly speaker to be so honoured. And Manning told the delegates:

> There are three basic reasons why we have invited Sir Roger Douglas to be with us ... and three reasons why we as Reformers should pay close attention to what he has to say ... Sir Roger is an authority in fiscal reform ... and has advocated and promoted many of the fiscal reforms necessary to deal with the fiscal crisis that is facing this country ... Secondly ... he has been in a position to actively implement those reforms. He is not only a reformer in word, he is a reformer in deed. Sir Roger deregulated the financial sector, phased down agricultural and other subsidies, ... phased out import controls and drastically reduced tariff levels. [He] instituted a 10% flat rate consumption tax [a G.S.T.] with virtually no exemptions. Thirdly, Sir Roger accomplished all these things ... as a minister of a labour party in government.

What Preston Manning and Roger Douglas did not tell their audience was the story of the impact of Douglas's policies on the people of New Zealand. Saskatchewan political economist, Dr. John Warnock, travelled to New Zealand to study the effects of what New Zealanders dubbed "Rogernomics." The figures tell a story of "devastation" — a word used by New Zealand's own agriculture minister to describe the state of agriculture in four years after the "reforms": a 40 per cent drop in farm income; a 50 per cent drop in the value of farm land; a policy of paying 3,000 farmers incentives of $45,000 to leave the land and the suggestion that another 15,000 (out of 79,000) should follow them. Unemployment, which had been 4 per cent before Douglas's reforms, jumped to over 12 per cent in just over a year and is still increasing.

Douglas completely eliminated regional development grants and subsidies to rural services. Says Warnock, "They had things like subsidized petroleum — regardless of where you were the price was the same — subsidized train service, bus service, airport service. They privatized all these things and the prices immediately skyrocketed." A massive de-population of the countryside resulted, and approximately 40,000 New Zealanders per year have since left their country for Australia to find work since "restructuring" took effect.

Conclusion

You can tell a great deal about a person — and a political party — by who their friends are. This chapter describes some of the individuals and groups who support Preston Manning and his Reform Party. These organizations and associates were not chosen to represent a careful selection of the social classes, groups, or individuals who are close to or influence Preston Manning and his party. Rather, they are the key individuals and groups which do so. There are no others: no labour unions, farm organizations, women's groups, native leaders or their organizations, no non-governmental organizations concerned about health care or poverty in Canada, nor cultural groups worried about the state of the arts in Canada. There are no groups concerned about the loss of rural post offices, VIA rail, or cutbacks to the CBC. These groups do not see the Reform Party as addressing their concerns. And Preston Manning did not go to them when he decided to launch his "populist" party.

Yet these are important sectors of the population, which deserve to be consulted. They and their organizations have been in the forefront of the fight against Brian Mulroney: they are the "grassroots" of the discontent in Canada.

Preston Manning says in the Reform Party's 1990 policy Blue Book that the old "left-right-centre" politics in Canada is "disintegrating ... To the young especially, left-right-centre formulations are simply inadequate ... " Yet, judged by the standard definition of right-wing — that is, very conservative — that label fits the Reform Party and its policies. Moreover, Preston Manning's long-time goal of creating an ideologically consistent conservative party has to raise serious doubts about his claim to have escaped the old political "formulations."

This view is clearly widely held — widely held, at least, by those groups in Canada which readily acknowledge that they are right-wing. These groups are either encouraging their members to join Reform or are praising the party in their publications. A comparison of the objectives and policies of these organizations demonstrates that they are nearly identical to those of the Reform Party. No other party in Canada, including the Conservative Party, has attracted the kind of open support which these groups offer to the Reform Party.

Preston Manning insists that his party is not right-wing. And it is not the fault of a party or its leader if unwanted elements are attracted to the party in error. But even if all these organizations and individuals on the policital right are somehow mistaken about the politics of the Reform Party, by endorsing it, joining it, and financing it, they help make it a right-wing party. And if its leader, Preston Manning, does not take measures to correct a false impression of his party — such as disassociating himself from the extreme views of Bill Gairdner — then it is reasonable for observers of the party to conclude that, denials aside, the Reform Party is what it appears to be.

6

Managing the Membership

It's amazing what you can persuade them to do once you convince them that it's the leader who is telling them.

Stephen Harper, Policy Chief, Reform Party of Canada

When Preston Manning decided in 1967 to wait until the next populist movement emerged, his plan for that movement was clear and had been developed in close co-operation with his father: the populist movement would be harnessed to restructure the Canadian political party system through the creation of a conservative party of the right.

That objective, however, contained within it serious contradictions. The kind of popular discontent that Manning wanted to harness could never reflect the kind of ideological purity to which he was committed. In addition, the specifically western alienation he had to use to build his western base was only marginally useful outside the West and his plan all along was for a national party. Last, the conservative social and cultural policies, which the party would adopt and which Manning supported, would inevitably attract a volatile and extremist sector of the electorate.

Preston Manning would not have any problems with the powerful corporate sector which backed his free-market economic agenda, so long as he could deliver continued success. But he would face very complex problems with the membership of his party. To succeed he had eventually to attract a broad base — not only of members but of voters. Unless he could control the former, he would fail to attract the latter. Referring to troublesome members, Stephen Harper said, "They do more damage to us than any media outlet, any other party, and any real enemy can do."

The need to manage the membership of the party would prove to be Preston Manning's biggest and toughest task of 1990-1991. In part this was because the party suddenly took off on the strength of two issues which must have seemed like outright gifts from the Conservative government in Ottawa: Meech Lake and the Goods and Services Tax (GST).

Catching a Second Wave

The free trade deal with the U.S. might have reduced the Reform Party to another western protest party that flared up and quickly died off. It gave the oil companies almost everything they asked for and promised even more. It seemed to put to rest forever the historic western grievance over tariffs. And it spoke to the strong pro-American sentiment felt by those Albertans that the Reform Party hoped to attract to its fold.

But what the free trade deal did for Brian Mulroney's Conservatives was quickly undone by Meech Lake and the GST. More than any other province, these issues touched the rawest of nerves in Alberta. Mulroney's perceived "kow-towing" to Quebec with Meech Lake was reaffirmed in spades, and his back room dealing and "roll the dice" approach reinforced the feeling among Albertans that they had no voice in Ottawa. The fact that their own Conservative premier, Don Getty, supported the accord further alienated Tory supporters from their party and governments.

The failure of Meech Lake at least removed it as an active irritant. The GST, however, would prove to be the death blow to the Tories in Alberta and to a lesser extent the rest of the West. Alberta is the only province without a provincial sales tax and no credible political leader has dared suggest one. It has been a defining characteristic of Albertans' self-image as a people and province different from the others. Low provincial taxes have always appealed to that considerable portion of the Alberta electorate for whom freedom from "big government" was an issue.

For many Albertans, the GST was the final straw. By the end of the year, virtually every Tory MP in Alberta was in trouble. Many were denounced by party members at their own constituency association meetings. While the hated tax brought Brian Mulroney and his government to the lowest point in the polls of any government in Canadian history, it was a gift to Preston

Manning. In concert with Meech Lake, it virtually doubled his party's membership in a year.

While most of Manning's support was still in the West, the GST issue gave him an opening in the East that no other single issue could have provided. The GST quickly raised concerns about accountability and democracy. Mulroney's determination to ram the tax through drove Canadians everywhere to distraction. His hurried appointment of twenty-four Tory senators, including eight for whom he had to get the Queen's approval, outraged a population who had come to believe that the Senate was simply a repository for political bagmen — and further exacerbated discontent in Alberta where the idea of democratic reform of the Senate is strongest.

The two opposition parties in the Commons were powerless to stop Mulroney and seemed inept at responding to the outpouring of anger in any effective way. As a result they began to share some of the blame for the crisis. Into this unprecedented political dilemma came Preston Manning with virtually ready-made solutions.

The old Social Credit direct-democracy mechanisms suddenly had appeal beyond the borders of Alberta. The principles of accountability, of less party discipline on MPs, and of direct votes on issues like the GST began to have real resonance for tens of thousands of Canadians. Many even went beyond the Reform Party to draw more from the American experience — buttons calling for the impeachment of Mulroney began to appear.

By mid-1990, Manning faced the prospect of being able to attract a much broader base than he had hoped for even six months earlier. Always a man to recognize the necessity of striking at the right time, the nation-wide unrest presented Preston Manning with an irresistible temptation to move East quickly.

While the 1989 Reform Party Assembly had begun the process of revising party policy to make its orientation less western and more mainstream, the party membership displayed an extremely narrow demographic base. As more than one observer has noted, Reform meetings present a "sea of white heads." The impression that party membership is made up largely of older, white, middle-class men was confirmed by a survey of the 1989 Assembly.

Based on a 75 per cent response to the survey, the membership profile showed that 72 per cent were men, 38 per cent were retired,

48 per cent were over 60, and only 19 per cent were between 30 and 44 years old. Under 2 per cent said they were students. Two-thirds of those not retired were either in business, professional, or management jobs. Seventy-five per cent had post secondary education or training. Just 15 per cent had jobs that paid wages. And for a party which claims to be the child of Social Credit, it had very few members who were farmers. Only 7 per cent identified agriculture as an important issue. In fact, the party is so urban-oriented that the survey neglected to include "farmer" under the occupation question. Twenty per cent identified themselves as ex-Social Crediters and 76 per cent said they were former Conservatives. While Preston Manning certainly had the numbers to claim a base, it was extremely narrow, politically and demographically.

Preston Manning had tapped into and nurtured powerful forces of western discontent in order to build his conservative project. His way had been made easier by a prime minister reviled in much of the country. But his calculated appeal to western sentiment was now part of his dilemma, and it wasn't simply worry about going East and the image of eccentricity. The party had deliberately used wide-spread anger at Don Getty to get Deborah Grey and Stan Waters elected. The side effect of that strategy was a desire among a majority of Alberta Reform members to run provincially.

Having used both traditional western discontent and provincial politics to build support, Manning through 1990 and into 1991 faced the difficult task of weaning the membership from those sentiments without losing their support. This task, as well as putting in place consistent free-market social and economic policies, dominated Preston Manning's efforts through the last half of 1990 and into 1991.

He was well placed to accomplish all his objectives. Few doubt that Manning is the Reform Party's biggest asset. Calgary political scientist David Bercuson went even further: "There's no party without Preston."

Members recognized this as well. John Ogilvie, president of the MacLeod constituency in Alberta said: "The strength of the party is Preston and the Manning name." Another party member was even more perceptive about Manning's role from the beginning. Adrian Berry, a former Calgary alderman, assessed it this way:

"If we look backwards and look at the Reform Party, it wasn't a group picking a leader; it was a leader picking a group."

Calming the Eccentrics

Preston Manning has given a whole generation of ultra-conservative westerners something that nearly a dozen protest groups and parties had failed to provide: the credibility and proven capacity to make an impact on the national stage. He promises them, their grievances, their fears, and their aspirations legitimacy. And for that, Reform Party members have proven willing to give a great deal in return.

Preston Manning has shown an uncanny ability to appeal to a number of groups. He speaks in such a way that very different people get very different messages from what he says — messages they want to hear. Fred Lennarson, an Edmonton consultant and long-time Manning observer, described this ability. "When Manning calls for a 'balanced' immigration policy, the racists hear 'We'll keep the Pakis and the niggers out.' Those hoping for something reasonable hear just that. 'Balanced' is a code word for true believers and a soothing reassurance to those who want reasonableness and moderation." A number of reporters covering Reform meetings have commented that they are more like revival meetings than political events, with Preston Manning as the preacher.

In terms of keeping the so-called "rednecks" in check, Manning's prestige and credibility served him well. So long as the racist language of the extreme elements did not enter into party policy, Manning could, as he has done repeatedly, get a lot of mileage from quoting his father: "A bright light attracts bugs."

The occasional outburst about "low blacks and low hispanics" (from an Alberta member) could be handled. And because the party had only two high-profile spokesmen — Manning and Stan Waters — there was a maximum of control over "official" party statements.

Whether or not this two-man show was orchestrated by Manning, it has very definite parallels with the Social Credit Party's view of mass party politics. Both Aberhart and Ernest Manning saw a restricted role for party members. They were to carry out two tasks — organizing and proselytizing. The rest, particularly

policy and the choosing of election candidates, were the prerogative of the party leader, his executive, and key advisors. The
Reform Party follows very much in its predecessor's footsteps.

Manning's personal prestige and his role as almost a parish
pastor among his flock gave him great power to soothe and quiet
individual zealots in the party. But he would need more than
personality to stop the rush into provincial politics. Manning tried
to play down the popular support for provincial politics, telling
the *Edmonton Journal* in February, 1990: "If you're a populist
party, you know you've got your own strategies, but if a third of
your people start talking about this sort of thing, we can't just
dismiss it."

In fact, Manning knew when he made that statement that nearly
twice as many members — and 48 per cent of Alberta voters —
wanted the party to contest the next provincial election. A party
poll of 5,000 members done just the month before found 60 per
cent in favour despite the fact that he had already urged caution
on the question.

Rumblings of Grassroots Discontent

By the fall of 1990, the provincial politics issue was turning into
the most divisive issue in the party and one which was breaking
into public view. Worse, the issue was focusing attention on the
party's central office and its alleged desire to control the membership.

Dissidents in the party, those angered at what they considered
"manipulation" of the provincial politics issue as well as Manning's eagerness to "go East," openly claimed the party was being
run by a "Calgary clique." "A lot of people are frustrated — we're
seeing the inevitable erosion of grassroots politics into a smaller,
more dominating group at the top," said Norm Gaskarth, a director
of the Wild Rose constituency, north of Calgary.

The charges against the party office were reminiscent of a
previous controversy which occurred in 1988. That also burst
loudly into the public arena. Doug Collins, a Vancouver broadcaster and columnist known for his right-wing views, had been
nominated by acclamation for the constituency of Capilano-
Howe Sound. Manning had warned constituency officials against
the nomination and had sought written and public assurances from

Collins repudiating racism. When Collins and his officials refused to comply, Manning, on his own and with questionable authority, refused to sign the nomination papers. While the action may have put Manning in a good light outside the party, it rankled inside, and not just in B.C.

The "clique" which was being criticized in 1990 consisted of Manning and four of his staff members. One of the key members was thirty-two-year-old Stephen Harper, a founding member of the party, its Chief Policy Officer, and the man who became known as Manning's chief political lieutenant. Though only a staff member, he often made speeches and was one of the two people, the other being Waters, whom Manning trusted to speak for the party. He spent four years working for the oil industry after arriving in Alberta from Toronto in 1978. Formerly active in the Tory party, from 1981-86, he was legislative assistant to Tory MP Jim Hawkes in 1985-86. Besides drafting the party's foundation policy document, "Achieving Economic Justice in Confederation," he also a ran for Reform in 1988, in Calgary West.

Diane Ablonczy, the party chairman, Gordon Shaw, a former Calgarian responsible for organizing in B.C., and financial officer Cliff Fryers, a corporate tax lawyer and one of the original Calgary group who gave Manning the business seal of approval, rounded out the group targeted by members as wielding too much power. They had easy access to Manning and, as staff people, worked closely with him on a day-to-day basis.

The charges of elitism and control of the party by a Manning clique struck a very sour note in an otherwise spectacular rise in party fortunes. Whether because of this serious problem or according to some long term plan, Preston Manning began in late 1990 to adopt — and adapt — many of the old Social Credit "direct democracy" techniques to persuade the party membership away from policies and directions he disagreed with. The various techniques would be applied to selected issues which he felt critical to his goals.

Managing the Members: Task Forces and the Leader's Word

The most urgent issues were the provincial politics issue, eastern expansion, and the GST. Manning had gained tremendous support in Alberta on this last issue. His fierce opposition to the tax led people to believe that the party intended to repeal it. In party surveys, members were asked to choose between alternative tax sources (half wanted a flat tax; almost a third increased corporate taxes). Repealing the GST, however, would have conflicted directly with Manning's conservative economic strategy. Another important issue was a Code of Conduct for all nominees for party election candidates: a screening process that would help prevent another Doug Collins incident. A third area of concern was the party's own constitution, which many members wanted to amend to give more power to constituencies. Yet another issue was the question of immigration policy — a political hot potato which Manning did not want to be juggling when he took his party into Ontario.

Despite the charges of elitism, the process of refining and shifting party policy was assigned to an even smaller group within the inner circle: the Party Policy Committee (PPC). The PPC was an appointed committee of the party's Executive Council. Chaired by Preston Manning and responsible to him as leader, the committee seemed designed to give him as much power as possible to control the policy of the party and the process by which it was determined. Its key members, besides Manning, were party policy co-ordinator Stephen Harper and Stan Waters — two men who had enjoyed critical policy roles from the beginning. Deborah Grey was also a member. The ten remaining party members were mostly unknowns. Not a single member sat on either the 1989 or 1990 national Executive Council, so that the only overlap in membership with the elected executive of the party was Manning himself.

One of the mechanisms Manning and his advisors used to get the party's policy house in order was the task force. It would become a principal tool to broaden the policy-making process but at the same time retain control over it. Most of the dozen or so task forces, appointed by the PPC, simply worked on policy areas and reported their findings back to the PPC. It would use the reports to write policies for the 1991 Assembly. While policies also came from the constituency level, those generated by the PPC's task forces dominated the assembly and the new policy book. Because they involved people picked for their knowledge of the area of policy they were examining, their work took on greater authority than policies developed by rank and file members.

The Task Forces

The first task force appointed was to examine the question of provincial politics. Its task reflected the consistency with which Preston Manning was pursuing the principles he and his father established in the mid-1960s. Partisanship was not to be allowed to interfere with the goal of social conservatism. Where genuinely conservative governments existed, the Reform Party would not interfere. But the Alberta Conservatives fell short of the mark. The party would have to reform itself to qualify.

To that end, Manning sent Premier Don Getty a copy of the task force terms of reference inviting his response. He had said previously that one of the determining factors in the provincial politics decision was whether or not the provincial Tories were prepared to " ... fall more into line with their right-wing cousins in Reform," according to Richard Helm of the *Edmonton Journal.*

Only the task force on provincial politics held membership meetings to gauge members' feelings on the issue. Simply changing policy on these key issues on the basis of reports by a committee chosen by Manning and his advisors would not have been enough to persuade those with strong contrary views to change their minds.

Before the formal task force meetings on provincial involvement were held and media events set up to announce them in Calgary and Edmonton, the party held a trial run in Camrose. Manning himself attended, intervening occasionally to ask a question or to direct discussion. The end result according to *Edmonton Journal* reporter Mark Lisac, reflected the same ambiguity on the issue as the October, 1989 Assembly. The members voted 51 to 42 to concentrate on federal politics for the time being and then voted 59–40 to enter provincial politics immediately.

Before the task force meetings were held, Manning took the surest route available to guarantee that the provincial politics issue would go his way: he announced publicly that no matter what the party decided, he would be sticking with national politics. The party used the trial run task force meeting at Camrose to fine tune the process. Each of the ten remaining meetings would use the same format: a task force member (all members were chosen by Manning and the PPC) would facilitate the meeting. Fourteen questions would be addressed with five minutes allotted to each for discussion and voting, within small discussion groups. The results for all the small groups would be added up to determine the overall position of those attending. There would be no plenary session where open discussion of the broad question could take place.

Saturday Night's Ian Pearson attended one of the meetings, at Red Deer, with 140 Reformers in attendance. After dealing with the likelihood of the provincial Tories changing their ways (assessed at fair to poor), the ten members in his group turned to the main issue.

Six Reformers thought the prospects for a new provincial party were good, four said fair. The questionnaire then asked, "What are the prospects for securing the workers, volunteers, campaign managers and qualified candidates necessary to launch a new provincial political party within the next two years?" Still optimistic, the group voted: good - 4, fair - 4, poor - 2. On the question of raising enough money, six thought the chances were good; two said fair.

Then came the key question: "What are the prospects for securing a trustworthy and dynamic provincial political leader capable of leading a new political party and a provincial government?" Still hopeful, four answered good and five fair.

Despite the relatively favourable answers to individual questions, the final vote gave Preston Manning what he wanted: nine out of ten said the party should not enter provincial politics at this time. The meeting as a whole voted, 106 to 27, to support their leader and stay out of provincial politics. Eight of the other nine meetings had the same result. The task force recommended that the Reform Party restrict itself to federal politics.

Said Pearson of the results: "Manning had brilliantly persuaded the grassroots of the party to change their reasoning and follow him — while they believed that they arrived at the opinion themselves." Lethbridge political scientist Peter McCormick sat on the task force as an observer.

The questionnaire was very skillfully done. Only one meeting failed to come up with the obvious answers they'd been fed ... The party leadership is very sincere in getting this kind of feedback, but they know the kind of answers they'd like to hear. The task force drew up the questions but there's no doubt that Preston had most of the suggestions and they just went along with him.

The issue of whether or not the party would run candidates in the East was far from over: it would come up again at the 1991 Assembly and would be subject to an internal party referendum. As well, the provincial politics issue wasn't dead and would still cause Manning considerable grief, not only in Alberta but in B.C. He had only taken the first of several steps to pull the majority of the party in his direction.

But it wasn't just the question of national versus provincial or West versus East which motivated Preston Manning. It was also a question of policies and platform. Manning had to have policies in place which had appeal broader than that determined by western alienation and moderate enough to escape the label of extremist. Equally important for Manning, for whom consistent political principles were nearly the equivalent of religious doctrine, his policies had to be uniformly free market in the areas of social and economic policy.

And they had to be in place for the April, 1991 Assembly of the party. That assembly, possibly the last before a federal election, would be the critical test of Manning and his party. Media scrutiny would be intense, looking for signs of the so-called "lunatic fringe," watching the debate on eastern expansion and searching out signs of dissent on the issue of provincial politics. Party policies could also be under a microscope.

Straw Votes and Pseudo-Referenda

Manning and his closest advisors used a number of "direct-democracy" mechanisms in late 1990 and early 1991 to bring the membership on board on key policy issues before the April assembly. They used the party paper, *The Reformer*, as a straw vote vehicle, creating what it called a "Referendum Column." The party, said the preamble to the column, "would continue to use the Referendum Column to monitor the opinion of Reformers on important public policy issues." While it cautioned members not to mistake this "monitoring" for the official main ballots provided for in the party constitution, it was clearly intended to capitalize on the principle of direct democracy that the term *referendum* implied.

In the November/December, 1990 issue of *The Reformer*, the party used the Referendum Column to poll the party on the GST. The ballot gave two options: revoke the GST or revise the GST. There was no detail on what revisions would be made. The ballot was not secret — there was a blank space for the voter's party membership number. For many members, the survey was the first they had heard that revising the GST was being considered.

A one-page report to members, entitled "The GST ... Reformers Want Revision," gave the results: "nearly 1,000 ballots were received" and "35.5% voted to revoke but a majority of 65.5% voted to revise it." At this time, the party had a membership of 60,000. Of that total just over 1 per cent had voted to keep the GST. At the subsequent 1991 Assembly, both Stephen Harper and Preston Manning would use this "straw vote" in personal interventions in the GST debate.

In addition to the "Referendum Column," the party headquarters conducted other straw votes on selected issues. In none of the reports to members on this party polling was it explained how some issues were picked for polling while others were not. In a two-page hand-out given to members at the assembly, entitled "Reform Party Membership Survey," members were told, "In October 1990, Reform Party members were given the opportunity to express their opinions on a wide range of issues. The following is a selection of the responses received ... this is not a scientific survey, as the respondents were self-selecting ... "

The survey reports on a number of issues, pointing out that "roughly three quarters of Reformers" were satisfied with the demise of Meech Lake, that 90 per cent of all respondents "agreed that the Rest of Canada (outside of Quebec) should now initiate steps to develop a new constitution ... " This was Manning's personal view, stated several times publicly and in *The Reformer*. As with the other issues dealt with in the report, there was no indication of how many people responded to the survey: only round number percentages were given.

On the issue of "across-the-board cuts in federal government spending, approximately 30% ... favoured a 10% reduction, over 20% ... favoured 15% ... and between 25 and 30% wanted a 20% cut ... " On some issues no figures were given. The report simply stated that respondents "indicated" that spending on "bilingualism, funding of special interest groups, and ... multiculturalism should be the first to go."

The hand-out also reported on members' ranking of "Major National Concerns." The choices were provided by the party and included some of the standard issues found in any such survey: unemployment (it placed sixth out of nine categories), environment (fifth), and aboriginal issues (seventh). Some issues were seemingly chosen to strike favourite chords: the federal deficit (first place), "Lack of Trust in Political Leaders" (second place), and "Lack of National Spending" (last place).

A third method for garnering support for party practices was used in the controversial issue of the "Code of Conduct for Reform Party Members of Parliament." There had been public criticism by party members who claimed the comprehensive code was far too invasive. In order to reduce the impact and likelihood of such criticism at the 1991 Assembly, the party sent the draft of the code to all members. The report of the results, mailed three weeks before the assembly, indicated that, "To date, 6,014 Reformers have replied!" Ninety-six per cent supported the concept and the wording of the draft.

Preston Manning and his advisors showed a lot of enthusiasm for the mechanisms of direct democracy in building support for their policy objectives among the membership. But they were less enthusiastic about the prospect of the members using them. The resolutions coming in from the constituencies regarding the party's own constitution were radically democratic — calling for far more control over the party and its executive by the grassroots constituency organizations.

This presented a problem for Preston Manning in one area in particular: his decision to expand the party into eastern Canada. Manning had known all along that "western alienation" would not translate neatly into Ontario support, and his efforts at revising Reform policy was meant to deal with this problem. A more immediate and potentially explosive problem was the party's lack of effective influence over who would run their Ontario constituency organizations.

With nearly ninety separate right-wing organizations in the province, party headquarters was very concerned about establishing a reliable local leadership, free of extremist elements. Manning's tour in March, 1990, was intended to introduce the party to Ontario. While he did have a handful of reliable people guiding the formation of unofficial constituency associations, Ontario was unfamiliar territory and had more ridings than all four western provinces combined. It was a huge job.

Stephen Harper, Manning's chief political operative, was particularly worried. He had written to Robert Matheson, chairman of the party's task force on expansion, in late 1989 urging caution on the question:

> The extreme democratic nature of Reform Party constitutional structures gives small minorities a great deal of potential power and public relations influence if we decide to expand.
>
> In parts of Ontario where extreme right-wing fringes are well organized, it is my view that the Reform Party could easily be hijacked before it becomes well established.
>
> We should continue to explore expansion through trusted individuals and affiliated organizations until we have some trusted individuals in place. In the meantime, the party must evolve less dangerous structures … With a proper constitution, areas of low support should present no danger of either bad publicity or resource drain.

Preston Manning had decided to expand eastward despite the slow pace of organizing in Ontario in 1990. But he apparently shared the view that early expansion presented some real dangers. He moved personally to ensure that the party's constitution was "less dangerous." The party had repeatedly used its paper to inform the membership of Preston Manning's personal views on crucial matters. But this time it took the form of a personal two-page letter to all members.

Dated February 5, 1991, and titled "Leader's Comments on Proposed Reform Party Constitutional Amendments," Manning addressed the members in the first person. After a preamble explaining exactly what a "democratic, grassroots party" was, Manning told members "There are three (3) questions for members and delegates to ask:

> 1 Do the amendments support majority rule ... or do they raise the spectre of minority rule?
> 2 Do the amendments encourage and reward the participation of grassroots people ... or do they treat elected volunteers as if they are professional politicians?
> 3 Do the amendments encourage the Reform Party to serve the public or to serve its own internal needs?

Each of the questions is followed by an elaboration of the implications of "failing the test." Manning then lists six constitutional amendments passed by Reform Party constituencies to be considered at the 1991 Assembly. All but one either involve procedures for the "nullification" of electoral candidates, or apply the principles of recall and referenda to party affairs. Manning introduced them with this instruction: "I believe members and delegates should ask serious questions about the following proposals of the Constitutional Committee, or any other proposals like them."

In effect, Manning instructed delegates to vote against six resolutions brought forward by the Constitutional Committee, a body appointed by the Executive Council, the ruling body of the party between assemblies. Manning, by not negatively identifying any other constitutional amendments, implied support for all other amendments being brought forward by the committee.

The result of this forceful intervention demonstrates the power of Preston Manning to influence his party. The delegates gave their leader almost everything he wanted. Three of the amendments he asked them to reject were duly defeated, one passed unchanged, and two were passed with amendments addressing Manning's concerns. Of the remaining seventy constitutional amendments on which Manning made no negative comment, delegates defeated only one, and enhanced the power of the executive by doing so.

The Party Policy Committee had taken no chances with the key issues facing the 1991 Assembly. The use of straw votes, appeals from the leader, and task force meetings which resembled "focus groups" used by marketing experts, virtually ensured that the results of the assembly would be in accord with Preston Manning's agenda for his party. As Stephen Harper put it "a wrong decision in any one of those areas could seriously hurt the party's chances in the next federal election."

Sanitizing Party Policy

Manning and Harper did not take any chances in the many other areas of policy either. Like their Social Credit forebears, they saw the need to guide the membership. Stephen Harper expressed the potential problem that Manning faced in this way:

> The biggest problem is that when you seek input from the bottom up, often the ideas are simple and low quality, or just slogans ... But if people feel you're listening to them, they'll have faith in you, and then they'll be very open to what you're trying to sell them.

The "selling" of Preston Manning's policies was accomplished through the process by which policies arrived at the assembly. Manning referred to this mechanism as "a new process for developing policy [which] allows the grassroots to put forward all the ideas, which are screened three times." The "screening" was to be done by the party and the members with a view to eliminating unacceptable policies. "A lot of these things will not get through the screening process," said Manning.

There were, in Harper's words, "two channels" through which policy reached the 1991 Assembly: local riding associations and the Party Policy Committee. These two streams of policies were then screened by the Party Policy Committee and reduced to 159, eighty-eight from the constituency associations and seventy-one from the committee itself based on task force recommendations. Only twelve constituency associations out of approximately eighty bothered to submit resolutions, demonstrating either great

trust in the party leadership or disinterest in the notion of government policy. These 159 resolutions, assembled in an "Exposure
Draft," were sent to each constituency which was then expected
to call a pre-assembly meeting to vote on them and submit the
results to the committee.

Much was made in the media of this last phase of the policy
process, yet, according to the party's own figures, very few members actually took part in it. Although fifty-four riding associations
met to discuss the draft, the total number of members taking part
was only 2,000. The average number of members attending the
Exposure Draft meetings was thirty-seven in constituency associations which averaged at least 700 members each.

The Exposure Draft itself was heavily loaded in favour of the
policies put forward by the Party Policy Committee. Resolutions
were ordered according to policy area. In most policy areas there
were two resolutions to choose from — usually one from the party
and one from a constituency. But in fifty instances, only party
resolutions were available for discussion. In many of these areas
— such as the environment — the party could simply generate no
interest among the members.

In all but eleven cases, the PPC made recommendations to
members about which resolutions to support. The structure of the
draft also reinforced the authority of the committee's resolutions.
Following the text of competing resolutions was a section called
"Rationale." Most of the constituency resolutions had not come
with an accompanying rationale, so for these resolutions this category was followed by the word "None" — a subtle hint that
perhaps the policy had not been well thought out. In every case,
the competing party resolution had a detailed rationale. Following
that was the "Party Policy Committee's Remarks," most often
criticizing the competing constituency resolution and making a
recommendation on which resolution to support.

Some of the remarks on constituency resolutions were harsh.
Some were dismissed as "nonsensical," "politically unacceptable," and, in the case of a resolution calling for the "con-
tinuance of universal medicare," a "serious contradiction of our
constitutional and fiscal policies." Of the eighty-eight resolutions
put forward by constituencies, only two were recommended by
the Party Policy Committee and only one of these was in com-

petition with a PPC resolution. The PPC recommended sixty-seven of its own seventy-one resolutions.

Preston Manning and his closest advisors, principally Stan Waters and Stephen Harper, had two objectives in fashioning party policy: to moderate the extremist resolutions and to purge any which were not in accord with strict, free-market economic principles. Agriculture and immigration, two key areas of policy, demonstrate this process most clearly. These two areas generated by far the most interest among the rank and file. Combined with the PPC's counter-resolutions, they took up nineteen and twenty-five pages, respectively, in the 172-page Exposure Draft — more than twice the space of the next longest policy section.

The agriculture section of The Exposure Draft demonstrated Preston Manning's determination to create a conservative party of the right with policies to match. All five resolutions from the constituencies called for increased government assistance to struggling farmers or for government programs to enhance the farm sector. Every one of them was opposed by the PPC and in their stead were thirteen party resolutions, each expressing free-market principles.

The first resolution in the draft was from Medicine Hat, Alberta. It read, in part:

> Resolved that the agriculture sector ... must be sustained through difficult times by government support. This support should be in the form of guaranteed fair market prices ... and guaranteed interest rates at a reduced percentage ...

Such a program would be funded by consolidating various other existing programs, said the resolution, which was backed up by a rationale which called for "fairness and equality." It could have been written in the 1930s; it expressed classic western populist sentiment.

The PPC responded with a 300-word rebuttal of the resolution and the sentiment behind it. As it did in many of its comments, it promoted consistency: "In the view of the Policy Committee, the Medicine Hat resolution is not consistent with the general policy direction of the Reform Party." Manning and his committee went even further to ensure that this policy would not be supported in the next round of discussions — and revealed that the leader was still troubled by the spectre of socialism:

> ... the Policy Committee believes the proposal would lead us further from market economics and ever closer to socialistic solutions to agricultural problems. It proposes a guaranteed income support program for farmers through price regulation. This is the opposite of a market-driven system, and it goes against the grain of the Policy Committee's and the Agricultural Task Force's entire package of proposals ...

Other constituency resolutions called for enhancement of existing government-run crop insurance (the committee opposed it, calling for private crop insurance); for the government to ensure that chemical companies provide "education and training" to food processors to protect their health and the environment (rejected as "too specific"); for maintaining or increasing "monies being spent to ... study ... alternate and drought-resistant crop development, natural pesticide and herbicide ... and improvements in soil conservation" (rejected by the PPC because " ... it is impossible for the Reform party to make financial commitments such as implied by the Lethbridge resolution").

A final constituency resolution called for a Reform government to "create new areas of water storage ... management and conservation." It was rejected because it " ... calls for a major public investment ... it is inappropriate for the Party to make commitments of development assistance ... "

None of the constituency resolutions made it into the delegates' resolution kit at the Saskatoon assembly. The policy committee's political interventions had succeeded. And in what was little more than sleight-of-hand, it effectively eliminated another, older policy which opposed further forgiving of Third World debts until "the Government of Canada has resolved the debt problems of Canada's farmers." The committee simply removed the reference to farmers' debts and then recommended that the resolution be moved to External Relations.

Preston Manning had, through his policy committee, success-fully prevented any interventionist agricultural policies from reaching the floor of the Saskatoon Assembly. But his problems with his own package of free-market farm policies were far from over. As described later in the chapter, he had to make an even more extraordinary intervention at the assembly to push through his agenda for agriculture.

The PPC's interventions in immigration resolutions paralleled those respecting agriculture, except that in the former the constit-uency resolutions were too far to the left; with the immigration policies they were too far to the right. Eighteen constituency resolutions were included in the Exposure Draft. All were extreme in one respect or another — a variety of restrictions and demands for ethnic balance, for the deportation of immigrants convicted of crimes, for immigrants to take out citizenship, and for the disal-lowance of dual citizenships were put forward.

One that would prove very controversial would have "en-courage[d] immigrants to settle in less populated areas ... " The policy committee "sympathized with the objective ... " but re-jected it as being "unenforceable." Another would have denied immigrants protection under the Charter of Rights.

While all of these resolutions were advised against or rejected, most of the committee's remarks were far less critical than they were of the agricultural resolutions. The immigration resolutions were not rejected as being in conflict with "the general policy direction of the Reform Party." They were rejected because they were open to "misinterpretation," "unenforceable," or created "administrative problems." The PPC pointed out that obligatory Canadian citizenship might cause "problems in the oil industry."

The flood of extremist resolutions on immigration caused real problems for Preston Manning and confusion as to how to deal with them. The media in Alberta had gotten wind of the issue. Manning told a reporter on February 12, 1991 that he wouldn't "stifle the rank and file Reform Party members even if they're proposing an extreme immigration policy."

But as the assembly approached, he apparently changed his mind. Party Chairman, Diane Ablonczy, announced on March 24 that the party was softening its immigration stance. Of nineteen resolutions on immigration only three — all drafted by the PPC

— would be brought forward, said Ablonczy, because there "was no support" for the others.

Once the Exposure Draft package was voted on by the constituencies they went again to the PPC where they were reduced to sixty, based on which resolutions received the most support. These were the resolutions which would be considered at the assembly. Of those final sixty resolutions — the result of three "screenings" — just seven had originated with the constituencies.

While thirty sample resolutions published in the *Reformer* just before the assembly indicated whether resolutions came from constituencies or the PPC, the resolutions in the delegates kit did not.

More Dissent

The interventions into policy-making by Manning and his closest advisors had not gone unnoticed among members — especially in the areas of provincial politics and eastern expansion. In October, 1990, the *Calgary Sun* reported that twelve Reform Party officials, "including several directors of federal riding associations" were secretly organizing a plan to establish a provincial party. The effort was centred in the Wild Rose riding where director Jim McCrae maintained that despite the results of the task force meetings, "up to 70%" of the 25,000 Alberta Reform members supported entering provincial politics. "The federal party — controlled by Mr. Manning and the executive — keep hedging on this issue."

Even the *Alberta Report*, whose favourable reporting helped the Reform Party make its early gains, noted that many in the party were upset by the "Calgary clique," which ran things from the centre, and were grumbling about "autocratic leadership."

The grumbling peaked towards the end of the 1990 as Preston Manning's efforts to push his own agenda were at their height. *Edmonton Journal* columnist, Don Wanagas, commented on the "perception [that] Preston Manning is trying to keep total control over the future of what was supposed to be a populist grass roots political movement." The discrepancy between the task force report on provincial politics and the apparently wide-spread support for running provincially had led, said Wanagas, to "charges that Manning and a handful of his closest followers have manipulated things to get the desired result." Similar and even more angry dissent was heard from B.C. over the same issue.

The determination of Manning to expand eastward caused more consternation. Dal Brown, a Reform candidate in the 1988 election, complained, "When I went knocking on doors ... I told people this new party was the voice of the West. I don't know how I can face them now ... It's not hard to see Ontario dominating the party."

Just a few months before the 1991 Assembly planned for Saskatoon, reform politics turned nasty in B.C. It was primarily the result of factional in-fighting over the provincial politics and eastern expansion issues. The twist was that in two Vancouver Island ridings, the "recall" provisions in the party constitution (by which petitioners can force a vote of confidence on executive members) were used to oust riding presidents. They resigned rather than face the public humiliation of a constituency meeting vote — providing graphic evidence of how divisive the recall mechanism could be. A third president was forced from office by an ultimatum from his own board of directors.

While the public airing of these disputes harmed the image of the party and probably reinforced the frustration felt by less vocal members, the dissension was far from fatal. Manning's personal authority was such that no open revolt would take place at the assembly, even if there were wide-spread frustrations and doubts about the party's direction. Manning and top party officials played down the issues, characterizing the dissenters as a small minority and claiming that all the issues would be fully aired at the 1991 Assembly.

The preparation and orchestration carried out by the party, however, left very little to chance and little likelihood of a "full airing" of the issues. The assembly was judged an almost complete success after its four very intense and jam-packed days of debate, inspirational speeches, and decision making.

The opening day of the assembly set the tone for the four-day event: it was strictly business, with no key-note speaker or any pep talks about the future. The first two hours were taken up with a meeting between constituency presidents and the leader. The afternoon was set aside for "Election-Readiness Seminars."

The second day was opened by Manning's closest advisor, Stephen Harper. He reviewed the policy process, stating what all delegates already knew: "The opinion of the leader on all resolutions was conveyed to the membership through the Policy Committee."

Harper was straightforward about the foundations of the new party: it was founded on the great dissatisfaction with current institutions and politics in Canada. "These developments have created a great opportunity for us, an opportunity for which this party was founded ... but public cynicism alone will not ensure the success of the Reform Party."

The last part of Harper's speech was a warning to the delegates to put aside any extreme views they held in the interests of success. He urged members to ensure that Reform policy was "free from extremism, especially on issues like language and immigration ... we must ... distance ourselves from those who are really focused on the race or ethnic background of immigrants ... Do not allow the Party to be shot in the foot on these issues by radical elements, as has happened far too often to new parties."

On questions of policy, Preston Manning, Harper and others in the inner circle of the party made every effort to ensure that the party would not "shoot itself in the foot."

Even with the extraordinary pre-assembly measures taken by Manning and his policy committee to ensure the right policies, they were still taking no chances with the delegates. Throughout the policy discussions either Preston Manning or Stephen Harper were at the head table at the front of the meeting hall. They were permitted by the assembly chairman to intervene at any time and to speak to resolutions before any discussion from the floor had taken place. When Preston Manning had to leave the convention floor for any reason, his place was taken by Stephen Harper. Throughout the debates, the two men repeatedly intervened to guide the discussion, caution delegates about the folly of alternative positions, and underline the leader's views on important matters.

The speaking rules were strictly enforced: delegates from the floor were allowed two minutes (a green warning light indicated one minute; a red one, thirty seconds remaining). At the two-minute mark the mike was turned off. While delegates were kept to this tight limit, Harper and Manning were allowed to speak for as long as they wanted. A motion to adopt *Robert's Rules of Order* at the beginning of the session was overwhelmingly defeated.

Reform rules gave more power to the assembly president, whose decisions — except on votes, where counts could be called for — could not be appealed.

The Party Policy Committee's resolution on the GST took the position that had been elicited from the membership through the "Referendum Column" of the *Reformer*. The delegates could choose either to rescind GST legislation or, in the final version of the committee's resolution, "reform" it "to make it more visible and easier to administer." Harper rose to speak before the discussion began, claiming that two-thirds of constituencies favoured reforming, a figure he did not explain.

After pro and con speakers addressed the GST resolutions, Manning repeated Harper's reminder of the straw vote in favour of reform, despite the fact that in his letter to members regarding constitutional matters, he underlined the supremacy of the assembly. Manning spoke in favour of keeping the GST, saying it would mean a spending cut of $25 billion. At no time was any alternative or any possibility of an alternative referred to. In the end, a delegate moved that the two alternative motions be tabled until the public's view of the question could be determined. The chairman ruled that the tabling motion failed. A request for a count revealed it had passed by 365 to 337. Preston Manning had failed to get a new policy on the GST.

The package of agricultural resolutions was substantial and detailed. There were eleven resolutions, all but one (rescinding an old policy) from the PPC. The lead resolution stated the philosophy of the new policy. It represented a reversal of fifty years of Canadian agricultural policy:

> Resolved that the Reform Party support an agricultural policy based on market mechanisms *with the objective of meeting the demands of consumers for safe, secure supplies of food at competitive prices* [italics added]. Where circumstances allow, this would mean a shift from a government dominated and supported agricultural industry to an industry shaped by the free operation of comparative advantage between regions and commodities, free entry into all sectors of production and marketing and free trade on a global basis.

This was a cheap food policy — a radical departure from the history of farm policy, especially in the West, where freight rate subsidies, price supports, and marketing boards were crucial to making farming viable. It revealed in dramatic fashion Preston Manning's absolute commitment to free-market economics. That it was hostile to the interests of western farmers, more particularly family farms, did not escape the notice of the farmer delegates attending the assembly. One farmer spoke in favour. Two others expressed dismay.

A delegate from the Yellowhead, Alberta constituency stated, "I have a real problem with these resolutions. In my constituency we discussed them for three evenings. We concluded that this policy will be unsaleable in a federal election." A delegate from Mackenzie reinforced that view: "We discussed these resolutions in my constituency. We concluded we can't win an election on this platform." He moved that the whole package be tabled. The resolution passed by a two-to-one margin.

There was then a motion from the floor to support Manning's address on agriculture. That motion contradicted the intention of the tabling motion because Manning's address had made the identical call for a cheap food policy. Nevertheless, it passed unanimously, revealing how delegates were often torn between their personal sentiment on an issue and their desire to support their leader.

For the most part, even controversial policies passed at the convention with very little debate and with the question being called early. Most votes were strongly in favour of the resolutions, especially when spoken to by Manning or Harper. But on a free-market agriculture policy Manning apparently believed special effort had to be made. In his draft statement and speech he cajoled the delegates on "essential truths" of the free market: "We are looking for an agriculture policy that will be frank and honest in communicating essential truths to farmers (what we need to hear as opposed to what we want to hear) about the new economic realities." After detailing the free-market policy, he again addressed any lingering doubts: "We may not like these facts. We may feel like denying or fighting them. But the practical, hard-headed common sense for which the Canadian farmer is famous demands we face up to them."

The delegates' vote to approve Manning's address was not satisfactory to Manning. The next day, he announced that he was calling a special meeting, for 5:30 A.M. the next morning, to hammer out an acceptable agricultural policy. At noon on Sunday, he counted once again on his members' willingness to follow. He had met with 140 delegates that morning, as scheduled, and worked out a policy. He addressed the assembly, stating that "the root of the problem seemed to be one of communication."

His proposal was seemingly bold: "We do not have time to reopen debate on agriculture policy. I propose instead that we put a simple motion on the floor for a straight vote with no debate." The motion called for acceptance of Manning's short speech and the revised resolutions as the basis for the new policy. Manning told delegates it was a matter of trust: "Do you trust the work that your colleagues did earlier this morning?" Copies of the revised resolutions were not distributed. The resolution passed unanimously.

There were only minor changes to the resolutions. One major change in wording was included. Both the key resolution on agriculture and Manning's address contained the phrase "secure supplies of food at competitive prices." It was the phrase "competitive prices" which the farmer delegates knew they could not sell. In a revised version of the speech later sent out to journalists, it was changed to "affordable prices," a phrase designed to offend no one. With this calculated ambiguity, Preston Manning had salvaged a key plank in his free-market economic policy.

In the areas of provincial politics and eastern expansion, the assembly went the way Preston Manning had hoped and planned for. As he had predicted, the assembly voted to hold a party-wide referendum on the expansion question, after passing resolutions designed to prevent Ontario's membership from dominating the party. A straw vote on expansion at the assembly was approved by 96.6 per cent of the delegates. Manning, appealing for a similar vote in the referendum, declared that he would announce the results at a huge rally in Vancouver later in the spring. The assembly also passed a resolution on provincial politics which was a complete victory for Preston Manning. It was unambiguous and slammed the door on provincial involvement:

... that the Reform Party of Canada not become involved in provincial politics and that it undertake all
legal means available to protect its name, logo, trade-
marks and membership lists from unauthorized use by
any political group and from any group passing itself
off as being associated in any way with the Reform
Party of Canada.

There were other policy areas in which either Manning or
Harper intervened — sometimes spontaneously when a policy
was in trouble, other times when trouble was anticipated. Harper
did this frequently, most often to "explain" the intent of a resolution.

On virtually every occasion of their intervention, with the exception of the GST and (temporarily) agriculture, delegates voted
with their leader or the man they recognized as his lieutenant.

Manning intervened when his policy of eliminating the Canada
Health Act came under fire. Winnipeg-St. James delegate, George
Van Den Bosch, saw the provincialization of medicare through
"unconditional" federal grants as a threat to national health care.
"It is absolutely essential that the Reform Party have a position
that is clearly in support of universal medicare." Van Den Bosch
and others tried to get support for an amendment guaranteeing
universal health care, but with the possibility of applying user
fees.

Manning took the mike and reassured delegates that universality was "implied" and that, in the case of user fees, " ... getting
specific about things like money ... just isn't smart politics." In
any case, he said, user fees would be possible under provincialization. His claim that universality was implied in the policy was
in direct contradiction to what he had said in The Exposure Draft.
Van Den Bosch's amendment was defeated. The resolution passed
with ten delegates voting against it.

When two delegates questioned the party's vague but seemingly moderate resolutions on native affairs, Manning was forced
to intervene again. One delegate stated, "This is a blank cheque
for the natives. Will we continue to fund aboriginal people
forever?" Manning, implying that this was not the case, explained
that the purpose of the native package was to do away with the

Department of Indian Affairs and its agencies. The policy was passed with thirty opposed.

On the issue of accountability of Reform MPs, Manning took the mike first. The resolution, regarding free votes in Parliament, dealt with a democratic reform that had been a key element of the party's appeal to Albertans who felt betrayed by their Tory MPs. They had been led to believe by the notion of "free votes" that their MPs primary allegiance was to their constituencies, not to the party.

But the resolution allowed only for free votes in the Reform caucus, with the results of the vote to be made public. After that, Reform MPs had to vote with the majority in the House of Commons, unless it was the clear "will of the constituents" that they not do so. This measure actually lessened caucus democracy. In other parties, caucus votes are secret. Reform MPs faced with publicly disagreeing with their leader might think twice about such an action.

Manning had anticipated the reaction to this virtual gutting of the "free vote" principle. Once again, he addressed the delegates. The sentiment during the following debate was for some control over MPs. But Preston Manning again prevailed. The motion, including the provision giving the executive council control over how "the will of the constituency" would be determined, passed overwhelmingly, with only fifty negative votes.

Manning had made his most forceful and direct pre-assembly intervention in the area of party constitutional reform. Six resolutions caused him concern, most of them because they applied Reform Party democratic principles a little too enthusiastically — and in ways which decreased the power of the party's Executive Council. One in particular would have allowed for the recall of Executive Council members. All but one of these amendments were either defeated, as requested by Manning, or amended to make recall and disciplinary actions against elected officials more difficult to carry out.

One resolution targeted by Manning would have reduced the power of the Executive Council to "nullify" candidate nominations. It would have allowed the candidate and representatives of the constituency to appeal a decision by the Executive Council. The resolution was defeated, as was a companion resolution, leaving Manning and the Executive with " … absolute discretion where it feels the overall best interest of the party is involved to nullify any candidate ... "

One of the most controversial measures proposed by Manning was the candidate questionnaire for party members seeking nomination for a federal riding. It brought negative comments not only from some media commentators — who called it an invasion of privacy, a "program of elitist intimidation" and a "blatant violation" of the party's democratic principles — but from members of the party. Dave Wylie, a party member from Calgary, stated publicly that "It bothers me a hell of a lot." A candidate in the 1988 election, Gerry Maloney, said such personal information "is none of the party's business." It reminded some commentators of William Aberhart's call for "one hundred good men" to run Alberta.

The questionnaire is part of a forty-page candidate recruitment package which provides a detailed description of what it means to be an MP — the time and energy demanded, the pressures on the MP and his or her family, the responsibilities. The recruitment package also contains a twenty-page candidate nomination form which requires any candidate running for nomination to reveal a great deal about his or her private live, beliefs, and even family members who might "embarrass" the party.

Easily one of the most detailed questionnaires developed by any party, it is divided into various sections: "Electability and acceptability to constituents," "values and motivation," agreement with "party platform," "skill requirement," "knowledge and experience," "political vulnerability," "health and fitness," and "implications for personal relationships." In addition to the questionnaire, the party code favours a candidate with "a demonstrated record of success" in his work and a salary "in the high half of job holders in that particular occupation."

The questionnaire often reads like a point-by-point summary of Preston Manning's conservative agenda. While the "free votes" in Parliament were virtually eliminated in an earlier policy decision, the candidate recruitment procedure reinforces the likelihood of a compliant caucus. Each candidate is required to answer "agree, disagree or modify" to every policy in the Blue Book. (The form urges members to "Please be frank.") In addition, under "Values and Motivation," they must go through what even party sympathizer and *Alberta Report* writer Ken Whyte called an "orthodoxy check." Based on the party's statement of principles, candidates are asked to confirm or deny their support for each. One establishes the candidate's degree of commitment to conservative economic policies: "We believe that the creation of wealth and productive jobs for Canadians is best achieved through the operation of a responsible, broadly-based, free enterprise economy in which private property, freedom of contract, and the operation of free markets are encouraged and respected."

In addition, candidates are asked to gauge how pro-American they are by responding to another statement: "We believe that Canadians should seek to maximize the benefits of our unique geographic and economic relationship with the United States."

The section on skills required might intimidate all but the most politically active citizens. Questions about media relations ability, public speaking, administrative skills, experience in government, analytical and legislative skills would eliminate many minority candidates and working people who have generally been denied access to such experience.

The questionnaire was to be filled out by each candidate. It would then be reviewed by the Constituency Nominating Committee which subsequently interviews the candidates. The committee would then advise the candidate to "proceed to seek a Reform Party nomination," to seek more experience, or not to run. The committee would then release a list of "recommended candidates" to party members.

As well, says the questionnaire, any party member can run for a nomination "regardless of the recommendations of the Committee." Yet, because all candidates must go through the process, it is clear to all party members that any candidate who has not been recommended has, in fact, been rejected by the committee because he or she failed in some unrevealed way to pass the test — a test devised largely by Preston Manning himself.

The candidate recruiting programme devised by Manning and his close advisors passed at the 1991 Assembly. It represented a virtual clean sweep of all the key elements of Preston Manning's agenda for the party and his conservative vision. Virtually all his free-market economic and social policy was in place; the ultimate say over who candidates would be was still in his hands and an unprecedented screening process provided even more insurance against potential dissension, particularly ideological dissent, in his caucus. The party would hold a referendum on eastern expansion in whose results Manning was totally confident. (He was right: the subsequent referendum supported expansion by over 90 per cent.) Rebels wishing to run provincially were also sidelined.

Manning's other main objective was also accomplished: the media scrutiny so many had expected turned out to be a mild affair. Most journalists from the East in particular had made it clear in pre-assembly stories that they would focus on Quebec, eastern expansion, and the question of provincial politics. For the most part this is just what they did.

The latter two issues had been settled long before the assembly through straw votes, special flyers sent to delegates and repeated public statements by the leader revealing his "personal" preference. And, as the party was not entering into the political debate within Quebec, there was little scope for members to say anything controversial about that issue. There were few embarrassing statements by delegates as they heeded Stephen Harper's call and did not shoot the party in the foot.

Reporters hoping to scrutinize Manning's main address found that he talked for two-thirds of his speech about Canadian constitutional history, federalism, and the role of Quebec in Canada. He made no mention at all of his commitment to conservative social and economic policy nor even to the party's democratic reforms. His speech seemed deliberately non-controversial and was certainly not inspirational in content or delivery.

Something to Cheer About

The media paid very little attention to one of the speakers at the assembly. Had they listened to William Gairdner they would have indirectly heard the political sentiments of the 1,200 Reformers gathered in Saskatoon at the peak of their party's success. They had just pleased their leader by endorsing his carefully crafted, moderate-sounding package of policy resolutions. Requested not to express any extreme views themselves, they were, nevertheless, permitted to cheer those expressed by someone else.

Bill Gairdner, author of the best-selling book, *The Trouble with Canada,* warmed up the audience at 8:15 Saturday morning. The cheers and whistles he evoked tell a separate story of the Reform Party's 1991 Assembly.

Gairdner thanked Preston Manning for personally inviting him to speak. Then he gave the Reformers what they wanted to hear. As Manning has done repeatedly, he attacked all "politicians." "In the mere space of a quarter century our beloved country has endured a wrenching economic, political and moral transformation ... by professional politicians from ... a classic liberal society into ... a social welfare state."

Gairdner went on to attack the whole concept of human rights and the funding of advocacy groups that "compete for government funding to get these rights." The attack on the "rights illusion" brought applause, but his attack on feminists brought a roar of approval: "Furthermore ... we fund ... radical feminist groups all over the country ... [extended applause] ... that publicly support social revolution ... of the most utopian kind and they vow to abolish the traditional family."

Again, going after women and women's rights, Gairdner suggested to more loud applause, that Canada "throw the Charter [of Rights and Freedoms] out and return to our common law heritage ... any Charter should only refer to citizens without distinction as to sex, colour or religion ... Women get special treatment but men do not. [loud 'boos']. Such favouritism by ranking cannot lead to a happy nation [more loud applause]."

Attacking the idea that the wealthy should be taxed more heavily, Gairdner attacked governments in general: "I see no way out of this unless we stop the politicians and the bureaucrats from continuing the wreckage ... Canada must be depoliticized" [applause].

The Reformers gathered in Saskatoon saved perhaps the loudest cheers, whistles, and applause for Gairdner's last shot: "And my favourite [proposal], by the way, is returning choice to education by privatizing every public school in the country."

Whether the cheers for William Gairdner more accurately reflected the delegates' views than the policies they passed is open to debate. In any case, Preston Manning was now prepared to take his party officially into the rest of Canada — excluding Quebec. His goal of a national conservative party of the right had been achieved. But the victory was still only on paper. There were those in the party, including some close to Manning, who had advised strongly against rushing into Ontario in particular. This advice was not due to the anxiety of alienating Reform's western base.

It had more to do with the fear of seeing the party hijacked — and embarrassed — by the extreme right in Ontario.

Manning had been begun preparing the ground in Ontario in the spring of 1990 when he made a tour to several centres there and in the Atlantic provinces. While the tour was supposed to be an informational testing of the waters, it was more than that. While the constitution prevented official constituency organizations from being set up, Manning did not discourage the selling of memberships or the establishment of unofficial constituency groups. Over a dozen such groups were set up and over 2,000 memberships sold in 1990 in Ontario.

The concern of the party was expressed by Stephen Harper in a long letter to the chairman of the task force on expansion. He addressed a number of questions but urged caution on the question of expansion: "We should continue to explore expansion and through trusted individuals and affiliated organizations until we have some reliable people in place."

Stan Waters was also reportedly wary about moving into Ontario too soon. And at least one high-profile Ontario organizer and long-time associate of Preston Manning has ended his active support of the party because of what is already happening in that province. Brian Hay, now a senior business executive in Toronto, has known Preston Manning since 1975 and attended the same church as Manning in the Edmonton suburb of St. Albert. He was a key party organizer for Manning throughout most of 1990.

> I helped Preston organize his first visit to Ontario, officially, in March of last year [1990]. I had provided him with advice and counsel on organizing and on some issues and [advised] some of his people through the fall of last year. I am a paid-up member of the Reform Party. I have nothing but the highest regard for Preston as an individual in terms of his intellect and ... his ethics. He is a very, very decent, bright person. Having said all that, I am irrevocably opposed to the Reform Party and what it's up to.

Brian Hay's alienation from the party has its roots in the kind of concerns expressed by Stephen Harper. Hay was worried about a number of groups, including anti-abortion organizations and the Confederation of Regions (CoR) party. But he was primarily concerned about the powerful presence of the Association for the Preservation of English in Canada (APEC) throughout the party in Ontario. "You've got some very, very interesting groups of people that are using the party as a cover for their own activity ... people start using [Reform's] criticisms of the system as code words for their own agenda."

Hay and four or five of the twelve-member Ontario Expansion Committee were concerned about going into Ontario too soon. "We didn't want to peak too soon," said Ernst Kneisel. "We wanted to peak about six months before the next election, sometime in late '92." Hay wrote to Manning: "I said don't rush the organization into Ontario, don't go in high profile."

The main source of Hay's concerns, and those of the original organizing committee's, was the new chairman of the National Expansion Committee, Reg Gosse. Questions about Gosse had been communicated to party headquarters and to Preston Manning personally by several people. It was Manning's refusal to deal with what his original organizers considered a crisis that caused Hay and others to withdraw.

After Manning's tour in March, 1990, six individuals, including Hay, Ron Peterson, Michael Dean, Ron Fisher, and others volunteered their services to the party. As a result, Gordon Shaw, party vice-chairman and Ontario organizer, called them together. Several meetings were held in May and June, and the group was given the mandate to organize the expansion in Ontario.

After several others turned down the position, Reg Gosse was appointed chairman of the committee. It was soon after this that problems began to develop. According to Hay:

> People were very concerned that records were not being kept, that people were being appointed without any credentials or background checks ... Others were being dropped along the way, new people being added without explanation of who they were. People were assigned responsibilities without the opportunity to carry them out, like a treasurer who didn't see the books for six weeks. Decisions were being made after meet-

ings and then being announced as though they were part
of meetings.

Ernst Kneisel tells a similar story. "When we would ask for an
accounting of Ontario funds, Gosse would tell us that Calgary had
the figures and we didn't need to know. Then he told one of the
other guys [in the organizing effort] that I was a spy for the
Conservative Party." After disagreeing with Gosse on an organizational matter, Kneisel was unilaterally dropped from the committee by Gosse.

The internal democracy issue came to a head at a meeting held
on November 28. A more formal organization, the need for
Robert's Rules of Order at meetings, and the positions of
secretary, treasurer, and vice-chairman of the committee were all
confirmed. Reg Gosse was confirmed as chairman.

Six days later, on December 4, Preston Manning wrote to all
members of the organizing effort in Ontario:

> In the past week I have received some good news and
> some not so good news from your fair province. The
> good news is ... that the Party is at 8 per cent in the
> polls ... The not so good news is that I understand there
> are some personality conflicts among you and ... dis-
> agreements on how to proceed organizationally.

Manning went on to offer counsel and, while admitting to
having had critical reports on Gosse, asked that he be kept on —
that he was a familiar name and that "changing horses in mid-
stream would raise needless questions about how the expansion
investigation is being conducted."

In a request with strong echoes of his father's approach to party
matters, Manning asked organizers to concentrate on two main
tasks. First, they were to distribute Reform materials to "interested
voters" at the constituency level and conduct preliminary membership drives. And second, they were to hold "coordinating meetings of key organizers from various constituencies called by Reg
Gosse ..."

Manning requested that the organizers put the organization
question on hold and "Put yourself to the immediate service of

'the cause' ..." Manning promised to deal with their "important" concerns later.

What the members of the Expansion Committee were not told was that Reg Gosse had already organized a parallel committee. This committee, consisting of regional co-ordinators, was put in place in September. "It was begun roughly parallel to the other committee," said Gosse. "By December it was pretty well set." It was in December, immediately following Manning's letter to the Expansion Committee, that Gosse unilaterally disbanded the original Expansion Committee. Its members never met again.

The committee members were shocked by the development. "What I had real trouble accepting," said Hay, "was that we were being dictated to; that we were not being permitted to organize ... in our own right." Ernst Kneisel wrote to Manning expressing his dismay at Gosse's action. "I consider it unfortunate especially in view of the recent adoption by the group of a new, I thought, very democratizing charter." He included correspondence which he hoped would give Manning "some insight into the current situation." He never got a reply.

Both Gordon Shaw and Reg Gosse deny that there ever was a serious problem. According to Shaw, "I'm not sure the problems haven't been dealt with. As far as I can tell, the issue has completely gone away. It's been dealt with to somebody's satisfaction." Gosse does not recall any controversy.

But the disaffected group clearly does and its questions about democracy go beyond the unilateral disbanding of the organizing committee — especially for Manning's friend Hay.

> I also have some difficulty with the notion that a party believing in decentralization will not contest elections provincially ... but more importantly will not even have provincial organizations dedicated to a federal purpose. The same party that accuses Ottawa of absolutely insensitive anti-regional centralism is a party which demands constituency by constituency uniformity from Calgary. I think there is a fundamental and fatal flaw between their philosophy and their organizational structure.

Preston Manning's promise of dealing with the "important issues" after the April assembly was never kept. Four of the six
original organizers have either ended their active participation or
withdrawn to local constituency work. When Brian Hay received
Manning's letter asking him and others not to rock the boat, "I
said, oh, oh, as soon as we've got that we've got a problem. It's
like giving up smoking for Lent. It was said to me that when
Preston got my letter he just didn't know how to deal with it. And
that was when I knew we had a problem with leadership. When
you don't know how to deal with a problem then you have a real
problem."

The organizational problems didn't take long to develop. In
May, just a month after the Saskatoon assembly, the hijacking of
the party which Stephen Harper and Brian Hay had feared, occurred in the Peterborough, Ontario constituency association.
Widely reported in the media, it had all the elements of a public
relations disaster.

The incident which brought the internal conflict to light involved Bruce Knapp, a seventy-two-year-old ex-sergeant-major
in the British army, and Len Bangma, a local Peterborough businessman and ex-policeman. Knapp had founded the local chapter
of Reform in early 1990, making him one of the first Reform
organizers in Ontario. He had willingly given up the presidency
to the younger Bangma but after doing so became alarmed —
along with others in the party — at the failure of the new president
to call regular meetings or to give an accounting of constituency
finances.

Speaking to a motion regarding local member input, Knapp was
literally shouted down by Bangma supporters. When Knapp refused to sit down as ordered, Bangma abruptly adjourned the
meeting. John Watson described the incident for the *Toronto Star:*
"It was a disgraceful procedure. Bruce was speaking to a legitimate point and he was howled down." Judy Steed of the *Star*
recalled speaking to Knapp and his supporters. "They had joined
because they believed in the grassroots nature of the party. They
suddenly discovered that the whole thing was tightly controlled,
so tightly manipulated — they were devastated."

Another member, Reverend Gordon Young, who knew Manning in Alberta, said in August, 1991 that there had not been a
treasurer's report for months. Says Young, "It's not just Bangma.

The whole CoR [Confederation of Regions] bunch came to the meeting that elected Bangma and they ran a slate. They got secretary, treasurer, and five or six of the ten executive positions."

What most disturbed Knapp, his supporters — and Brian Hay — about the incident was Manning's apparent inability to deal with the matter. Letters from Knapp and others to Manning and the Calgary office went unanswered. Manning left the incident in the hands of Reg Gosse and Jack Hurst, the party's central Ontario co-ordinator — and one of the men appointed in secret by Gosse. Hurst described Knapp as "a bothersome pest ... He wouldn't stick to the issue and he wouldn't shut up. As Preston says, bugs are attracted to a bright light and Bruce is one of them, in my opinion." Gosse concurred with Hurst's assessment.

The confusion and disappointment among those first Ontario organizers who had been inspired by Preston Manning is palpable. Ron Peterson comments: "Why would he trust a man like Gosse who he has known for three months over a man like Brian Hay whom he's known for fifteen years? It's just odd." For Hay, Manning's behaviour in dealing with Ontario issues reveals a fatal flaw in leadership. Hay believes that Manning is often unable to "define the problem and the solution, and if it doesn't work he tries to make reality fit the solution."

Conclusion

As one Alberta Reform member noted, the history of his party revealed that it was not a movement looking for a leader, it was a leader looking for a movement. The short history of the Reform Party confirms that assessment and confirms as well what Preston Manning has said about his enterprise. It had been his intention from the time of his and his father's social conservative project in 1965 to harness the power of popular discontent as the vehicle for an ideologically consistent conservative party.

The role that Preston Manning sees for the party vehicle he has created is remarkably similar to that envisioned and fashioned by William Aberhart and Ernest Manning in the Social Credit Party. They, like Preston Manning, saw the role of the membership in very restricted terms. They were to "proselytize and organize." Policy was, for the most part, the prerogative of experts and the leader.

And so, while the structure of the party is democratic and delegates to the 1991 Assembly were well versed in the policies on which they were voting, the party's central organization ensured that the policies put forward at the assembly were consistent with a free-market philosophy. The use of straw votes, mini-referenda, task forces, and flyers and letters explaining the leader's position on key issues all demonstrated Preston Manning's use of old Socred techniques of persuasion.

The Exposure Draft, more than any other single party document, demonstrated the limited role that the membership was allowed on policy matters. Throughout the draft, constituency resolutions are rejected for their inconsistency with free-market enterprise. At the convention, too, Preston Manning and his closest aid, Stephen Harper, guided the membership on policy matters, explaining why certain policies were necessary and others unacceptable because they contradicted the overall thrust of the party's philosophy.

The letter to Ontario organizers reaffirmed Preston Manning's view of the role of the membership: he asked them to set aside matters of democratic structure and concentrate on "distribut[ing] party materials and preliminary membership drives and preliminary constituency organizations." All other issues were to be decided by party headquarters.

The Reform Party may be no less democratic than other parties in Canada. All practice varying degrees of control over policy and routinely ignore many policies duly passed at delegate conventions. But the Reform Party and its leader place themselves outside and above the standards by which other parties are judged. Attacks on traditional parties, their leaders, and their practices are a key element in the Reform Party's appeal to its members and to potential voters. Grassroots control of the party is seen by the members and the public as a fundamental part of "reform."

The membership of the party remains dominated by aging, white middle-class men. While Preston Manning rejects the label *right-wing* when it is applied to his party, its own membership surveys and the response of delegates to very conservative keynote speakers suggest otherwise. The party has almost no input from sectors of the population which account for millions of Canadians: single mothers, young unemployed people, aboriginal people, immigrants, ethnic communities, the poor. Even working people are not joining the Reform Party in significant numbers.

As described in the previous chapter, the connections the party has with conservative business lobby groups, think tanks, and business circles in the West and, increasingly, the East, suggest that it is not only a party with very conservative members, but it is a party of big business. And it is judged by big business to be so.

The Reform Party stands out as a party dominated by its leader and its central headquarters. Preston Manning, as leader and founder of the party, has an extraordinary ability to sway the membership. He has demonstrated his tremendous influence — over how the party is run, who will occupy key posts at the centre and locally — and his willingness to use his stature among his members to fashion a consistent set of free-market policies as a platform for the next election.

Reform Party Policy

Most Canadians know very little about the social and economic policies of the Reform Party. In effect, this means that Canadians do not know how the Reform Party would affect their everyday lives if it formed a government or became part of a coalition government.

Media coverage of the 1991 Assembly, when the party got the most attention in its history, focused on a handful of issues: the party's position on Quebec, on immigration, on becoming active in Ontario and the Maritimes, and on contesting provincial elections. A few western reporters did question how a populist party from the prairies could take a stand against marketing boards and price supports for farmers. But in their analysis of a political party that claims to provide a radical alternative to the ruling Progressive Conservative Party, the national media have not enabled Canadians to understand the difference between Reform and Conservative social and economic policies.

The key to understanding Reform's social and economic policies is to grasp the underlying principles. These principles, which form a coherent conservative ideology, help to explain why the party would ignore massive public sentiment against the Mulroney government's policies on free trade and cuts to social programs to opt for even "freer" trade and more extensive cutbacks.

A Pure Ideology

The first article in the party's Statement of Principles asserts what may sound obvious: "We affirm that political parties should be guided by stated values and principles which are shared by their members and rooted in the beliefs of Canadians." Seen in the context of Manning's political writing, however, the statement takes on added meaning. Manning has consistently argued that political parties must adhere to "a clearly defined set of meaningful political ideals and principles." The thrust of *Political Realignment,* the book he helped his father write, is the call for an ideologically pure party, one that would stay the course regardless of political pressure.

The evolution of the Reform Party over its four-year history can be viewed as the successful effort of Manning and the Party Policy Committee to establish for Reform a coherent conservative ideology. As the Reform Party gained increasing credibility under Manning's leadership, his particular priorities and personality have become more dominant. As members began to realize that their party's success was bound up with that of their leader, they gave him ever more leeway to formulate party direction and image.

Departures from Manning's views, such as government debt relief for farmers, have progressively been eradicated from policy documents. Proposals to change the political process — free votes in Parliament, for example — that might have impeded a Reform government's ability to implement a right-wing strategy have been watered down.

The core of Reform ideology as expressed in its 1991 Blue Book is laissez-faire economics. Principle Eight of the Blue Book states, "We believe that the creation of wealth and productive jobs for Canadians is best achieved through the operations of a responsible, broadly-based, free enterprise economy in which private property, freedom of contract and the operations of free markets are encouraged and respected." The role of government, described in Principle Seven, is "to foster and protect an environment in which initiative and enterprise can be exercised by individuals and groups." Other Reform principles contained in the Blue Book argue that society's responsibility to the poor and disadvantaged should be met through private enterprise and charity; governments should only intervene to help the most destitute.

Following the American Model

The particular kind of economy Canada should be striving for, according to Reform, appears to be exemplified by the United States. In his address to the 1991 Assembly, Manning talked about his preference for an American-style market economy, although he did not think that entrenching such a model in the Constitution could "be sold to the Canadian people at this point in time."

Throughout his political career, Manning has expressed his admiration for American institutions and values. He has argued for a two-party system and for the creation of an American-style Constitution. His speeches make frequent references to American historical figures such as Lincoln and Washington and to events such as the Civil War. Canada itself sometimes disappears in his terminology, becoming merely the "northern half of the North American continent," as it did three times in his address to the 1991 Assembly.

In a speech he made in New York City to the Americas Society, Manning promised to translate this affinity for the U.S. into economic reality. Under a Reform government, said Manning, Canada would be "a better U.S. ally." Reform would also extend the Free Trade Agreement into areas currently not covered. While Manning did not offer specifics, Reform Senator Stan Waters called for the sale of Canadian water to the U.S. While this is technically permitted now, more specific inclusion of water in the agreement would make it impossible for provincial governments to prevent such exports.

Reform's commitment to bring Canada closer to the United States and its economy goes beyond expressions of policy. It is elevated to the status of philosophical principle in the party's Blue Book. The party's concluding Principle 21 states: "We believe that Canadians should seek to maximize the benefits of our unique geographic and economic relationship with the United States, and that the establishment of more positive relations with the U.S. need not in any way impair Canada's national sovereignty or cultural identity."

Free Trade

It can be argued that the Free Trade Agreement negotiated by the Mulroney government and supported by the Reform Party already works to impair Canada's national sovereignty. The agreement takes precedence over any other piece of Canadian legislation, federal or provincial, past or future. It has been described as having the effect of an amendment to the Constitution. Canadian legislators cannot implement any policy that runs counter to the agreement without cancelling the entire deal.

For example, with the Free Trade Agreement no Canadian government can ever decide to conserve natural gas supplies for future Canadian use rather than exporting them to the U.S. Canadians are now committed, forever, to selling the same proportion of our gas production to the U.S. that we currently sell, even if we face a shortage at home that imposes hardship on Canadians. Should our exports increase at any time, the U.S. can then demand this higher rate in perpetuity. Canadian politicians can never, without cancelling the agreement, choose to foster domestic industries by setting lower energy prices for them than we charge the U.S.

As Maude Barlow described in her book, *Parcel of Rogues: How Free Trade Is Failing Canada,* the energy part of the deal was "the irresistible bribe our government used to lure the Americans to the table." In advance of the deal, "The vital-supply safeguard, the requirement that there always be a twenty-five year surplus of natural gas before export applications could be granted, was first reduced to fifteen years and then abandoned." The Free Trade Agreement's provisions on natural gas apply to oil and hydro-electricity as well. The least that could be said about these provisions is that they severely restrict Canadian sovereignty over energy resources.

As it stands, the deal affects virtually every aspect of social and economic policy: medicare and social programs, labour law and wage levels, regional development, agriculture, the fisheries, natural resources, and taxation. American trade representatives have stated their intent to challenge Canada's social programs, such as medicare and unemployment insurance, as unfair subsidies and barriers to implementation of the agreement. And because industries can now relocate to any place in North America offering the lowest tax rates, the federal government was obliged to create a "level playing field," bringing corporate taxes down to U.S. rates. Since these rates are the lowest in the western world, the Canadian government's ability to continue to pay for programs such as medicare is jeopardized.

In addition to supporting the Free Trade Agreement, the Reform Party passed a resolution at its 1991 Assembly stating that "The Reform Party supports a comprehensive effort to realign

Canada's economic policies to be consistent with our trade requirements. This realignment must include industrial development policies, regulatory policies, taxation policies, transportation
policies, education policies, and fiscal and monetary policies."
This policy would seem to indicate that trade will be the overriding consideration for Reform in the formulation of policy in contrast to other possible goals, such as job creation or regional
development.

The Reform Party's expression of support in 1991 for the Free
Trade Agreement indicates more than a commitment to the ideology of the free market. It also demonstrates the extent to which
the party will adhere to Manning's insistence on following a
"clearly defined set of meaningful political ideals and principles,"
in this case against majority public opinion in Canada that now
opposes free trade. In the years following the signing of the Free
Trade Agreement, Canadians were subjected to almost daily an-
nouncements of plant closures. The Canadian Labour Congress
has estimated that the agreement has cost a permanent loss of
226,000 jobs to the end of 1990. Although the deal's supporters
have questioned how many of these job losses can be attributed
to free trade, opposition to the agreement has grown with the
increasing relocation of Canadian manufacturing plants south of
the border. Despite the extent of this opposition, the Reform Party
has risked losing public support by coming out unambiguously in
favour of the Mulroney government's agreement.

Medicare

The party's resolution on this issue begins with the assurance that
"The Reform Party recognizes the importance of ensuring that
adequate health-care insurance and services are available to every
Canadian ... "

However, three additional clauses in this resolution assert that
"it is the provinces which currently possess the legal and constitutional responsibility to provide such insurance and services,"
that "federal funding in support of such insurance and services
should be unconditional," and that this funding should "recognize
different levels of economic development in the provinces." A
policy based on these clauses would effectively allow for extra
billing, user fees, progressive erosion of the number and types of

services offered, the end of "portability" (the ability to have insurance from one province provide for coverage in another province), different standards of care between rich and poor provinces, and the discretionary use by individual provinces of federal health care monies for non-health care purposes. In short, the Reform Party's policy for all practical purposes would put an end to "medicare" as a Canada-wide, universal health insurance program with national standards.

Reform Party spokesmen tend to deny these conclusions can be drawn from their policies. A letter sent by NDP MP Lorne Nystrom to his Melville-Yorkton constituency in Saskatchewan, criticizing Reform policies on medicare and other issues, prompted an angry rebuttal in the local newspapers from Lyle Mund, president of the local Reform chapter. Mund directs Nystrom to read his party's policy Blue Book to correct his impression that Reform is in favour of "taxing the sick."

Mund correctly states that the Reform Party's policy on medicare does not call explicitly for the sick to be taxed. What it does do, though, is call for health care funds to be transferred without conditions by the federal government to the provinces, so that individual provinces can introduce user fees or "tax the sick." Reform Party policy on social programs calls for an end to universality — "those able to pay all or part of the costs themselves need not be fully subsidized."

Currently, the Canada Health Act guarantees nation-wide medicare standards by allowing the federal government to withhold funding to provinces who refuse to conform to national guidelines — such as the prohibition on extra billing and charging user fees. The federal government has already had to invoke the Canada Health Act to preempt precisely these kinds of challenges to medicare by the provinces. Reform's policy of unconditional federal funding would require repeal of the Canada Health Act and open the door wide to erosion of the medicare program.

Making federal funding "unconditional" is only one way Reform would "provincialize" medicare. The wording of the resolution on medicare makes the claim that according to Canadian law it is the provinces' exclusive responsibility to provide health insurance services. This claim ignores the fact that the specifics of health care jurisdiction have been a matter of ongoing constitutional interpretation and federal-provincial negotiation. But the resolution, originally put forward under the heading "Provincial-ization," seems to go beyond just describing what is to prescribing what should be. The party's general policy on social services states that "The Reform Party opposes the increasing use of the spending powers of the federal government in areas of provincial jurisdiction, such as medicare, education, and the like." It calls for transfers of the tax base from the federal to the provincial govern-ments "so that the content and particulars of provincial policy would be set provincially by provincial governments clearly ac-countable to the electors of each province."

The policies on shifting responsibility for social programs in-creasingly to the provinces does not explain why the "contents and particulars" of some aspects of social policy that affect Canada as a nation should not be set nationally by the federal government "clearly accountable to the electors" of the entire country. Reform does not discuss the problems that would result from an elimination of nation-wide standards for medicare. The potential exists for ten separate programs with their own criteria, no constraints on extra billing, and surcharges. Nor does Reform discuss how this would affect portability. Party documents do not explain why provincial control of health care is more desirable as an underlying value for policy than the ability of Canadians, regardless of their income, to receive an equivalent standard of medical care from coast to coast.

Deborah Grey, Reform Party MP, has suggested that equitable treatment for rich and poor should not be an objective of medicare. In May, 1989 she said in the House of Commons, "Regarding medicare, we feel that medicare is for the sick and not for the poor."

Reform policy on medicare, with its opposition to "increased federal funding" for the program, gives an inaccurate picture of what is actually happening with medicare spending under the Conservative government. Far from increasing federal funding, the Conservative government has been implementing cuts by not keeping funding levels up to increases in inflation. Bill C-69 made this practice law, so that by the year 2005 the Conservative government would eliminate federal funding for medicare alto-gether.

The Reform Party's policy does not explicitly demand the elimination of medicare; instead, it calls for the jurisdictional and

funding changes that would allow for medicare's complete transformation. Reform's preference for the kind of transformation this
should be is hinted at in the party's policy on "Alternatives to the
Welfare State: The Reform Party opposes the view that universal
social programs run by bureaucrats are the best and only way to
care for the poor, the sick, the old, and the young."

This statement seems to recommend turning over health care
programs to the private sector. The policy supporting "adequate
health-care insurance and services" does not specify that this need
be a public health care program.

Reform Party members are by no means unanimous in their
opinions about medicare. Interesting insights into the differences
can be gained by reading The Exposure Draft, an internal party
document that provides all of the resolutions submitted for consideration by constituencies in preparation for the 1991 Assembly,
the rationale behind them, and the Party Policy Committee's remarks.

A resolution proposing that the Reform Party endorse the con-
tinuance of universal medicare did get submitted by a constituency association for inclusion in The Exposure Draft. However,
the Party Policy Committee objected to it, saying "The issue of
medicare creates distinct policy problems for the Reform Party. If
the Reform Party endorses universal medicare as proposed in the
Swift Current resolution, it will then have to indicate how it
intends to do this. This will invariably lead to Reform taking
substantive legislative positions in a major area of provincial
jurisdiction, which will lead to serious contradictions with our
constitutional and fiscal policies."

Social Programs

The implications of the Reform Party's antagonism to universal
social programs run by *bureaucrats,* the term Reform uses pejora-
tively in referring to government, are more clearly spelled out in
respect to the social safety net than for medicare. Reform Party
policies on "Alternatives to the Welfare State" talk about ending
Family Allowance payments, Child Tax Credits, Spousal Exemptions, Child Exemptions, federal contributions to social assistance
and retirement plans, federal social housing programs, day care
deductions, and minimum wage laws. All these programs "might"

be replaced by "a family or house-hold oriented comprehensive social security system administered through the income-tax system."

Eliminating these existing programs and replacing them with changes to the tax system would significantly alter their present purpose. Take, for example, the elimination of minimum wage laws. To replace these laws in a way that would not hurt the working poor would require a Reform government to compensate fully anyone whose income fell below a minimum level. Existing legislation compels all employers to pay their workers a minimum wage. Reform's policy could result in employers being indirectly subsidized with public funds; they could cut wages below the minimum people needed to live on knowing that the government would make up the difference. With Reform's overriding emphasis on balanced budgets, however, it is unlikely that the party would ever make the kinds of changes to the tax system that would cancel entirely the damaging effects on the poor of eliminating minimum wage laws.

The substitution of taxation policy for government-run programs and regulations is not a new policy. The United States under Ronald Reagan instituted similar changes. In the field of housing, for example, the U.S. government was spending $31 billion on social housing when Reagan took office in 1981. By the end of his term, Reagan had cut that figure by 70 per cent. The U.S. now has, according to Peter Dreier, Director of Housing for the Boston Redevelopment Authority, more than three million homeless people and thirteen million who are "one rent increase, one accident, one layoff away from becoming homeless." U.S. reliance on the free market seems to have failed that nation's homeless.

Child Care

Reform policy on child care "opposes state-run day care." This statement is misleading, since the government does not organize and administer day care centres in Canada. Reform opposes government programs designed to foster non-profit as opposed to profit-making day care. They oppose any extension of child care programs of any type if they will cost more money. They support "expenditure reduction or elimination" for "universal and bureaucratic social policy in areas such as daycare." And, according to Reform MP Deborah Grey in a speech made in Parliament in May, 1989:

> The people of my riding, supported by the Reform Party and its platforms and policies, feel that universality, if I could speak specifically about child care, is probably a waste of money and that these programs should be targeted to people who need them. In other words, we may be discriminating against parents who choose to raise their children at home. We believe firmly that these programs should be targeted to those who need them ...

Reform's dislike of government-administered programs emerges in a resolution on how social policy should be administered. So that such policy can be implemented with "greater compassion," the party would "actively encourage families, communities, non-governmental organizations, and the private sector to reassume their duties and responsibilities in social service areas." The policy suggests a shift away from a concept of social services as a citizen's right to dependence on the provision of such services as charitable acts. The policy is reminiscent of Preston Manning's study in 1970 recommending privatization of many public services.

Women's Issues

In November, 1990 a task force on women's issues headed by Sandra Manning, wife of the party leader, concluded that there were no distinctively women's issues. Diane Ablonczy, at the time national chairperson of the Reform Party, was quoted in *Alberta Report* as saying the work group came to the consensus that women's issues should subsequently be considered social and family issues.

Reform leaders have shown considerable hostility to the National Action Committee on the Status of Women (NAC), an umbrella group that works on women's issues. Stan Waters repeatedly singled out the organization as typical of interest groups whose government funding should be cut. Deborah Grey answered a request from NAC for the party's position on women's issues by saying the Reform Party refuses to appeal to interest groups so "we will not be responding to the questions."

The issues that NAC sought a position on included violence against women, equal pay for work of equal value, and provisions to prevent discrimination against women. Although these issues have implications for society in general, they obviously do have a more direct impact on the lives of women. In coming to the conclusion that there are no issues that are specifically women's issues, the Reform Party's women's work group made a political statement on the significance of the concerns raised by groups like the National Action Committee. The fact that issues like equal pay for work of equal value have not re-emerged under any category in Reform policy seems to indicate that the party's position on such issues is guided more by ideology than by concern for categories.

One policy suggestion that the women's task force did make was for laws and programs to deal with the problems of family violence and child abuse. At the 1991 Assembly, this suggestion was approved as Reform policy, along with a commitment to making programs aimed at prevention a priority. The resolution was passed despite opposition from one delegate who argued that this was an intrusion into the family and it was such intrusions that caused family violence. An amendment proposing that abusers be held accountable for their acts, however, was overwhelmingly defeated. There is no mention of violence against women outside the family context, nor is there any reference to sexual harassment in the workplace.

Aboriginal People

Reform Party policy on aboriginal peoples focuses on how to increase their self-reliance and decrease their dependence on the federal government. Given aboriginal experience with the federal government in general, and Indian Affairs in particular, Reform emphasis on native independence from government is a goal many aboriginal people might share. But this independence would largely rest on the realization of another Reform resolution supporting "processes leading to the early and mutually satisfactory conclusion of outstanding land-claim negotiations," some-

thing that is much easier said than done. Only a handful of significant land claims have been successfully negotiated, and some
have dragged on for decades. Reform would have to devise some
very radical new processes — or free up more federal financing
— to achieve "early and mutually satisfactory conclusion" of all
the outstanding claims. Yet, they do not elaborate on these
processes in their policy documents.

Reform policy also calls for the "replacement of the Department of Indian Affairs with accountable agencies run by and
responsible to aboriginal peoples, [and] the replacement of the
current economic state of aboriginal peoples by their full participation in Canada's economic life and ... a state of self- reliance."

Preston Manning's personal history in working for oil companies in Alberta suggests that self-reliance for native people is not
a goal he actively promoted when he was in a position to do so.
When aboriginal leaders attempted to secure jobs for their communities, called for in a specific oil sands agreement, Manning
worked for the oil companies to assist them in getting around the
agreement. His 1980 consultant's report on native business
development criticized government-sponsored approaches to
economic development because they "have tended to give highest
priority to the support of group enterprise with employment as the
major goal, rather than assisting the individual native entrepreneur
and emphasizing the importance of wealth creation and return on
investment."

The kind of economy the Reform Party would have aboriginal
people participate in is the unregulated free-market economy
which drove them off their land in the first place.

Reform's policy states "The Reform Party supports the principle that aboriginal individuals or groups are free to preserve their
cultural heritage using their own resources. The Party shall uphold
their right to do so." The Party Policy Committee deliberately
formulated this resolution to correspond to the party's policy on
multiculturalism.

Reform policy on native peoples is consistent with the party's
drive to reduce the role of government to the greatest degree
possible. When a delegate at the 1991 Assembly expressed concern that proposed policies meant continuing "to fund aboriginal
people forever," Manning reassured him that the purpose of the

policies was "to do away with the Department of Indian Affairs and agencies."

In the key area of self-government, Reform policy and the leader's statement indicate a fundamental conflict with the consensus view of aboriginal leaders. Manning has ruled out any form of sovereignty and has stated that self-government would be limited to municipal authority — a policy which would make even current aboriginal control over family services, education, and economic development difficult.

Multiculturalism

Reform policy on multiculturalism has evolved significantly. As it came out of the 1991 Assembly, the policy now appears as another cost-cutting measure with proposals to rescind the Canadian Multiculturalism Act and eliminate the Department of Multiculturalism. As with native people, Reform wants groups to pay for preservation of their culture without help from government. The Party Policy Committee, in recommending the resolution in The Exposure Draft, explained it in economic terms: "it should result in administrative simplicity and reduced cost to taxpayers."

In terms of the non-economic content of multiculturalism policy, the revised party statement criticizes the Conservative government for pursuing "hyphenated Canadianism" and for its "current concept of multiculturalism." In contrast, Reform policy "stands for the acceptance and integration of immigrants to Canada into the mainstream of Canadian life."

This terminology is a departure from Reform's previous statement on multiculturalism. According to the Party Policy Committee which devised the new wording, it makes a "more positive statement" than the previous policy that called for the state to "promote, preserve, and enhance the national culture and ... encourage ethnic cultures to integrate into the national culture." References to a unitary "national culture" left the party vulnerable to accusations of intolerance while the phrase "mainstream of Canadian life" does not. From a policy that was antagonistic to other cultures, it emerges transformed by the Party Policy Committee into a statement of apparent tolerance.

One certainty emerges from an examination of the evolution of Reform Party policy on multiculturalism. The Party Policy Committee will prevent inclusion of statements of racism in public documents. The Edmonton East chapter attempted to get a resolution to the 1991 Assembly stating that "immigrants must accept and respect our Canadian Heritage and institutions." In The Exposure Draft, the Party Policy Committee recommended against it, saying that "the Reform Party cannot credibly demand that people have certain attitudes nor, in a free society, can law enforce such a thing."

Immigration

Save for its policies on democratic reform and Quebec, more critical attention has been paid to the Reform Party's immigration policies than perhaps to any others. It is here, as well as in aboriginal affairs and multiculturalism, that the racial intolerance of some Reform members threatens to undermine Preston Manning's efforts to build party credibility. When Stephen Harper, Manning's young lieutenant, asked 1991 Assembly delegates not to shoot the party in the foot, one of the bullets he might have worried about was their opinion on immigration.

The extent of concerns the party has about members' views on immigration is demonstrated by the way resolutions from constituencies were dealt with prior to the assembly. The Party Policy Committee took the extraordinary step of pulling all eighteen immigration resolutions submitted for consideration by constituencies in advance of the assembly and replacing them with three moderate resolutions of its own. Explaining its decision, the committee said "The Policy Committee received a large number of immigration resolutions which were not well drafted or considered, negative in orientation, or very different from current policy directions."

One example of these rejected resolutions came from the Calgary North constituency. It said, "RESOLVED that we should maintain ethnic/cultural balance as of September 1990." The response of the policy committee was scathing: "The Policy Committee believes strongly that we cannot avoid the 'racist' label if we adopt immigration policies that make ethnicity/culture a key element. This resolution is extremely ill considered and must be rejected."

Some of the resolutions prepared by the Party Policy Committee that did get presented and ratified at the 1991 Assembly contrast sharply with the ones rejected from constituencies. For example, the Blue Book states that "The Reform Party opposes any immigration policy based on race or creed" and supports "immigration policy that has as its focus Canada's economic needs and that welcomes genuine refugees." The Policy Committee's preoccupation with the economic aspects of immigration emerges in another policy stating, "The Reform Party opposes the use of immigration policy to solve the crises of the welfare state through forced growth population policy." An older policy could be interpreted to mean that a Reform Party government would restrict immigration to middle-class professionals or otherwise privileged individuals: "Immigrants should possess the human capital necessary to adjust quickly and independently to the needs of Canadian society and the job market." The needs of Canadian society are not spelled out.

The gap between Reform's official immigration policy and the resolutions submitted by its members raise questions about the future of Reform immigration policy. While the party harshly rejected explicitly racist resolutions from its members, it invites Bill Gairdner to speak to its assembly and rallies. Gairdner's views on immigration — eagerly taken up by Reformers who buy his book and applaud his speeches — are much more explicitly racist than those contained in the rejected resolutions, leaving the party open to the suspicion that it wishes to attract the anti-immigration vote but be officially committed to a moderate policy.

The Environment

In The Exposure Draft, the Party Policy Committee expresses concern that Reform members are not motivated to submit resolutions on the environment despite public interest in environmental issues. Most of the policies published in the environment section of the 1991 Blue Book date back to the 1989 convention.

Reform environmental policy states that "the Party supports sustainable development because, without economic development and income generated therefrom, the environment will not be protected."

Some of the party's environmental policies do seem to depart from its overall tendency to promote an unfettered free market and reduce the role of government. They suggest tough penalties for polluters, encouragement of regional development to make industrial activity less concentrated, and a country-wide program to improve municipal sewage treatment facilities. These particular policies predate the 1990-1991 round of resolution debates, and seem to have survived despite antagonism from the Party Policy Committee.

A resolution the committee proposed that does not appear in the Blue Book recommends "harnessing market forces to address environmental issues" to be used "in place of regulations wherever possible." The rationale behind this resolution was that "it must be recognized that stiff penalties and environmental laws may be costly in terms of enforcement and the competitive ability of our industries ... We believe that more will be accomplished through self-directed, cooperative efforts by industry, reinforced by market mechanisms."

Writing in the *Edmonton Sun* in March, 1991, Don Wanagas described Reform environmental policy as "purposely vague." He questioned whether the party could retain its credibility on this issue when Senator Waters had opted in favour of water exports.

Agriculture

In shaping the Reform agenda to conform to free-market ideology, the Party Policy Committee achieved perhaps its most impressive victory in the area of agricultural policy. Only resolutions drafted by the committee made it into the delegates' package for the 1991 Assembly and, through some complicated manoeuvring, Preston Manning overcame opposition from delegates who stated that the policy as presented would not be saleable to the farm community.

Key aspects of the Reform agricultural policy ultimately approved at the 1991 Assembly are support for "an agricultural policy based on market mechanisms ... a shift from a government-supported agricultural industry to an industry shaped by the free operation of comparative advantage between regions and commodities ... free entry into all sectors of production and marketing

... free trade on a global basis ... phased reduction and elimination of all subsidies, support programs, and trade restrictions."

The harshness of this policy, at a time when Canadian farmers are experiencing one of the worst crises in the history of farming in this country, prompted Netty Wiebe of the National Farmers Union executive committee to comment: "They are looking at abandoning those kinds of structural supports that farmers have come to depend on where international prices and the weather are certainly not dependable. Institutions like the Canadian Wheat Board have given farmers some bargaining strength within the agricultural industry and [with the Reform Party] we will be left as individual farmers to take whatever price is dealt to us in a hostile environment."

The Party Policy Committee did try to soften the impact their free-market approach would have on farmers by adding phrases such as the need for "transitional support," a "step-by-step" approach to the elimination of agricultural programs, proceeding only when other sectors and countries agreed to do the same, and a *voluntary* (the Party Policy Committee's emphasis) income averaging program. The committee, however, fiercely rejected any program that would help farmers out of the current crisis. Without exception, the committee recommended against proposals from the party's constituencies.

Tax Reform

The Reform Party's tax policy has three basic elements: the "elimination of special treatment, credits, write-offs and deductions," opposition to the GST, and the replacement of the current income tax system " ... with a simple and visible system of taxation, including the possibility of a flat tax."

But the simply stated opposition to the GST that appears in the Blue Book does not reflect the extent of disagreement about the tax inside the party. Preston Manning and his aide, Stephen Harper, intervened repeatedly at the 1991 Assembly to argue against repealing the GST. Manning pledged he would reform the tax by reducing exemptions, extending its scope even further. In introducing guest speaker Sir Roger Douglas, the former New Zealand cabinet minister, Manning made a special point of praising him for his success in implementing a 10 per cent value-added tax (similar to the GST) with no exemptions.

According to explanations provided in The Exposure Draft, the Party Policy Committee sees expression of opposition to the GST as an important short-term measure "to keep the pressure on the Mulroney government to reduce spending."

However, an alternative policy the committee put forward in order "to broaden the discussion" within the party is that the "Reform Party support reforming the Goods and Services Tax to make it more visible and easier to administer." The party felt it had to have an "honest" position to present to the Canadian public should they hold the balance of power after the next election.

A key principle in Reform Party policy is simplifying the tax system. In contrast, a constituency resolution based on the principle of fairness calling for a surtax on high-income earners was criticized by the Party Policy Committee in The Exposure Draft. Manning, arguing in favour of retention of the GST, said that its repeal would mean a loss in government revenue of $25 billion. The inequity of charging everyone the same tax, regardless of income, was not raised; neither was the Mulroney government's reduction of corporate taxes from 36 per cent to 28 per cent at a time when there is supposedly a crisis in government revenues. The continual shift in the burden of taxation from corporations to individuals was also not addressed. In 1950, corporations and individuals paid equal amounts to the government. In 1990, corporations paid 11.9 per cent and individuals paid 88.1 per cent of the total tax bill.

Neil Brooks, Osgoode Hall professor of tax law, has proposed a number of tax reforms that could both replace revenues lost through the GST and be more equitable. Eliminating the ability of corporations to defer their taxes interest-free, in itself could net an estimated $4 billion annually. A tax on all capital gains and a European-style wealth tax could raise a similar amount. However, Manning follows Brian Mulroney's lead in portraying the GST as a tax that is inevitable and that the Canadian people must learn to accept.

Fiscal Policy

The responsibility of governments to balance their budgets is an article of faith for the Reform Party. Reform leaders persistently attribute serious consequences to government deficits, to the extent that Stan Waters promised that, on being, elected, a Reform government would immediately move to put the country into a state of "voluntary receivership" and institute a 15 per cent across-the-board spending cut. "Resolution One" states that "all ... increases in revenue must be exceeded by reductions in expenditures." None but the most critical services would be funded until Reform had satisfactorily reduced the deficit.

Reform Party targets for reduction or elimination include day care and other social programs, foreign aid, grants to advocacy groups, and "thick layers of middle management in federal administration." Since it is this component of the civil service that traditionally is responsible for making new program initiatives workable, Reform's targeting of this particular group of civil servants reveals their general bias against government intervention.

The overriding value Reform places on balanced budgets means government would have no role in attempting to moderate economic crises. Reform's view of the problems with the Canadian economy is exclusively that governments have interfered with market forces.

Labour Policy

The Reform Party's labour policy consists of three paragraphs and has not changed since 1989. In some respects the policy appears to be one of moderation: the party "supports the right of workers to organize democratically, to bargain collectively and to strike peacefully."

But it is also ambiguous, seeming to contradict its first policy statement with its second: "The Reform Party supports the harmonization of labour-management relations ... " This is an admirable sentiment, but it does not reveal a great deal about what sorts of policy would emerge from it.

Unfortunately, the term "harmonization" can have many meanings — including the provision for binding arbitration, more complex labour legislation which would make strikes more difficult and costly for unions, or even legislated restriction on what could be bargained, such as wage controls.

The Reform Party has already indicated in its policy on "Alternatives to the Welfare State" that it intends to eliminate the minimum wage, replacing the income security of that law with a "household oriented ... social security system administered through the tax system."

This policy reveals more about Reform labour policy than the specific labour-management relations section of the policy book. The legislated minimum wage is the cornerstone of what has come to be known as "labour standards" legislation. Along with the minimum wage, labour standards acts across Canada legislate such things as the number of hours that can be worked in a week, overtime regulations, and the amount of notice an employer must give to an employee for cuts in hours, pay, or lay-offs.

Reform Party labour policy also has nothing to say about health and safety legislation or about the whole area of pay equity: the principle of equal pay for work of equal value designed to reverse pay discrimination against women. It says nothing about affirmative action programs for aboriginal people. Given Reform's general pro-business policy thrust, lack of policy in these areas is potentially more worrisome than having policies which can be assessed. This is particularly true for pay equity, given the party's open hostility towards women's issues and towards the National Action Committee on the Status of Women, a prime advocate of pay equity.

The last article of Reform labour policy states that "Unions and professional bodies may ensure standards, but should not block qualified people from working ... " This policy is aimed directly at the unionized construction trades and is designed to facilitate the use of non-union workers for wage rates much below union standards.

Preston Manning has stated that he supports the Forget Report on Unemployment Insurance (rejected by the Mulroney government as too Draconian) as a guide to assessing other social programs. The party's policy on Unemployment Insurance reflects Forget's recommendations, calling for the end of " ... regional entrance requirements and regionally-extended benefits ... "

While it has a policy on Unemployment Insurance, the party has no policy on addressing the problem of unemployment itself or on the retraining of workers whose jobs have been eliminated through the restructuring of free trade. Both Preston Manning and Stan Waters openly supported the principle of across-the-board cuts to the civil service of 10-15 per cent. Waters put it more bluntly: he would have laid off 75,000 federal civil servants, throwing them onto a private sector labour market already devastated by huge job losses.

Privatization

While Reform policy on privatization technically leaves the door open for crown corporations, it is open only a crack. It says that "corporations should be placed in the sector" where they perform best "with the least likelihood of incurring public debt ... We believe that there is overwhelming evidence that this would be the private sector in the vast majority of cases."

The only specific crown corporation targeted for privatization by Reform policy is Petro-Canada, an apparent good-will gesture to the oil industry in Calgary. But one of the three criteria for judging a crown corporation's suitability for sale is whether or not it incurs a "public debt." This criterion alone would mean the end of the CBC, what remains of VIA rail, and a host of other agencies and services.

While they do not call for the sale of Canada Post, Reformers do call for "free competition for the post office ... [with] no restrictions on private competition in the delivery of mail." While the party also has a policy of ensuring "Rural and remote areas comparable service ... " it doesn't say how it would accomplish this when Canada Post's private competitors wouldn't have to service high cost areas.

The policy on privatization is deceptive in that it leaves out a large area of government services which the Reform Party intends to privatize. As described earlier, the party's "Alternatives to the Welfare State" call for the massive privatization of social services. And under its "Income Security and Income Support" policy the party proposes to establish a negative income tax or some similar approach to social security — a form of guaranteed income. This is designed to replace all transfer payments, such as family allowance, spousal exemptions, and so on.

Together, these two Reform Party policies would create a new field of operation for the "free market." The poor and disadvantaged would be free to spend their negative income tax on whatever services they could afford on the social service open market. Day care is one service explicitly targeted for privatization elsewhere in Reform policy. This aspect of Reform privatization policy is reminiscent of Preston Manning's 1970 study, "A Strategy to Enhance the Role of Private Enterprise in Canada."

Culture

The Reform Party has no policy on culture. While it considered it important to search for members who would put forward resolutions on the environment, it didn't feel compelled to make the same effort on cultural policy. But its other policies and the unambiguous statements by some of its key spokesmen leave little doubt about what Reform would do in this field. First, privatization would almost certainly eliminate not only the CBC but also the Canada Council.

Another aspect of its free-market policies would have a major impact on cultural industries. Manning pledged to an American audience in New York just two weeks after the assembly that he would extend free trade with the U.S. One of the few areas not covered already are cultural industries: Canadian books, magazines, television, films, and music still enjoy a somewhat protected market. All would likely be cast onto the "level playing field" of free trade.

Stan Waters's attacks on the Canada Council for funding "books that shouldn't be written and music that shouldn't be listened to ... " and Reform Party members' thunderous applause suggest that federal funding to cultural agencies would be eliminated. The National Film Board, the National Ballet, the National Art Gallery, the Museum of Civilization, and the National Archives might sustain cutbacks or disappear altogether.

All of these areas are, of course, in addition to Reform's policy of eliminating the Department of Multiculturalism, which spends much of its money on cross-cultural education to combat racism.

Aboriginal people would have all their cultural funding eliminated as well.

The only cultural institution that is given protection in the Reform Party's policy book is the RCMP uniform. The Reformers state: "the distinctive heritage and tradition of the RCMP [should be preserved] by retaining the uniformity of dress code."

Reform Party Policy: Tories in a Hurry

What is striking about the Reform Party's social and economic policies is the extent to which they are negative. They are the policies of a party and a leader who nurture a long-standing hostility to the idea and purpose of modern government. Reform Party policy reveals a party which does not want to form a government. It wants to form an anti-government: a government reduced to as minimal a role as the limits of political credibility will allow. It is a role inspired and defined by an American model of free enterprise.

A summary of Reform Party policy reveals the consistency of its free-market principles. In the area of social programs it wants to end universality and give much broader access to private enterprise in servicing social needs. In medicare, it sets the stage for ending both national standards and universality and opens the door to private insurance schemes. Its intention to extend the free trade agreement with the U.S. and to eliminate exemptions from the GST indicated that rather than oppose unpopular Mulroney government initiatives in these areas, Manning will extend them. The party's commitment to a flat tax — a tax, like the GST, which is among the most regressive — would be a continuation of Conservative tax reform aimed at reducing the tax burden on corporations.

In addition to committing itself to getting rid of all agriculture subsidies, the party has said it will eliminate protection for all industries. While party members support penalties for polluters, Preston Manning's preference is to use market mechanisms to solve environmental problems. In areas of language policy, multiculturalism, and immigration, the party is guided by policies which would either eliminate any government programs or would reduce them to a bare minimum. And with no explanation of what would happen to services now funded by the federal government,

Reform policy hints at a fifteen per cent across-the-board cut in federal spending.

This anti-government thrust of Reform Party thinking is revealed not only in its policies but in the key areas in which it has no policy at all. The most poignant example is poverty and child hunger. The figures on poverty in Canada are appalling and one in five children in Canada live its consequences. Yet Reform Party policy has nothing to say about poverty and Preston Manning never mentions it in any of his speeches.

The majority of Canadians support a generous program of foreign aid, both through governments and through personal contributions to independent agencies. Yet the only mention of foreign aid in Reform Party policy targets current foreign aid as one of nine areas of "expenditure reduction or elimination."

In its support of the free trade deal and its policy of eliminating interprovincial trade barriers, grants, and tax breaks as regional development tools, the Reform Party all but abandons economic development in the poorer provinces. Eliminating regional "slush funds" as politically motivated is a worthy objective. But Preston Manning has said that equalization payments would also be eliminated eventually — suggesting that Atlantic provinces would no longer require them if they take advantage of trade with the U.S.

Other than dealing with family violence, the party has no policy for supporting the family. There is no mention of energy conservation as a goal. In other areas, such as foreign affairs, policy statements are very vague: "The Reform Party supports foreign policy guided by the values and principles of Canadians — political democracy, economic freedom and human rights."

Despite referring to it with respect to foreign policy, there is no mention of human rights anywhere in its domestic policy. The party has no position on institutionalized racism, sexism, and discrimination against lesbians and gays. Would the Reform Party cut the Canadian Human Rights Commission's budget as a deficit-reduction measure?

There are many other policy areas, already described, that seem characterized by a calculated ambiguity designed either to camouflage the party's true intentions or permit it to deny claims against it by those who disagree with their policy. This is true in the areas of medicare, aboriginal affairs, the environment, labour policy, and tax reform.

Reform Party social and economic policy is consistent throughout with a conservative, free-market philosophy. It is consistent as well with Ernest and Preston Manning's long-term plan of creating a political party guided by strict adherence to "essential truths." That these policies have been adopted and accepted by a party built on the discontent over the nearly identical policies of the current Conservative government reflects the distemper of Canada in the nineties. But it does not change the fact that its policies reveal the Reform Party to be Tories in a hurry.

Quebec and Constitutional Reform

The Reform Party is the only party in Canadian history to declare itself a national party and state its intentions not to engage in the political process in Quebec. This decision suggests that Preston Manning and his party recognize that Quebec is, in fact, a "distinct society"; a "nation" within Canada that is different in such fundamental ways that policies that are good for the rest of the country cannot be applied to Quebec. It also suggests that Preston Manning believes that a political party founded in the West cannot have relevance in Quebec. Yet its policy on Confederation takes the opposite position:

> The Reform Party supports the position that Confederation should be maintained, but that it can only be maintained by a clear commitment to Canada as one nation, in which the demands and aspirations of all regions are entitled to equal status in constitutional negotiations and political debate, and in which freedom of expression is the basis for language policy across the country. Should these principles of Confederation be rejected, Quebec and Canada should consider whether there exists a better political relationship ...

There is no ambiguity in Reform Policy, as Preston Manning has stated repeatedly that he and the Reform Party cannot support special status for Quebec. He defines Canada as a strict federation of completely equal provinces. Over half of his speech to the 1991 Assembly was devoted to attacking the idea, the institutions, and the constitutional arrangements of Canada as a marriage of two founding nations. "A new Canada must be a federation of provinces *not* a federation of founding races or ethnic groups."

Despite his insistence that Canada jettison the notion of two founding races or nations, Manning goes on to propose that Quebec, this province-like-any-other-province, should be left out of the political process of defining what a new Canada will look like. Canada — without Quebec — should define what a new Canada is, and Quebec should define what a new Quebec is. At the 1991 Assembly, Manning stated:

> First of all, let the people and politicians of Quebec define the new Quebec ... But at the same time we say with even more vigour and insistence, let the people of the Rest of Canada (and federalists in Quebec if they so wish) clearly define New Canada.

Manning invites " ... genuine Quebec federalists to contribute to our Vision of Canada." Yet there is no mechanism for them to do so in a party which has decided not to engage in political dialogue in Quebec. Manning's speeches on the Quebec issue and constitutional negotiations are expressed in Reform policy:

> The Reform Party supports a bottom-up process of public consensus building in the next round of constitutional negotiations. This would begin with elected Constitutional Conventions at the provincial or regional level.

In his address to the 1991 Assembly, Manning expanded on this process. Delegates would be elected to regional or provincial conventions and a National Convention would have delegates chosen from the regional conventions. Each convention would produce a draft constitution. These would be " ... presented to the Provincial and Federal governments for modification through a federal-provincial conference ... " The result would then be put to the population "through a Constitutional Referendum."

None of this would involve Quebec. Quebec would determine its own version of a new constitution for Canada. Yet Manning has also indicated how Quebec's decision must be made. He has stated on several occasions that a referendum on sovereignty in Quebec is not good enough: an election would be needed to validate Quebec's decision to separate. In the rest of Canada, however, elections are not good enough. We have to have a referendum.

After the conventions, referenda and elections would be held, " ... once the New Quebec and the New Canada are clearly defined ... the stage will be set for the conclusive Constitutional negotiation" between Quebec and the rest of Canada.

Preston Manning has set further conditions on these negotiations. According to Manning, none of the leaders of the current national parties are fit to negotiate for Canada because they also try to speak for Quebec. That puts them in a "conflict of interest" situation:

> Either you represent the Rest of Canada in this or you represent Quebec. But you can't represent both ... As long as you are playing for votes on both sides you can't be trusted by the rest of Canada to articulate its interests.

Manning has repeatedly stated that his approach to conflict resolution is guided by his Christian beliefs: "I have always been interested in relating religion to business, science, politics and conflict resolution." Yet his approach to resolving the conflict between Quebec and Canada seems to make resolution impossible. According to Dr. Ronald J. Fisher, a professor of psychology at the University of Saskatchewan and a member of the International Association for Conflict Management

> Preston Manning's approach to dealing with the potential separation of Quebec from Canada is both curious and ultimately counterproductive. His strategy is deceptive and contradictory in that it appears to strongly acknowledge Quebec's right to self-determination, which Quebec is demanding to remain a part of Canada, and yet it sets up a self-fulfilling scenario for the dismemberment of Canada. Combined with the Reform Party's unappealing policies on bilingualism and

multi-culturalism, Manning's strategy will render 'New
Canada' highly unattractive to many Quebecers.

Given the strong nationalist sentiment in Quebec, leaving the
job of defining the New Quebec entirely to Quebec nationalist
politicians would seem ill-advised. Manning's refusal to engage
politicians like the Parti Quebecois's Jacques Parizeau, who
would take Quebec out of Canada, strengthens the separatist ar-
gument. It reinforces both the notion that Quebec is separate and
different from other provinces and the feeling among French Quebecers that the rest of the country doesn't care. It seems designed
to smooth the way for Quebec's separation. As Don Wanagas of
the *Edmonton Journal* put it: "Manning can see the opportunity
to be prime minister in a Quebec-less Canada, with a new constitution based on Reform party policies."

Decentralization

The Reform Party's position on decentralizing power to the provinces is often ambiguous, and that ambiguity is enshrined in the
party's actual policy. It simply calls for "a re-examination and
re-establishment of a clear division of powers between constitutional levels of government. Legislative authority should rest with
the level of government most able to effectively govern in each
area, with a bias to decentralization in cases of uncertainty."

Manning has stated on numerous occasions that he does not
want to gut the national government, that he is not for complete
decentralization of power to the provinces. Yet, in some instances,
he places "provincialization" as a first principle — overriding all
other considerations. This is most clearly demonstrated in his
policy towards medicare, which was examined in the last chapter.

The party's policy on medicare simply states that, because it
was a provincial matter in the original division of powers in 1867,
it should be transferred back to the provinces. Beyond this rationale, there is no explanation of why medicare should be the exclusive preserve of the provinces. Nowhere does Manning judge this
important policy shift on the basis of the party's own criteria —
that "authority should rest with the level of government most able
to effectively govern." In the end, Canadians must decide on what
they want in a medicare program: if they want such a program to

be national in scope guaranteeing identical standards and coverage for Canadians no matter where they are, then clearly the national government is the one which can "most ... effectively govern."

Manning gives no rationale for his call for re-examining the division of powers. He seems to want to eliminate the results of years of de facto constitutional change, implying that somehow all these changes were not done properly. In fact there is nothing to suggest that this assessment is true. While changes have been piecemeal, it is not true that they have been undemocratic or in violation of provincial rights. In the medicare example, a national health care system was established because there was popular demand for it — and it was duly worked out between the two levels of government.

The same lack of political or philosophical rationale exists with respect to the Reform Party's policies calling for the transfer of responsibility for education, social welfare, child care, and other unspecified responsibilities, to the provinces.

The Triple-E Senate

The Reform Party's support for a triple-E Senate is one of its most consistent constitutional policy proposals. In combination with its package of political reforms, discussed in the next chapter, it is designed to deal with what many in the West feel are regional grievances. But given the widely perceived abuse of the current parliamentary system by the Conservative government of Brian Mulroney, the idea of Senate reform is now supported by many Canadians who seek greater safeguards for democracy, not just regional fairness.

The proposal for Senate reform calls for a Senate that would be elected, equal, and effective, hence the triple-E. Each province would have an equal number of senators — six is the number most often suggested — elected by province-wide elections. The new Senate would have the power to stop some of the legislation passed in the House of Commons.

Western proponents of the triple-E Senate claim it would have prevented the passage of the National Energy Program, the awarding of the CF-18 contract to Quebec, and the imposition of the GST. They also claim that it would not only be more democratic than an appointed Senate, but would make federalism work more fairly.

Preston Manning most often refers to the U.S. government as an example of how regional interests have been successfully accommodated by such a second house. But Australia, which has a parliamentary system similar to Canada's, has a triple-E Senate. According to Desmond Morton, writing in the *Toronto Star,* it has not changed federalism in Australia and "won't change federalism here either."

First, says Morton, a triple-E Senate has the potential to be undemocratic, too. Under Manning's proposal, Prince Edward Island, with a population of 120,000, would have the same number of senators as Ontario with eight million people. And in the National Energy Program example, Morton points out that eight of the ten provinces would have benefited from the program. Consequently, senators might have had difficulty explaining to their constituencies why they voted against it.

Morton sees a secret agenda on the part of Reformers and other supporters of a triple-E Senate.

> [It] would be a bastion for right-wingers and the wealthy. Who else would have the big bucks needed for a province-wide campaign? Even if senate districts were created, they would be enormous. If political parties were excluded ... the race would be open strictly to the wealthy. That helps explain the passionate backing from Preston Manning's Reform Party. A triple-E senate would fulfil Sir John A. Macdonald's 1865 promise: "The senate would exist to protect the minorities, and the rich are always fewer than the poor.' "

There are additional problems with the triple-E proposal. It would create a third centre of power alongside the two which already exist: the provinces, which have taken an increasingly active role in national affairs, and Ottawa. Already complex federal-provincial relations would be complicated by yet another factor, with the prospect of federal-provincial conferences becoming federal-provincial Senate conferences.

One possible alternative is to have a house of the provinces, similar to the federal state in Germany. Given that the provinces have already assumed a greater role, it would be reasonable to suggest that it be formalized. The body would be made up of representatives from the provincial governments, which are responsible for carrying out domestic policies funded by the federal government.

What is missing, argues Morton and others, is the representation of minorities. "Why not," says Morton, "a 'house of minorities?' " The Spicer Commission heard dozens of people similarly suggest that a constituent assembly made up of women, aboriginal people, ethnic minorities, the poor, and young people, give direction to the next round of constitutional negotiations.

The role that popular organizations have played at the national level since the days of "participatory democracy" in the seventies reinforces such an idea. The Reform Party, however, has effectively said "no" to such a proposal. It does not support a constituency assembly involvement in constitutional negotiations and has a policy on its books of eliminating all federal funding to the very minorities — which it refers to as "interest groups" — which would make up such an assembly.

Property Rights

Property rights are a key component of the U.S. Constitution and have been part of Preston Manning's agenda for constitutional change for many years. In 1977, Manning produced a paper on the issue for the Business Council on National Issues, a conservative business lobby. Entrenching property rights in the Canadian constitution is part of Reform Party policy. "The Reform Party supports amending the Charter of Rights to recognize that in Canada there has existed and shall continue to exist the right of every person to the use and enjoyment of property ... "

The notion of property rights is unfamiliar to most Canadians because very few Canadian political parties have ever called for it — including Conservative governments. There was little support for it in past constitutional negotiations — and for good reason.

According to University of Saskatchewan constitutional law professor Howard McConnell, property rights in the U.S. have generally been interpreted as the right of corporations to a certain return on their investment. A "person," for the purposes of property rights, includes corporations. Property rights rarely protect individual property: if someone owns a mortgage on a house or farm, property rights favour the bank, not the borrower occupying the house.

The number of areas in which property rights have been used in the U.S. is, says McConnell, "prospectively legion." For example, any effort to place a moratorium on farm foreclosures or to set maximum interest rates would be ruled unconstitutional — as they were in the U.S. Similarly, efforts by public utility boards to set rates for consumers have been overturned if the court decides they are too low and represent an "unconstitutional divestment, or taking of, property rights" of the utility.

All levels of government could be hamstrung by such an amendment. Zoning by-laws, designed to separate residential areas from industrial or commercial areas, could be successfully challenged. Even restrictions on building heights near an airport could result in a developer successfully demanding a huge compensation package.

Any attempt to place restrictions on foreign ownership of land or minerals such as oil and gas or forests could also be found to be unconstitutional. As well, says McConnell," ... if a government environmental agency set effluent controls on a riverbank at 'too low' a tolerance ... a chemical company [might] argue that it was being deprived of property rights ... because its operations were being 'unreasonably' curtailed." Others have argued that pay equity laws, workers' health and safety regulations, and measures protecting workers from sudden plant closures could also be successfully thrown out by the courts.

Property rights were originally conceived to promote small business so that increasing numbers of ordinary people could enjoy the fruits of "property." Our economy, however, is dominated by huge corporations whose influence with governments already provides a formidable level of protection of their rights to property.

Conclusion

Preston Manning's proposals for constitutional reform are inspired by and modelled after American constitutional arrangements and institutions. His position on Quebec reflects this: all provinces, like all U.S. states, must be exactly equal in status.

Calling for wide-spread public participation in the constitutional debate, he states: " ... the more that the *people* of Quebec and the *people* of the rest of Canada are involved, the higher will be the probability that the two visions can be reconciled." Yet Manning's proposal appears to have the potential to isolate these two peoples from each other. The effect is likely to be just the opposite of the reconciliation that Preston Manning suggests: two peoples, their suspicions of each other at a historic high, talking not to each other but amongst themselves, reinforcing their suspicions and their defensive postures.

Preston Manning says that giving " ... constitutional status to the French and English as 'founding peoples' ... relegates the nine million Canadians who are neither French nor English ... to the status of second class citizens." These nine million Canadians, however, do not have fewer democratic rights, fewer economic opportunities or access to fewer or lower quality social programs than the French or English. Consequently, it is hard to see in what sense they are "second-class citizens."

The people with a genuine grievance about the "two founding nations" concept are aboriginal people. They rightly point out that they are the first nations of Canada. But they have stated clearly how they wish this injustice to be addressed through constitutional change and the establishment of self-government. This does not require, and they do not demand that, Quebec be denied special status as a distinct society. The demands of the first nations for the settlement of their grievances are rejected by the Reform Party. With respect to their demand for sovereignty, Preston Manning has refused it outright. He has also said that he hopes that aboriginal people "might be willing to trade constitutional status for self-government," according to the *Globe and Mail*'s Miro Cernetig. Self-government, however, would take the form of municipal governments — not constitutional governments.

On the Charter of Rights, Manning takes the position that Canada should have, like the U.S., a concept of rights which makes no mention of race, gender, or language.

His support for triple-E Senate is modelled after the U.S. Senate and is proposed for Canada in spite of the fact that a similar model "often makes government impossible" in Australia, according to Desmond Morton.

Last, Preston Manning wishes to emulate the U.S. by including a provision for property rights in the Canadian Charter of Rights. This concept is rooted in American individualism and free-enterprise culture. However, it may be less appealing in Canada, which has had a more co-operative and collective approach to life and to government.

9

The Reform Party's Democratic Reforms

As Brian Mulroney's Conservative government became increasingly unpopular through 1989 and 1990, the conditions for the resurgence of a Western protest movement ripened. Then, after more than six months mired at 14–16 per cent support in the polls, the Tories found themselves in last place. The Reform Party had taken off.

The cross-country hearings into Canada's future, held by the Spicer Commission, provided poignant evidence of the connection. Appointed to find out what Canadians thought about constitutional issues, it had instead provided a forum for an outpouring of "dissatisfaction with the state of the country." Commission members concluded that as a result of this dissatisfaction people were demanding "responsive and responsible political leadership" and the "powers to help them oust bad leaders."

Preston Manning, capitalizing on the mood of the times, has proposed what are traditional right-wing populist reforms: the ability to recall MPs; the lessening of party discipline in the House of Commons to allow "free" votes where MPs vote according to their conscience or the wishes of their constituency; the use of plebiscites and referenda to determine the will of the people. Many of these same proposals were presented to the Spicer Commission hearings as ways to reform Canadian democracy.

The state of Canadian politics in the early 1990s is unique in a number of ways. The Conservative government has the least support of any party in power in Canadian history. An August, 1991 Gallup poll put support for the Mulroney government at 12 per cent across the country — and 7 per cent on the prairies. Dislike for the prime minister is particularly intense. Sheila Copps, Liberal MP for Hamilton South, has commented that for the first time in her political experience constituents openly talk about violence as the only way to stop what the prime minister is doing to the country. When anti-GST activists talked to people across Canada to organize opposition to the tax, they heard similar disturbing expressions of hatred for Brian Mulroney.

Preston Manning's Democratic Reforms

Preston Manning's Reform Party has responded to the democratic crisis in two ways. It has cultivated an image of a grassroots, democratic "populist" party which it deliberately contrasts with the three "traditional" political parties. More important for Canadians, it has presented a whole range of suggestions for reforming the parliamentary system to make it more responsive and accountable to citizens.

Some of these reforms are relatively straightforward and are aimed more at enforcing current rules and long traditions breached by the current government: the more prompt calling of by-elections; ending the current abuse of Orders-in-Council by the cabinet; making parliamentary committees more effective; and, more of a departure from current practice, setting firm election dates every four years. These kinds of reforms are fairly standard proposals for parliamentary changes and most have been called for by the opposition parties. But it is more radical reform that has become the trademark of Preston Manning and the Reform Party.

In its statement of principles introducing its "Political Reform" policies, the party speaks to the frustration of Canadians who feel their democracy has lost its meaning. The statement is cast in classic populist language:

> We believe in the common sense of the common people, their right to be consulted on public policy matters before major decisions are made ... and to govern themselves through truly representative and responsive institutions, and their right to directly initiate legislation for which substantial public support is demonstrated.

That statement of principle provides the basis for two of the party's major reform initiatives: referenda and new rules of Parliament which would make MPs more accountable to their constituents. These broad areas of reform have their roots in Alberta. The idea of referenda and plebiscites are mainstays of populist philosophy, particularly of the right.

The issue of accountability has more recent Alberta roots. There, more than anywhere in Canada, anger at the GST created a universal outpouring of anger at elected MPs. All but a handful of Alberta MPs are Conservatives, and the continued refusal of these representatives to speak for their constituents on the question of the hated sales tax created a fury not seen since Trudeau's National Energy Program.

The appeal of allowing MPs to speak for their constituents and to have an allegiance to them that outweighs allegiance to the party is powerful in Alberta. Albertans who feel betrayed by Brian Mulroney — referred to on popular buttons as Pierre Elliott Mulroney — see this idea as insurance against yet another betrayal by a party claiming to speak for the West. With the provision of free votes in the House of Commons, political parties would be less inclined to ignore election promises. MPs, with their first allegiance to those who voted for them, could actually stop legislation which, for example, ignored Western interests.

Two reforms are needed to establish this principle. One would have to change the nature of votes of non-confidence. Currently, any defeat of a major piece of legislation results in the fall of a government. Reform Party policy would change this: " ... the defeat of a government measure in the House of Commons should not automatically mean the defeat of the government. Defeat of a government motion should be followed by a formal motion of non-confidence ... " which would determine the fate of the government.

Support for such a measure can be found right across the political spectrum. But for it to be meaningful, the strict party discipline which now characterizes the House of Commons and was used with particular ruthlessness by Mulroney to pass the GST, would have to end. In other words, MPs would have to have the right to vote against their party on substantive issues.

While Preston Manning often focuses on this party discipline issue, his party's policy is essentially the same as the other three national parties. The only difference is that Reform Party caucus votes will be made public. Once Reform MPs have expressed their views in caucus they must vote with the party. Reform Party policy states: " ... having had the full opportunity to express their views and vote freely in caucus, with such caucus votes always made public, Reform MPs shall vote with the Reform Party majority in the house ... "

This article, passed at the 1991 Assembly, reaffirms the principle of strict party discipline. It was put forward by Preston Manning's Party Policy Committee and it was one of the resolutions to which Manning spoke before debate began. It was prompted by a resolution from the constituency level calling for all MPs to be allowed a "free vote on all issues presented ... " The Party Policy Committee recommended against this resolution in favour of its own, calling the constituency resolution "naive."

There are provisions for MPs breaking the policy directive. They must vote with the majority " ... unless a Member is instructed to abstain or vote otherwise by his/her constituents." Getting such instruction would be difficult at the best of times because it would imply a consensus among a normally diverse population. It is made even more difficult by the remaining sentence in the resolution: "The Reform Party of Canada shall provide criteria for proper processes to elicit the will of the constituency and such processes shall be initiated by the constituents or by the Members."

In this context, "The Reform Party of Canada" means the party headquarters. It is not surprising that Preston Manning and his advisors moved to take control of the "free vote" idea and its practice. It would be extremely difficult for one party to follow an open-ended free vote policy. To attempt to reform parliamentary rules to permit free votes would be nearly impossible: in effect, it would be trying to apply rules taken from the U.S. Congress that are part of a completely different political system.

In the U.S., the powers of the Congress and the president are completely separate, and free votes are an integral part of the system. Applying them to the parliamentary system would make governing difficult. Such a rule in Canada would likely be regularly ignored by the party in power or eventually repealed. Manning's efforts to control this reform may well be reasonable —

but it was he who promoted it in the first place and gave people hope that it would provide redress.

Under "Parliamentary Reform," Reform Party policy has several reforms to parliamentary procedures — broadening the oath of allegiance to include constituents as well as the Queen. It also calls for "restrictions and limitations on the number and types of Orders-in-Council permitted by a government in its term of office." The latter is an important reform, given the Mulroney government's overuse of this procedure.

Recalls, Referenda, and Initiatives

One of the most popular democratic reforms put forward by the party is the idea of "recall": "The Reform Party supports the principle of allowing constituents a recall procedure against an M.P. they feel has violated his/her oath of office."

It is not clear from this policy whether the party would press for parliamentary reform to implement a recall procedure. It is also unclear just how it intends to apply the principle to its own MPs. Manning ensured with the "free vote" policy that the party had the power to define the "proper processes" for such an event. The fact that the recall provision is supported only "in principle," and doesn't stake out its authority to define the provision further, suggests that it will not actually be implemented as a procedure.

A resolution in The Exposure Draft proposing a relatively moderate procedure for recalling MPs was recommended against by the Party Policy Committee because it didn't have "a cost estimate … a major factor in the execution of recall procedures."

The party's reluctance to follow through on its promise of this radical reform is not surprising. Such a provision, while appealing to voters who feel they have been disenfranchised, would again create chaos in practice. Any opposition party or determined group of any kind could embarrass a party leader or a prime minister by implementing the recall provision in their constituency. The first major political leader to pass such legislation found this out. It was none other than William Aberhart, the founder of the Social Credit Party, who was threatened by his own recall legislation. When his constituents began to gather names on the required petition, he moved quickly to repeal the legislation.

An equally radical departure from normal Canadian parliamentary practice is provision for referenda and plebiscites. Plebiscites
are non-binding and are meant, according to their proponents, to
be a gauge of "the public will" and a guide to governments.
Referenda can be either binding or non-binding votes. Both can
be initiated either by governments or, if provisions allow, by
citizens through petitioning.

Under the Reform Party's "Direct Democracy" policy, both
plebiscites and referenda are called for. Citizen-initiated legislation is enshrined in the party's Statement of Principles: "The
Reform Party supports the mechanism of binding referenda on the
current government of Canada by a simple majority vote of the
electorate, including a simple majority in at least two-thirds of the
provinces (including the Territories)."

This is more a statement of principle than a policy because it
provides no guidelines for who would initiate the referenda, how
they would be initiated nor whether they would be held during the
term of office of a government or at the time of a general election.
Presumably, however, it means that the Reform Party would push
for legislation allowing for binding referenda after the next election.

The party is more clear on the question of plebiscites — non-
binding votes. It sets out the procedure: "The Reform Party supports voters' initiatives by way of a plebiscite, if three percent
(3%) or more of the eligible voters of Canada sign a petition …
requesting that a question or legislative proposal be put before the
people."

Referenda and plebiscites will not likely be available unless the
Reform Party forms a majority government after the next election.
None of the other three parties have shown much interest in these
reforms. It is possible, of course, that as part of an agreement to
form a coalition government or to support a minority government,
the Reform Party could try to bargain for plebiscites on some
issues.

The state of California may provide the best example of the
effects of citizen-initiated referenda. Since 1982, it has had 141
such initiatives — called propositions — on the state ballot. It has
a population of twenty-seven million, about the same as Canada's,
and has also experienced a political crisis of confidence in the
traditional representative institutions.

One of the strongest criticisms of the referenda technique is its offering of a deceptively simple solution to complex issues through appeal to voter emotion. Nowhere has this been more dramatically demonstrated than in the issue which got the referendum ball rolling in California: Proposition 13. Prop 13, as it is called, was undertaken in 1978 to deal with rapidly increasing property taxes. The result was a landslide victory for the proposition, which called for limiting taxes to a percentage of appraised property value.

Murray Campbell, California Bureau reporter for the *Globe and Mail*, reported in February, 1991, that the long-term effects of Proposition 13 was a state fiscal crisis. After cutting services to the bone, the state government, legally bound to present a balanced budget, still found itself $7 billion short of "making ends meet." The $55.7 billion could not finance services even at the existing levels. Previous boom years had made budget balancing easier. The recession, combined with the legal requirement to balance, has created a crisis which has crippled representative government.

Public demands for increased health spending and other services are further hampered by another legal requirement: that the state spend 41 per cent of its budget on education. Yet politicians from both parties — relying increasingly on opinion polls as a way of predicting potential referendum results — are loath to implement tax hikes that the public says it does not want.

The tax limits set by Proposition 13 have caused California to fall dramatically in social spending comparisons with other states. High spending on education, which ranked the state tenth in per capita spending, is over. California now ranks thirty-first and its class sizes in primary and high schools are the largest in the country.

These effects on California — which include infrastructure as well as services — are the unintended results of Proposition 13. But even the intended impact has been denounced as unfair ever since it was implemented. Because property taxes are based on the assessed value at the time of purchase, Proposition 13 benefited older home owners and the wealthy: young and working people wanting new homes face the prospect of paying up to five times the property taxes of people next door with houses of identical assessed value.

Complex referendum questions have their own problems as democratic instruments. In October, 1990, California voters received a 144-page book of solid, very small type detailing the eighteen different "propositions" they would be asked to vote on in their November 6 election. The decline in reading by Americans and their 25 per cent functional illiteracy rate is cited as a major problem in the proper functioning of "direct democracy" and an open door to the domination of campaigns designed by public relations experts using television and direct-mail advertising.

Ironically, the use of referenda has put the democratic process back in the hands of vested interests — the very problem it was created to address. The citizen initiative process — binding referenda initiated by a set percentage of voters — was introduced in California in 1911 as a way of reducing the power of the rail barons who dominated the legislature. Today, according to Campbell, "Critics charge that special interests with big bankrolls have hijacked the process and that the public policy it creates is putting a straight jacket on elected representatives."

One example of that "hijacking" took place in 1984. The largest manufacturer of lottery tickets in the U.S. provided $2.2 million of the $2.6 million spent by a pro-lottery front group called Californians for Better Education, to promote a lottery proposition. They won — and the manufacturer got the contract to print the state's lottery tickets.

Larry Berg, a political scientist from the University of Southern California, states that it goes beyond just big money: "The trend since 1978 has not simply been one of the initiative process falling prey to well-financed interests, but also of a growing professionalization of the process." The 1978 Prop 13 fight relied on massive volunteer support for its success and it could at least be argued that it involved thousands of people in the political process. No more. A whole new sector of the economy, serving the needs of the initiation process, has sprung up: signature gatherers, political consultants, lawyers and initiative writers are now an integral part of the process. Those referenda supporters who argue that it takes the political process out of the hands of elites and their high-paid lobbyists have been proven wrong, at least in California.

Industry groups and other financial interests have learned from some of their defeats. " ... leading corporate groups ... realize that it is cheaper and often more successful to mount counter-initiatives, rather than to saturate the airwaves with negative advertisements," says Murray Campbell. Industry groups front organizations which place deliberately confusing initiatives on the ballot to counter grassroots efforts. In California, the "Big Green" environmental initiative — calling, in part, for stricter standards for pesticides — was countered with a "Big Brown" initiative which called for increased pesticide testing.

A coalition of law enforcement, health, and consumer groups sponsored an initiative calling for dramatic increases in alcohol surtaxes to pay for treatment programs for drug and alcohol abusers. The alcohol industry responded with its own initiative calling for much lower tax increases.

Referenda and plebiscites are appealing because they seem to offer quick and easy solutions to political crises. But there are no quick and easy solutions. Citizen-initiated referenda in California have resulted in taxes which are just as unfair as the ones the referenda were designed to reform. They have also resulted in a process dominated and distorted by powerful interests in that society — interests which already have an advantage in the traditional democratic system through lobbyists and large contributions to political parties.

Rather than increase the average citizen's influence over government, referenda, plebiscites, and initiatives have done just the opposite: opened the allegedly flawed system to another level of manipulation and actually made governing on behalf of the majority even more difficult.

There is every reason to believe that Canadian democracy would face the same dangers from allowing citizen-initiated referenda. The willingness of the largest Canadian and multinational corporations to intervene directly in the 1988 free trade election, their record of spending hundreds of thousands of dollars to lobby against and otherwise oppose progressive tax reform, social spending, and environmental and other regulations suggests that they would use the citizen-initiative process in the same manner that their business counterparts have in the U.S.

The simple answers promised by referenda, plebiscites, and the initiative process also tend to cover up the real basis of conflict in society. The divisions in society which people experience every day cannot be boiled down to "people who support taxes" and "people who don't support taxes." Everyone supports some level of taxation, especially if it benefits them personally.

The issues involved in taxation are complicated, and they necessarily involve differences between social classes. Trying to solve these differences by asking a single, simple question will not solve the underlying dilemmas. As in California, referenda and these other processes often create far more misery than they eliminate and intensify the conflicts they concealed in the first place.

The Reform Party is vague about the use of these techniques. It supports, in principle, the use of "citizen initiation" of legislation with no guidelines. But in its policy statement, it suggests restrictions. While Preston Manning and other party spokespersons have repeatedly promised the use of these measures to decide "important national issues," it is revealing to examine what they consider important. The policy book of the party gives very clear guidelines regarding the use of these "direct democracy" techniques: "The Reform Party supports a direct democratic process without partisanship or suppression on moral issues such as capital punishment and abortion, and on matters that alter the basic social fabric such as immigration, language and measurement."

To the Reform Party, then, capital punishment, abortion, immigration, bilingualism, and metrification appear to be the most important national issues. There is no mention of the Free Trade Agreement, poverty, unfair taxes, a cheap food policy for agriculture, the universality of social programs, or the GST as issues which are part of the "basic social fabric" and therefore worthy of referenda.

Preston Manning's view of democracy is very consistent with that espoused by the Social Credit Party and its leaders, including Ernest Manning, his father. It contrasts sharply with the participatory democracy advocated by left-wing populist parties such as the Co-operative Commonwealth Federation (now the NDP). It focuses on "results" not process. Manning's tight control of the formation of party policy and the choosing of candidates, and his determined efforts to change the minds of a majority of Alberta members about running provincially, reinforce this conclusion.

Preston Manning's package of democratic reforms are as notable for what they do not propose as for what they do. One of the clear abuses of Parliament for which the Mulroney government has been cited is the unprecedented use of time limits on debate and closure. The Mulroney Conservatives have used closure twenty-one times since 1984 — more than all governments between 1913 and 1984. Surprisingly, the Reform Party does not mention this in its reforms.

A reform often suggested is the proposal for proportional representation. This electoral reform would see each political party receive seats in the House of Commons in proportion to the percentage of votes it received nationally. If Canadians are looking for democratic reforms that would be effective in stopping the kinds of changes imposed by the Mulroney government, this single change would be more effective than any other.

The 1988 election was fought almost exclusively on the issue of free trade. But because of the current "first past the post" system of representation, the Conservatives won a majority of seats, and implemented the free trade deal even though most Canadians voted against it. Had a system of proportional representation been in place, the will of the majority would have held sway and there would have been no free trade deal.

Preston Manning does not support the use of proportional representation. This position very likely has to do with his long-term political agenda as laid out in his and his father's book, *Political Realignment*. That agenda includes the creation of a polarized, two-party system in Canada. Proportional representation, which gives much more effective power to smaller parties, would make the formation of a two-party system virtually impossible.

Participatory Democracy

It is the declared intention of the Reform Party to eliminate all funding to popularly based advocacy groups. This move would affect organizations working on behalf of native people, women, the poor, the disabled, the environment, and peace. It would extend the Mulroney government's elimination of federal grants to hundreds of advocacy groups.

The election of Brian Mulroney's Conservatives marked the end of an era of experimentation in "participatory democracy" in Canada. It had begun in the sixties: aboriginal people, students, anti-war activists, women, and welfare rights advocates confronted a complacent and placid Canadian political scene. Charging that democracy was a sham because it left them out of the process, increasingly militant groups demanded to be heard by government.

And they were. At first the response was a routine of meetings with bureaucrats. But as the movements grew and their leaders became more articulate and sophisticated, the relationship with government became more formal and official. The movements, consisting mostly of young people, had enough of an impact that Pierre Trudeau was swept to power in part on young people's response to his slogan calling for a "Just Society."

Gerard Pelletier was given responsibility for what he called citizen participation and multiculturalism. Asked why this was happening in the late sixties, Pelletier replied: "It was in reaction to people who said that liberal democracy was democracy in form and not content. I remember quoting a writer who said, 'I judge a social law on the basis of the advantages it gives the poor people I know.' Our mandate was social animation."

By the early 1970s, the result of this "animation" was the decision to fund a wide variety of community advocacy groups across the country. Provincial governments soon followed suit. Until this time, the only groups whose lobbying was subsidized were corporations who deducted their costs as business expenses.

Many in the movements concerned became disillusioned as their own organizations became bureaucratized. Yet for the first time, many groups in society had an effective voice. They had regular negotiations with government leaders, and programs addressing their concerns were developed. The place of these organizations became a recognized and accepted part of the governing of the country.

There were real results from this new dimension of democracy. The acceptance of aboriginal rights and land claims, the creation of human rights commissions, affirmative action programs, the breaking of many barriers for aboriginal people and women — all of these were the result of social movements and the formal organizations which they created.

While activists would argue that things did not change enough, the fact that progress was made is evidenced today by the anguish felt at the reversal of those gains. The practice of democracy did change. One permanent result was the notion that governments are expected to respond to citizens between elections, not just in the six months preceding them.

Brian Mulroney began the process of reversing two decades of greater democratic participation, and the Reform Party intends to continue this trend. Their policy formally calls for "expenditure elimination" of "grants to interest groups for the purpose of political lobbying" as a way of reducing the deficit.

Judy Rebick, President of the National Action Committee on the Status of Women, an organization which was repeatedly attacked by Stan Waters and other Reformers, views with dismay the Reform Party's commitment to cut funding to advocacy groups:

> [The cuts] will be a serious threat to democracy as we know it in Canada. This will mean that only groups like the Business Council on National Issues will be able to make their voices heard on the national level. It pretends to be for the "little person" but in fact the Reform Party's policies favour the most powerful forces in society.

How would the Reform Party respond to the needs of those groups in society who are still marginalized within the political system? Without government funding, effective representation to government is extremely difficult for disadvantaged groups who have few resources, precisely because they are disadvantaged.

As Lise Corbeil, Executive Director of the National Anti-Poverty Organization, puts it:

> If we live in a democracy, then all the groups have to have fair access to the system. The government has a responsibility to give them the means to have their voice heard and grants are part of that responsibility. Poor people don't have professional organizations — people aren't 'professionally' poor.

If groups speaking for poor people, for example, cannot raise the money themselves to keep an office open in Ottawa and hire

staff to meet regularly with government, then their voices simply
will not be heard.

Reform Party policy towards more participatory democracy is
consistent with right-wing populist parties of the past, such as
Social Credit. It assumes a kind of homogeneous, classless society
whose will can be determined by simple questions — typically
put to people in a plebiscite or referendum.

Reform's policy of eliminating grants to groups speaking for
the disadvantaged is also consistent with their social reform policies. Just as the burden of making themselves heard in the decision-making process has been thrown back onto the meagre
resources of the disadvantaged, programs to meet their needs
would be thrown back onto " ... families, communities, NGOs
and the private sector ... "

Last, Reform Party policy towards marginalized groups is consistent with its philosophy of unrestricted free market economics.
An examination of the grievances and demands of most of the
groups affected by the elimination of funding reveals the failure
of the market to provide fair treatment. The real focus of these
movements is not government, but the economic system which
marginalizes them. They have gone to government to plead their
case for moderating the market economy to make it more fair. It
is not surprising that a party calling for a much less restricted "free
market" would be unsympathetic to those calling for even more
restrictions and government intervention.

Conclusion

Some of the Reform Party's minor parliamentary reforms are
genuinely needed, but in the face of the crisis currently experienced by Canadians, they amount to tinkering with the system.
Of their three major parliamentary reforms — free votes, recalls,
and referenda — the first two have been diluted or modified out
of existence. The third has been initially targeted for "moral questions" such as abortion and the death penalty but left as a possibility for broader citizen initiatives. The latter leaves the door
open for powerful interest groups to dominate the process.

The Reform Party's policy with respect to democracy would
reverse previous democratic reform efforts of the 1960s and early
1970s through the elimination of the funding which allows dis-

advantaged minority groups to have their voices heard in the day-to-day decision-making of the federal government.

It is debatable whether or not the Reform Party's promise of democratic reforms would address the current concern that Canadians feel regarding their right to be heard. That concern focuses largely on the widely held conviction that Brian Mulroney has repeatedly lied to Canadians, either about the impact of the policies he did promise, such as free trade, or about actions he promised not to take, but did, such as cuts to medicare, education, and Via Rail.

That anger increased because of Mulroney's refusal to listen to people between elections. His declaration that he would always choose the right thing to do rather than the popular thing further confirmed for Canadians that their views did not matter. The passage of the GST against the clearly expressed will of 80 per cent of the population was the ultimate rejection of "participatory democracy."

None of the Reform Party's stated reforms would have stopped Brian Mulroney from doing what he has done to Canada. Preston Manning would not support a referendum on free trade — not simply because he supports the deal, but because issues of broad economic policy are ruled out by his own guidelines on the use of referenda. He also rejected a constituency resolution at the 1991 Assembly calling for a referendum on any GST increases for the same reason: as a part of budgets, they are a government's pre-rogative.

The democratic reforms proposed by the Reform Party do not address the crisis facing Canada because they were not designed to address that crisis. They are the old Social Credit proposals which even that party quickly abandoned once it achieved power. They have appeal for those who hope for simple answers to complex questions. The examination of actual policy demonstrates that even Preston Manning, like his father before him, has little real faith in them.

It may be that the main reason for Preston Manning's support of referenda lies somewhere other than in parliamentary reform. The promise of referenda, recall, and free votes "in principle" solves a potentially difficult problem for the party: it helps eliminate the need for explicit policies responding to anti-abortionists, death penalty advocates, and those opposing metrification, who make up a good part of the party's base and might otherwise complain about the party's lack of commitment to their issues.

Preston Manning's commitment to democracy should be judged, as well, by his open admiration for Sir Roger Douglas and his government's massive restructuring of the New Zealand economy. In Douglas's advice to Reformers to ruthlessly implement their restructuring and build a consensus later, we hear the voice of Brian Mulroney: doing the "right" thing rather than the "popular" thing.

Preston Manning has shown in his political beliefs and his behaviour within his own party that he has an even greater ideological commitment to doing the "right thing" than the man he wants to replace. His father put it best in *Political Realignment,* the book he wrote with Preston Manning:

> Government actions and decisions should always reflect the pursuit of essential truths and goals rather than the unco-ordinated, spontaneous, administrative reactions to political pressures and vague symptoms of unrest.

Where Would Preston Manning Take Us?

C anadians believe that their country is facing a crisis. The gulf between Quebec and English Canada has never been greater and threatens "to tear the country apart." The democratic system is seen as either a failure or at least a system so open to abuse that it must be transformed. The prime minister of the country is not simply unpopular but reviled by millions of citizens. The leaders of the two opposition parties, while clearly more popular than the prime minister, are viewed cynically by many because of their apparent inability to deal effectively with the crisis.

People want a change. But there are many things they do not want to change. In fact, the many changes wrought by Brian Mulroney are responsible for much of the rage and cynicism across the country. Canadians did not want Via Rail gutted, nor CBC stations closed, nor rural post offices boarded up. Those who voted for free trade did so because they were told it would mean jobs, and that social programs and medicare were sacred trusts. Having now experienced free trade first hand, most of these people have joined those who voted against it in the first place.

Because Canadians want change does not mean that they have changed their values. There is no indication that Canadians concerned about poverty or child hunger have quit being concerned, nor that they have decided that government has no role in dealing with this moral issue. Women have not suddenly revealed that they no longer want to be treated equally.

Most Canadians, according to the polls, believe that there has been a historic injustice done to aboriginal peoples and that their demands for justice should be dealt with fairly. There is no evidence to suggest that Canadians in richer provinces now oppose their tax dollars going to support fellow Canadians in disadvantaged parts of the country. There is, equally, no evidence that people want a "New Canada, built on the rubble of the old," as promised by Preston Manning.

But there is a very real danger that in response to the current crisis, Canadians will get much more than they bargained for. When nations reach historic crossroads, the great questions of the day revolve around how they deal with the crisis they are facing. What will Canadians draw on to meet the challenge facing the country?

It is certain that many Canadians will respond mostly out of anger, expressing, in the words of Calgary historian David Bercuson, "We don't give a shit who we get in. We just want to get rid of this bastard." This kind of "election catharsis," Bercuson reminds us, also happened in 1958 and 1984. In those cases, we got much less and much more, respectively, than we had bargained for.

The alternative is for Canadians, in a time of crisis, to take their responsibility even more seriously than they normally do: to examine their values and those of the previous generations who built this country, to determine how best to solve the existing crisis without risking the creation of a far worse one.

It is tempting to go along with Preston Manning's assessment that all Canadian politicians — except him — are corrupted by their desire for power and responsible collectively for all our problems. If the problem is cataclysmic, then we can somehow escape responsibility. The most satisfying response to the alienation people feel may be a vengeful response: a vote against "the system." A vote for Preston Manning.

It may be the most satisfying response — a kind of instant gratification in the polling booth. But it may not be the best response. Right or wrong, it is very clearly the response that Preston Manning is hoping for. From the beginning, the creator of the Reform Party has openly acknowledged that he intends to "ride the wave" of Canadian anger and discontent to build his party. His success will be directly proportional to the degree of frustrated rage expressed by Canadians at election time.

What will we get if we vote for Preston Manning and his Reform Party? What kind of leader will Preston Manning be?

How should we judge his character and his fitness to govern this country, based on what we know about him? What is the character of the political party which Preston Manning leads?

Most importantly, perhaps, what kind of policies is this leader and his party offering Canadians as a response to the dilemma we face? Last, given the answers to these questions, what can we expect of the Reform Party in a Parliament which may, in the future, be more divided than it has been for years?

Assessing Preston Manning

Preston Manning is something of a malcontent. Alienated from the mainstream of Canadian politics and marginal to the modern society that Canada has become, Manning deliberately remained on the sidelines for twenty years, clinging to a vision of Canada that was increasingly at odds with the social reality developing around him. A self-proclaimed student of history, Preston Manning has learned little from it. History is change, and Canada, like other countries, has changed in the fifty-odd years since Ernest Manning became premier of Alberta. Preston Manning says he is the man to take us into the twenty-first century, but the path he would have us follow will take back us through the nineteenth century to the world of the free market and the survival of the fittest, where the individual, in Preston Manning's evangelical view, must be "essentially alone" to seek the grace of God.

History is a living, dynamic process, a complex mix of human plans, historical accident, and local, national, and international forces and trends. But Preston Manning does not seem to see history in this way. Rather, he sees history through the eyes of the systems analyst, doing long-range planning. Manning identifies trends, collects political techniques, and examines the psychology of discontent. It is a technician's understanding of history, unconnected to the lives of actual people.

Preston Manning claims to speak to the sense of crisis that Canadians feel. He claims to have a vision of a "New Canada" which responds to that crisis. But when he plans the dismantling of medicare, the elimination of universal social programs, the enforced free market for already desperate farmers, or constitutional amendments for the foetus, Canadians should question what crisis he is addressing. When he repeatedly calls on Bill Gairdner, a man who preaches racial and ethnic hatred, as his key-note speaker, we should ask what his vision — and values — are. When he calls for a completely unrestricted free-market economy in which people in Atlantic Canada are encouraged to let go of their East-West ties and look South for progress, in which other Canadians will have to leave their communities because they are not economically "rational," we should ask how many Canadians agree with his vision of the future.

Many people would say that Preston Manning is an opportunist. He has deliberately waited for a period of political crisis to launch the Reform Party. He systematically manipulates and nurtures the fears that Canadians have about the future in order to build the political machine that he will use to "advance" his agenda. That agenda has not changed since he and his father and a handful of wealthy businessmen worked it out in the late 1960s. In order to achieve power, that agenda has been carefully blended with those issues most likely to rouse the emotions of the maximum number of Canadians: Quebec, immigration, racial and ethnic differences, the hatred of Brian Mulroney, and disillusionment with our democratic system.

Preston Manning has been judged by the media and other observers to be an honest man. Yet he says we must discard the old political labels of left, right and centre when, by any definition, he leads a party of the conservative right. He calls his party populist, yet it was created by a group of extremely wealthy and powerful individuals.

Manning claims to operate at a grassroots level, but proved willing, in his dealings with aboriginal peoples in Alberta, to assist giant oil companies in their efforts to subvert grassroots organizations. In addition, he misled aboriginal leaders about oil company intentions and his role in promoting their plans. He told his western followers that they were joining a party that would fight for a fair deal for the West, when he was, in fact, implementing a long-term plan to create a new conservative party with a view to revolutionizing national politics. He denounced the Mulroney government's Goods and Services Tax and gained tens of thousands of supporters on the promise of rescinding it. Yet he now plans to keep the tax.

Manning criticizes politicians who rely on public relations techniques, yet he has hired an American pollster, and Ronald Reagan's campaign strategist, Frank Luntz, an expert at how to plan election campaigns years in advance. Luntz credits Richard Wirthlin for his help — the architect of Reagan's image-not-issues campaigns. He has hired Hayhurst Communications, a professional political image-maker, to develop an advertising campaign. And he has had his own appearance professionally made-over for television.

In his careful fashioning of Reform policy, Preston Manning and his advisors have often used the technique of calculated ambiguity in order to give different messages to different constituencies: Reform may implement a flat tax (but they may not); they may make an across-the-board budget cut of fifteen per cent; they will reduce GST exemptions, but will not say which ones; and extend the free trade agreement, but will not say how. The party sanitized its immigration policies but repeatedly used anti-Asian immigration author, Bill Gairdner, as a key-note speaker. Preston Manning — who has opposed universal medicare for twenty-five years — plans to eliminate the national medicare system, but will not say so. Instead, he elevates provincial jurisdiction to a philosophical principle and calls for unconditional funding. He similarly disguises his plan to privatize many social services by saying that the party would "actively encourage ... the private sector to reassume their duties ... in social service areas."

Manning frequently characterizes Canada's social and regional development programs — almost all the result of social movements — as "top-down" policies and the result of "executive government." Yet he and his closest advisors have devised virtually all of the Reform Party's policies, imposed many of them on that party and run what many, both in an out of the party, have described as top-down control by an elite.

Preston Manning claims to be a democrat, yet a small handful of people run the Reform Party, most of them unelected and all of them hand-picked by Preston Manning. Using old Social Credit techniques, he has manipulated the people who have joined his party in order to persuade them to change their minds on a whole range of issues: purging the policy book of embarrassing resolutions on issues like immigration, which they supported, and adding to it orthodox right-wing policies which they did not ask for.

A majority in the party wanted to run provincially in Alberta and did not want to become a national party, but this grassroots sentiment was in conflict with Manning's objectives and he set out on a determined and carefully executed campaign to impose his will. He inspired his party faithful by promoting the principles of direct democracy and openness, and then proceeded to dilute those mechanisms within the party, adding power to an executive loyal to him. He set up a procedure for ideologically screening electoral candidates to ensure their acceptability.

Preston Manning promotes his party as a grass-roots democratic party, but he and his closest advisors have created a structure which disallows provincial organizations. Constitutencies next door to each other in a province have no mechanism for communicating with each other; they can only communicate with the Calgary headquarters. Preston Manning regularly attacks the Canadian political system for being centralist and ignoring the different needs of individual provinces. Yet he violates that principle within his own party, further concentrating power in his own hands.

Manning puts "the people" on a pedestal, and yet is an admirer of New Zealand's Roger Douglas and his record in government. Douglas's speech to the 1991 Assembly of the party consisted almost exclusively of advising Reformers to implement their free-market agenda as quickly and ruthlessly as possible and to ignore all public protest, building a consensus after implementation.

Manning's background demonstrates a clandestine approach to politics rooted in his and his father's belief in left-wing conspiracies. From the earliest days of the National Public Affairs Research Foundation and the behind-the-scenes efforts of the Social Conservative Society, to "co-ordinating" the machinations of the oil companies in their efforts to undermine aboriginal organizations, to Ernest and Preston Manning's secretive Movement for National Political Change, the leader of the Reform Party has often revealed a preference for the covert. It continues to the present.

This clandestine thinking extends to the founding of the Reform Party and to its current behaviour. Preston Manning discussed his plans for a conservative party of the right with some of the most powerful and influential men in Canada before he went public. He and a virtual handful of people — Stan Waters and Stephen Harper for the most part — worked and reworked Reform Party policy behind the scenes to make it fit their agenda. This approach was used on their own members (as well as the Canadian public), as Stephen Harper so frankly admitted when he told a reporter: "It's amazing what you can persuade them to do once you convince them it's the leader who is telling them."

His twenty-year wait for just the right political moment suggests that he discovered that Canadians would not accept his agenda in normal times, through the normal working of the political system. It suggests that he has found his agenda can only be implemented under extraordinary conditions of great disillusionment with that system. His avoidance of democratic politics under normal conditions implies a lack of respect for democracy. That lack of respect is further revealed in how he treats his own party members.

Also critical to Preston Manning's qualifications to run the country is his experience and the quality of the judgements he has made regarding his associates and advisors. Manning is in the unusual position of seeking the highest post in the land without ever having held any office. That makes judging how he might behave as a prime minister a very difficult task.

Part of that task involves assessing his judgements of people and how he delegates authority. It is an area of responsibility where the Reform leader has very limited experience. Before he founded the Reform Party, he was rarely involved in organizations with formal structures. Even his own firm, Manning Consultants, was very small. His experience over the years has been with people he has hand-picked, who have identical views to his own. Until now, he has never faced delegating authority or choosing and judging individuals on their appropriateness for a given task in any sizeable organization.

But it has been his judgement about people which many have questioned. His choice of Stephen Harper is one example; Harper was closer to Manning than any other advisor. He proved to be a willing aide in getting the membership on side, but was such an eager practitioner of back-room politics that he could not resist comments about how easy it was to manipulate Reform members.

Harper has been replaced by Tom Flanagan, a University of Calgary political scientist known in academia for his extreme right-wing views. A former American citizen, he has written several books and many articles on the Métis. In recent years he has attracted the wrath of the Métis for his questionable revision of Métis history, which completely absolved the government of John A. Macdonald for any responsibility in the 1885 North-West Rebellion and which denies that the Métis have any aboriginal rights. He is the party's Director of Policy and Communications, yet his only evident qualifications for the position are ideological.

More alarming for those in the party was Manning's response to an organizational crisis in Ontario. Despite numerous reports of very questionable political behaviour on the part of Reg Gosse, the man appointed to run the Ontario effort, Manning simply declined to act at all.

Brian Hay, a friend of Preston Manning's who shares his political philosophy and his religious convictions and once helped him build the party, no longer supports him as a future, potential prime minister:

> I have nothing but the highest regard for Preston Manning personally but — if I can use a medical analogy — if all of a sudden my body needed a quadruple bypass, would I call a dentist or a preacher to do it? [Would it] matter how much integrity or intelligence they had?
>
> The problem that I have is that Preston Manning has never held public office, whether at the municipal level, the school board level or the provincial level. I have trouble envisioning him playing a leadership role in holding the country together or, conversely, building a new country out of the pieces that might be left.

The Reform Party and Parliament

The extent to which the political crisis in Canada is the result of Brian Mulroney and his government is open to debate. But one thing is clear from this examination of Preston Manning and his party: while Reform claims to address the political crisis in

Canada, its policies are almost identical to those of Brian Mulroney's Conservative government.

In every substantive area of public policy, Preston Manning's Reform Party supports the policies of Brian Mulroney: on free trade, on ending the universality of social programs, on tax policy, on "provincializing" medicare, on the role of the "free-market," on the de-regulation of industry, on the privatization of crown corporations and social services, and on transfer payments and regional development. In all the policy areas which most affect the daily lives of ordinary Canadians, Preston Manning's Reform Party and Brian Mulroney's Conservatives are on the same track. The only important distinction is that Preston Manning would get us to the same place much, much faster.

In other important policy areas, we simply do not know what Preston Manning would do. His policies regarding agriculture, labour, tax reform, foreign policy, social policy, and immigration are so muddied by calculated ambiguity that they leave the Reform Party and its leader enormous flexibility in fashioning actual policy.

In addition, the democratic reforms of Preston Manning's party have been whittled down to the point where the only reforms the party is now clearly committed to are referenda and plebiscites. American experience has shown that these measures allow already powerful business interests another legitimate mechanism with which to intervene, with almost unlimited resources, in the democratic process. The close ties between the Reform Party and the National Citizens' Coalition — which is planning a national campaign in support of referenda — demonstrate that, far from being committed to curbing the unfair advantage of large corporations, Preston Manning sees their lobby groups as key supportive players in his "reformed" Canadian democracy.

While the Reform Party leader has been coy about what his party would do in Parliament — saying he would avoid formal coalitions "at this time" — he has made it clear on numerous occasions that he and his party will make whatever alliances are necessary to "advance the Reform agenda." There are a limited number of ways that Preston Manning can accomplish this goal.

He has never left any doubt about which party is the natural ally of the Reform Party. Indeed, had he and his father been successful at earlier efforts to reform the Progressive Conservative

Party, there would probably be no Reform Party. The objective, then and now, is to move Canadian politics to the right. Exactly what strategy and tactics the Reform Party uses in any future Parliament will simply be decided by the particular balance of power in that Parliament. If any future election produces enough Reform and Conservative seats, in combination, to form a majority, Canada will almost certainly have another "conservative" government. The formation of this government would be accomplished either by the Reform Party supporting a minority Conservative government or by a formal coalition government, which Preston Manning has not ruled out. It will have the same agenda as the Mulroney government, but with a renewed authority and mandate.

There is, of course, a great irony here. For Preston Manning has built his remarkable success on popular loathing for Brian Mulroney and his government. There is the possibility that angry voters will go to the polls to seek revenge against Brian Mulroney by voting Reform, only to find the next morning that they have given him a new lease on life.

The Reform Party has, in fact, already had considerable success in moving the Conservative government to the right. The success of the Reform Party in the polls and its ever-increasing membership has caused alarm in the Tory ranks. As a result, the Mulroney government has moved to reclaim some of the lost support by implementing or promising policies promoted by the Reform Party. This shift to the right reduces their policy differences even further, making an alliance that much easier and more likely.

On July 12, 1991, the government announced its Spending Control Act, which would limit government spending to 3 per cent increases from now through 1995. This approach to budget-making is a radical departure for a parliamentary system because the government party already has all the authority it needs to control spending: in effect the Mulroney government has proposed a law which "forces" it to implement its own policies. This budget law is right out of the Reform Party policy book and is modelled by them after the U.S. Budget Enforcement Act.

The Tories are giving signs of moving in the direction of Reform in other areas as well: they are reviewing multiculturalism, considering giving the provinces more taxing powers, reviewing medicare and social assistance plans, and proposing a parliamentary reform, which would actually reduce the effectiveness of question period.

Quebec: The Key Issue in Preston Manning's Strategy

The difference between the Reform Party winning thirty to forty seats and winning closer to eighty rests squarely on the issue of Quebec. From the time of the failure of the Meech Lake Accord, Preston Manning's strategy for his new party has been to position himself as the spokesman for English Canada on the question of Quebec and the Constitution. He has gradually established his negotiating stance: he is the man who will "stand up to Quebec." The more volatile the situation becomes between Quebec and the rest of Canada, the more successful Manning's strategy becomes. It is a classic model of "the worse the better" strategy.

In outline, it is made up of the following strategic pieces: Manning washes his hands of Quebec, speaking only for "New Canada." He states boldly that the current national party leaders are disqualified from speaking for Canada because they also claim to speak for Quebec — a conflict of interest. As these current leaders are unfit to speak for Canada, a national election must be held to determine who will have a mandate to speak for the rest of Canada.

Preston Manning's political future depends on the failure of Canada and Quebec to resolve the current constitutional impasse. If it is resolved before the next election, the critical distinction between him and the other national leaders — particularly Brian Mulroney — evaporates. No longer the spokesman for English Canada, Preston Manning is reduced to the status of just another leader of another party. In the political calm which would follow a resolution of the Canada-Quebec impasse, the actual policies of the Reform Party would come under greater and more rational scrutiny — to the certain disadvantage of that party.

In the formal sense, Preston Manning has no direct input in the constitutional process in the near future. But by positioning himself as the man who will stand up to Quebec — if given the opportunity — Manning accomplishes two things: he puts pressure on Brian Mulroney to take a tougher stand to protect his political base, making resolution more difficult and conflict more likely, and he continues to present himself to a frustrated English Canada as the country's saviour.

Preston Manning is not averse to raising the spectre of violence when he discusses the Quebec issue. He does not raise the possibility of violence often, but when he does, he does not elaborate on what he means — another use of deliberate ambiguity. He has, however, planted the seed, evoking the image of violence often enough to establish it in the public mind.

One of the first references to violence occurred early in the party's history, before the Meech Lake Accord was even an issue. At the November, 1989 Reform Party Assembly, Manning staked out his tough stance on Quebec, ending his speech with the following words, in reference to his terms for accepting Quebec in Canada: "Such terms will be judged satisfactory if they are fair and advantageous to Canada [and] if the new relationship can be established and maintained without violence ... "

No one in Canada was anticipating violence over Quebec at this time, and there was little evidence that the Meech Lake impasse was about to dominate the politics of the country. Preston Manning was already positioning himself as the man who would, in his own words, "call Quebec's bluff."

Manning raised the possibility of violence again at a time of maximum national media exposure — the 1991 Assembly in Saskatoon. This time he used his favourite analogy: the conditions which led to the Civil War in the U.S. While clearly establishing that his way, "the Canadian way," of dealing with Quebec, was through negotiations, he once again tossed out the spectre of violence, asking the rhetorical question, "Surely no Canadian wants our secession crisis to come to this [civil war]?" No one but Preston Manning had suggested it might.

Preston Manning's fondness for quoting Abraham Lincoln in reference to Canada's "secession" crisis is well established: in speeches to businessmen in Toronto, at the Americas Society in New York, in his address to the 1991 Assembly, and in many interviews. He is fond not only of the compelling parallels; he is an admirer of Abraham Lincoln and has repeatedly suggested that the Reform Party under his leadership might accomplish what Lincoln did under the Republicans: displace one of the old-line parties.

So far he has not taken his quotations of Lincoln much beyond his favourite: "A house divided against itself cannot stand." But his repeated, if muted, reference to violence may be explained by reading Lincoln further. Is he is patterning his approach to Canada's "secession crisis" after Lincoln's? In a speech, at Galena in 1856, Lincoln staked out his position:

> ... the Union ... won't be dissolved. We don't want to dissolve it, and if you attempt it, we won't let you. This government would be very weak indeed, if a majority, with a disciplined army and navy ... could not preserve itself ... We *won't* dissolve the Union and you *shan't.*

Is Preston Manning positioning himself in such a way that, given the right circumstances, he will utter the words, "We won't and you *shan't*"? Some — like the *Edmonton Sun*'s Don Wanagas — have suggested that Preston Manning sees himself as the future prime minister of a Canada that does not include Quebec. But in the speech he made to the 1989 Assembly, there are echoes of Abraham Lincoln. On "behalf of western Canadians," Manning said, "We do not want nor do we intend to leave this house ourselves. We will, however, insist that it cease to be divided."

The party's position on negotiating with Quebec is ambiguous. But it will, Manning has said many times, be tough. This position puts him in the same camp as the Alliance for the Preservation of English in Canada (APEC) which, like Manning, alludes to the use of violence, giving its reference constitutional back-up by speaking in terms of "self-defence." If the issue of Quebec sovereignty does become volatile again, the Reform Party and APEC may join forces. In Ontario alone, that could mean the strength of a combined paid-up membership of nearly 80,000.

Brian Mulroney is unfit to negotiate for the country, not because he is from Quebec — this should be an advantage — but because he is not trusted. If he "rolls the dice" again on Quebec — and there is a high probability that he will — the potential for rekindling the mutual hostility between Quebecers and English-speaking Canadians, which followed the failure of Meech Lake, will almost certainly be realized.

Thus, Preston Manning, playing a dangerous brinkmanship politics within his own country, positions himself to play his Quebec card one of two ways: establish a bargaining position that is so tough and uncompromising that it either helps intimidate Quebecois into voting no in a referendum, leaving an unresolved bitterness for years to come, or results in such protracted, bitter negotiations on sovereignty-association that the possibility of violence may, in fact, become a reality.

Preston Manning does not have to wait until the next election to play his card. By speaking publicly on the issue, he will play to the nationalist Quebec media as the true voice of English Canada — a voice they will eagerly promote. And if Quebecers are persuaded that Manning does speak for Canada, their position will harden. This, in turn, will play into Manning's hands in English Canada. Getting tougher each time he speaks, in supposed reaction to Quebec's "hard line," Manning will push the other parties into tougher positions in order to protect their political base.

Dr. Ron Fisher, an authority on conflict resolution, describes Manning's approach to managing conflict with Quebec as:

> ... a win-lose strategy, likely designed to gain votes from tough-minded and frustrated English Canadians. In combination with the competitive and provocative style of many Quebec separatists (also a win-lose strategy), Manning's attempt to use the Quebec issue to pole vault onto the national stage could result in a lose-lose outcome for all Canadians.

The Appeal to the Irrational

The lives of Canadians in Alberta or Ontario or any other province would not be changed if Quebec was recognized as a distinct society and was, as a province, given different powers. The Quebec people would not suddenly have an economic advantage over the rest of us, nor would they enjoy greater freedoms. Their different status, in fact, would not entail any disadvantage or impact in any negative way on the daily lives of Canadians outside Quebec.

Cancelling the $28.9 million spent on multiculturalism will improve neither our debt nor deficit situation nor improve our quality of life as Canadians. An immigration policy designed to allow in, at best, only the already-privileged or, at worst, only so-called "traditional" white immigrants will not make Canada a better place to live. These are just easy targets in difficult times.

The crises that Canada faces have no easy solutions and if we try to apply such solutions, we will with certainty make things even worse. There are no messiahs who will lead us out of the problems we have. No single leader and no so-called "new" party will solve our problems for us. Democracy cannot thrive or even survive through its citizens handing over their responsibility to a "leader" who promises to save them from themselves.

Democracies, like it or not, progress by muddling through, hit and miss, with the problems of the day. There is no other way. And by doing just that, Canadians over the decades created a more tolerant, democratic, and humane society.

People rightly sense that what they have built is being destroyed. But "leaders" arriving out of nowhere, claiming to be "different," with master plans for our future, should not be embraced as saviours. They should be seen for what they are: a warning sign that something is very, very wrong and that we must make an exceptional effort to set it right again. That exceptional effort means exercising tolerance, thoughtfulness, and sound judgement. Only if Canadians genuinely involve themselves in the political process — flawed as it is — will we preserve what we have and make it better. That means, minimally, examining the political parties as carefully and dispassionately as possible — their leaders, their records, their history, their policies, and those who finance them — and supporting the one which most clearly and honestly speaks to our values.

NOTES

All entries in these notes begin with a numerical reference. The first number is a page reference for this book and the second number is a paragraph reference. Thus, 2.2 refers to page 2, paragraph 2.

CHAPTER 1

2.2: John Howse, "On the March," *Maclean's* Oct. 29, 1990. All references to *Maclean's* are from this issue of the magazine.

2.3: Ian Pearson, "Thou Shalt Not Ignore the West," in *Saturday Night* Dec. 1990. All references to *Saturday Night* or Ian Pearson refer to this issue of the magazine.

3.1: John Barr, *The Dynasty* (Toronto: McClelland and Stewart, 1974) 155.

3.2: *ibid.*, 154.

3.4: Ian Pearson, *Saturday Night.*

3.5: John Howse, *Maclean's.*

4.3: Barr, *op. cit.* 154.

4.5: Pearson, *op. cit..*

5.2: Howse, *op. cit..*

5.3: Fred Walker, interview with the author.

5.5: Howse, *op. cit..*

6 - 7: Observations on the service at the First Alliance Church.

8.2: Alvin Finkel, *The Social Credit Phenomenon in Alberta* (Toronto: University of Toronto Press, 1989) 29.

8.5: Finkel, 141.

8.6: Ben Smillie, *Beyond the Social Gospel: Church Protest on the Prairies* (Toronto: The United Church Publishing House; Saskatoon: Fifth House Publishers, 1991) 131.

9.2: Finkel, 136.

9.3: *ibid.*, 137.

9.4: Larry Colle, "Religion and Policies: Canada's New Right," *Catholic New Times* Nov. 14, 1982.

9.5: Smillie, 131.

10.1: Martin Marty, "Modern Fundamentalism," *America* Sept. 27, 1986.

10.2: Smillie, 13.

11.2-5: Manual of the Christian and Missionary Alliance, (distributed by Christian Publications Bookstore, Calgary, 1990) 100-108.

12.3-4: Roger Gibbons, "American Influence on Western Separatism," *Western Separatism: The Myths, Realities and Dangers,* eds. Larry Pratt and Garth Stevenson (Edmonton: Hurtig Publishers, 1981) 195.

13.2-4: *ibid.* 203.

14.6: C. B. Macpherson, *Democracy in Alberta* (Toronto: University of Toronto Press, 1953).

15.4: Macpherson, 162.

15.5: Finkel, pp. 31-32.

16.3: David Laycock, *Populism and Democratic Thought in the Canadian Prairies* (Toronto: University of Toronto Press, 1990) 218.

16.5: Laycock, 216.

16.6: *ibid.* 220.

17.2: *ibid.* 215.

17.3: J. S. Osborne and J. T. Osborne, *Social Credit for Beginners* (Vancouver: Pulp Press Book Publishers, 1985) 136.

17.4-5: Finkel, 106.

18.1: *ibid.* 107.

18.3: *ibid.* 136.

19.1: *ibid.* 148.

20.2: *ibid.* 212.

20.4: Alfred Hooke, *I Know, I Was There* (Edmonton, Institute of Applied Art, 1971) 259.

20.5: Barr, 57.

CHAPTER 2

23.3: Barr, 143, and interviews by the author with John Barr, Don Hamilton, Owen Anderson and Erick Schmidt.

24.2: Hamilton, interview with the author.

25.2: *The Gateway,* Feb. 14 and Feb. 21, 1964.

26.4: *Edmonton Journal,* Nov. 3, 1965.

26.5: *ibid.* Oct. 1, 1965.

27.2: *ibid.* Oct. 15, 1965.

27.2: *ibid.* Oct.1, 1965 and Ian Pearson, *Saturday Night.*

27.4: Ian Pearson.

27.5: *Maclean's* Nov. 16, 1987.

28.2: Finkel, 161.

28.4: Hooke, 221.

29.1: Hooke, interview with the author.

29.4: Finkel, 162.

29.5-6: Don Sellar, *Calgary Herald* July 21, 1967.

30.2: A. M. Shoults, R. J. Burns, interviews with the author.

30.4: Finkel, 157-158.

31.4: *ibid.* 159.

32.3: Ernest Manning, *Political Realignment: A Challenge to Thoughtful Canadians* (Toronto: McClelland and Stewart, 1967) 22-23.

32.4: *ibid.* 26.

32.5-6: *ibid.* 40.

33.3: *ibid.* 86 and 47.

35.2: Don Sellar, interview with the author.

35.2: Owen Anderson, interview with the author.

35.4: Interview with Frank Booth, TRW Systems, Redondo Beach, California.

36.1: *ibid.*

36.2: Owen Anderson, Erick Schmidt, John Barr, interviews with the author.

36.3: *Maclean's*, October 29, 1990; *Defense News*, July 22, 1991.

36.4: *Fortune* February 1963; *Business Week*, September 24, 1966.

36.5: Barr, *op. cit.* 170.

32.1: Lenny Segal, interview with the author.

37.4: Neil Sheehan, *A Bright Shining Lie* (New York: Random House, 1988) 733.

37.5-6: Segal, *op. cit.*

38.2: *Maclean's, op. cit.*

38.3: Ron Wood, conversation with the author.

38.4: Barr, 171.

38.5: Owen Anderson, Don Hamilton, Erick Schmidt, interviews with the author.

39.2: *ibid.* Hamilton.

39.3: Finkel, 180.

39.4: *ibid.* 181.

39.6: *ibid.* 182 and interviews with author.

40.2: *ibid.* 183.

40.4: *ibid.* 184.

40.6: *ibid.*

41.3: *ibid.* 185.

41.4: Don Hamilton, interview with the author.

41.6: Ian Pearson.

42.2: *Calgary Herald*, July 22, 1967.

42.4: Ian Pearson.

42.5: Don Hamilton and Ian Pearson.

CHAPTER 3

44.2: Allan Hustak, *Peter Lougheed, A Biography* (Toronto: McClelland and Stewart, 1979) 130.

45.4: John Barr, interview with the author.

46 - 49: All quotes and references in this section are from the two versions of the "Requests for Proposals — Social Contract" paper produced by M and M Systems Research in 1970.

49.3: The Reform Party of Canada, *Principles and Policies 1990*.

49.4-5: Reform Party biographiess on Preston Manning, dated 1987 and 1989.

49.6: *Edmonton Journal*, December 23, 1978.

50.3-4: Reform Party biography on Preston Manning.

50.4: Rob Fricker, interview with the author.

50.5: Party biography.

51.1: Various Canada West Foundation documents.

51 - 52: References are all to the study "A Realistic Perspective on Canadian Confederation (Canada West Foundation, 1977).

52.2: *Edmonton Journal* February 1, 1991.

53.2: Reform biography.

53.4: *Western Report* supplement, 1989.

54 - 55: Various press reports and author's interview with Bruce Thomas, editor of *Scope* newspaper.

54.2-5: Bruce Thomas, interview with the author.

55.1: *Edmonton Journal*, 1973.

55.2: *ibid.*

55 - 60: This section of the chapter is based on interviews with Fred Lennarson and Rob Fricker by the author, documents of the Indian Association of Alberta prepared by Fred Lennarson, and press reports.

56.1-3: Fred Lennarson, interview with the author.

56.4: Rob Fricker, interview with the author.

57: *ibid.* and Lennarson, *op. cit.*

58.2: "Report on the Native Business Development Convention, BANAC and the VCC. Report prepared by F.M. Lennarson, Mimir Corporation, April 3, 1981, 6.

58.2: *ibid.* 7.

58.3: *Edmonton Journal*, April 9, 1981 and April 7, 1991 and Sam Sinclair, interview with the author.

58.4: Fricker, *op. cit.*

59.2: Preston Manning, "Native Business Development in Alberta: An Analysis of Requirements and Proposals for Action" Draft 4, July 21, 1980.

59.3: Fred Lennarson, "March 25, 1981: Meeting with Frank Halcrow and Preston Manning" 1 - 3.

59.6: *ibid.* 3.

60.1: *ibid.* 1, and Lennarson, "Report on the Native Business Development Convention ..." *op. cit.*

60.2: Lennarson interview, *op. cit.*

60.4-5: Elmer Ghostkeeper, interview with the author.

60.1: Lennarson, "Report on the Native Economic Development Convention" *op. cit.* 3, and Fricker interview, *op. cit.*

61.2: Ian Pearson interview with Preston Manning, unpublished.

63.3: Lennarson interview, *op. cit.*

CHAPTER 4

65.4: Don Wanagas, interview with the author.

67.1: Brian Hay, interview with the author.

67.3: *Edmonton Journal*, December 23, 1970.

68.1-3: *ibid.*

68.5: *ibid.*

69.1: Hay, *op. cit.*

71.3: Don Hamilton, interview with the author.

71-73: Ted Byfield, interview with the author.

73.5: Allan Tupper in Ian Pearson, *Saturday Night.*

75:4 Pearson, *op. cit.*

76.4: *ibid.*

76.5: *Toronto Star* October 31, 1987.

77.1: *ibid.*

77 - 79: Four-page advertising supplement, *Western Report* February and March, 1987, and "A Conference on the Economic and Political Future of Western Canada," The Reform Association of Canada, Draft, January 7, 1987.

78.5: Preston Manning address.

79.1: "A Conference on ..." *op. cit.*

79.4: *Western Report* November 9, 1987 and *Maclean's* November 16, 1987.

79.5: *Western Report op. cit.*

80.1: *ibid.*

80.2: *Western Report op. cit.*

80.2-3: Elections Canada.

81.2-3: *ibid.*

81.5: Reform Party policy book, 1989.

82.5: Reform Party biography on Deborah Grey.

83.1: Barb Boneau, interview with the author.

83.2: *Hansard*, May 3, 1989.

83.3: Reform Party biography on Stan Waters.

83-85: Party policy books, 1989, 1990.

CHAPTER 5

87 - 90: John Richards, Larry Pratt, *Prairie Capitalism: Power and Influence in the New West* (Toronto: McClelland and Stewart, 1979). Unless otherwise indicated the source for this section is Richards and Pratt, 155 - 173.

90.3: *Calgary Herald*, August 1988.

90.5-6: Nick Taylor, interview with the author.

91.4-5: Reform Party biography on Stan Waters.

91.5: Author's interview with Canadian general who wished to remain anonymous.

92.2: Senate election records, Alberta Government.

92 -93: Ian Pearson, *op. cit.*

93.3: *Edmonton Journal*, October 29, 1989.

93.4: *Edmonton Journal*, April 7, 1991 and *Globe and Mail* March 10, 1990.

94.2: *Edmonton Sun*, March 31, 1991.

94.3: Reform Party biography, *op. cit.* and *Consensus*, National Citizens' Coalition, August 1990.

94.4 - 5: *City* Spring 1984.

95.2: *Who's Who*, 949-950.

95-96: Except where otherwise indicated, the information on the National Citizens' Coalition is derived from two magazine articles: Nick Fillmore, "The Right Stuff," *This Magazine* June/July 1986, and Fred Gudmundson, "Canada's Right Wing Zealots — The National Citizens' Coalition," *Canadian Dimension*, April 1986.

95.5-6: *Edmonton Journal* April 20, 1991.

97.6: *ibid.* and *Consensus* February 1991.

98.1: *Edmonton Journal*, *op. cit.*

98.2: *Consensus*, April 1990.

98.3: *Edmonton Journal op. cit.*, and *Consensus* April, 1991.

98.4: *Edmonton Journal*, *op. cit.*

99.3: Ted Byfield and John Scrymgeour, interviews with the author.

99.4: Byfield, *op. cit.*

99.5: Mark Lisac, *Edmonton Journal*, January 9, 1990.

100.4: "The Continuing Crisis," *Quarterly Journal of the Northern Foundation* Winter 1990.

101.4: *Speaking Up for Canada's Silent Majority*, organizing pamphlet, Northern Foundation.

102.1: *Northern Voice*, Spring 1991.

102.5: Gairdner, *op. cit.* 151-52, 254, 259, 262-63, 265-67, 410.

102.6: Ted Byfield, "Is it True?"in *International Conservative Insight* April 30, 1988.

103.2: Jacquie McNish, *Globe and Mail* April 24, 1991, and Jacquie McNish and Lansing Lamont, Americas Society staff, interviews with the author.

103.4: Arthur Child, interview with the author; Elections Alberta; and "Board of Directors," Canadian-South African Society/La Societé Canadienne-Sud Africaine, Toronto.

103.5: Child, *op. cit.*

103.6: *South Africa Report* October 1985.

104.2: *ibid.* and Child *op. cit.*

104.3: *South Africa Report*, *op. cit.*

104.4: Norman Wallace, interview with the author.

104.6-105.1: Walter Davis, unpublished research paper, May 1987.

105.3: "The Persuaders," *The Fifth Estate*, Canadian Broadcasting Corporation, November 14, 1989, transcript, and Donovan Carter, interview with the author. All references to Carter come from these two sources.

106.6-107.3: Carter interview, *op. cit.*

107.1: *Who's Who op. cit.*, and Maurice Tugwell, interview with Mark Bidwell for the author.

107.2: *South Africa International* July 1991, and *Vancouver Sun* September 5, 1991, and *Vancouver Sun* October 13 and December 15, 1987.

107.3: Doug Collins, "Mere Skeleton of Truth," *International Conservative Insight,* April 30, 1988; Collins's name appears on C-FAR's letterhead as one of the "Regional Associates," and on an information sheet of the Canadian Friends of South Africa Society (Vancouver), as a member of their Advisory Board.

107 - 108: Various issues of the Foundation's publication, *Northern Voice.*

108.6: Rosie DiManno, *Toronto Star* June 19, 1991.

109.1-2: *ibid.*

109.3: Numbers come from APEC Chairman, James A. Morrison.

109.4: From informational pamphlet, "Alliance for the Preservation of English in Canada."

110.2: James A. Morrison, interview with Keith Rimstad for the author.

110.4: Morrison, *op. cit.*, and Ron Peterson, interview with the author.

111.3: Dust cover, *The Trouble with Canada,* William Gairdner (Toronto: Stoddart, 1990), and *Saskatoon Star Phoenix* June 22, 1991.

111.4: Gairdner, 389-421, 410.

112.1: *ibid.* 412 - 13.

112.2: *ibid.* 419.

112.3: *Edmonton Journal* June 13, 1991.

112.4: Sir Roger Douglas, address to Reform Party "Assembly '91." April 5, 1991, author's transcription.

113.2: Preston Manning's introduction of Sir Roger Douglas, "Assembly '91," April 5, 1991, author's transcription.

113.3: Figures derived from the research of John W. Warnock, University of Regina.

114.2: John Warnock, interview with the author.

CHAPTER 6

116 (epigraph): Stephen Harper, *Globe and Mail,* April 13, 1991.

116.3: *Alberta Report* March 1, 1991.

119.1: Party membership survey, 1989.

119.4: *Saturday Night op. cit.*

119.5: Richard Helm, *Edmonton Journal* February 10, 1990; Mark Lisac, *Edmonton Journal* April 15, 1990.

120.3: Lennarson, *op. cit.*

121.2: *Edmonton Journal* February 10, 1990.

121.3: Reform Party poll, January, 1990.

121.5: *Alberta Report* November 5, 1990.

121.6: *Vancouver Sun* October 19, 20, 1988.

122.2: Reform Party biography on Stephen Harper.

122.3: *Alberta Report* November 5, 1990.

123.2: *The Reformer,* February 1991 lists the members of the Party Policy Committee; Executive members' names appear in the 1989 and 1990 policy "Blue Books."

124.5: *Alberta Report* April 15, 1990.

124.6: Ian Pearson, *Saturday Night op. cit.*

125 - 126: *ibid.*

129.3-4: Stephen Harper, letter to Robert Matheson, August 24, 1989.

130.2: *Alberta Report* March 18, 1991.

131.3: Ian Pearson, *Saturday Night.*

131.4: *Edmonton Journal* February 12, 1991.

132-135: All references are to The Exposure Draft.

135.5: *Edmonton Journal* February 1, 1991.

135.6: *Edmonton Journal* March 24, 1991.

136.4: *Calgary Sun* October 14, 1990.

136.5: *Alberta Report* November 5, 1990.

136.6: Don Wanagas, "All Not Right With Reform," *Edmonton Sun* February 20, 1991.

137.3: *Alberta Report* November 5, 1990.

137.3: *Alberta Report* March 11, 1991.

137.7: Party agenda pamphlet.

137.7 - 138.1: Media Draft of Stephen Harper's speech, April 4, 1991.

138.5: John Warnock, *Briarpatch* reporter, interview with the author.

138.6: Taped proceedings of Assembly, author's transcript.

139.3: Reform Party, Official Record of Assembly Results.

139: All references to resolutions at the Assembly refer to the delegates' package: *Building a New Canada; Assembly '91; April 4-7, 1991, Centennial Auditorium, Saskatoon, Saskatchewan.*

140.2: Assembly's taped proceedings.

141.1: *Saskatoon Star Phoenix* April 8, 1991.

141.2: John Warnock, *op. cit.*

142.4: *Regina Leader Post* April 6, 1991.

142.3: *ibid.* and The Exposure Draft.

143.5: All results referred to are contained in the party's *Official Record of Saskatoon Assembly; Reform Party of Canada; April 4 - 7, 1991.*

144.2: *Edmonton Journal* February 27, 1991.

144-46: All references are to "The Reform Party of Canada - Candidate Questionnaire."

146-47: All quotations are from the author's transcription of the taped address of William Gairdner, April 6, 1991.

148.3: Stephen Harper, letter to Robert Matheson, August 24, 1989.

148.4 - 151: Brian Hay, interview with the author. All references to Hay are from this source.

150.4: Preston Manning, "Memorandum; To: Ontario Organizational Volunteers;" December 4, 1991. All references to the Manning letter are to this memo.

152.4: Judy Steed, *Toronto Star* June 18, 1991; Judy Steed, interview with author; Bruce Knapp, interview with author.

152.5: Gordon Young, interview with author.

153.2: Steed, *Toronto Star op. cit.*

153.3: Ron Peterson, interview with author.

CHAPTER 7

Most references in this chapter are to Reform Party policy following the 1991 Assembly. Unless otherwise indicated the source is the 1991 policy "Blue Book."

158.1: Preston Manning, "The Road to New Canada, An Address to the 1991 Assembly of the Reform Party of Canada," April 6, 1991.

159.3: Jacquie McNish, *op. cit.*

159.3: Maude Barlow, *Parcel of Rogues: How Free Trade is Failing Canada* (Toronto: Key Porter Books, 1990) 131–132

160.2: Bruce Campbell, researcher, Canadian Labour Congress.

162.3: Deborah Grey, *Hansard* May 3, 1989.

165.1: Grey, *op. cit.*

165.3: Kenneth Whyte, *Alberta Report* December 10, 1990.

166.1: Deborah Grey, letter to Judy Rebick, National Action Committee on the Status of Women, May 31, 1991.

167.6: *Edmonton Journal* September 9, 1990.

168.5: Policy book, 1990.

169.3-4: The Exposure Draft.

171.4: *ibid.*

172.2: Nettie Weibe, interview with the author.

173.5: Neil Brooks, *Paying for a Civilized Society* (Ottawa: Centre for Policy Alternatives, 1990).

177.5: Ian Pearson, *Saturday Night, op. cit.*

CHAPTER 8

181.1: The Reform Party of Canada, *Principles and Policies 1991.*

182.2-4: Manning, Assembly '91, *op. cit.*

183.2: *Edmonton Journal* February 1, 1991.

183.4: Ronald J. Fisher, analysis of Reform policy on negotiations with Quebec done for the author.

184.2: Don Wanagas, *op. cit.*

186.2 - 187.2: Desmond Morton, *Toronto Star* June 21, 1991.

187.6 - 188.5: Howard McConnell, *Saskatoon Star Phoenix* August 9, 1988.

189.3: Manning, address to Assembly '91, *op. cit.*

CHAPTER 9

192.4: Reform policy book, 1991. All policy references come from this source unless otherwise indicated.

195.5: The Exposure Draft.

197.2: Murray Campbell, *Globe and Mail* February 13, 1991.

197.5: *Los Angeles Times* June 13, 1991.

198.1 - 199.3: *Globe and Mail* September 29, 1990.

202.3: Gérard Pelletier, interview with the author, 1987.

203.3: Judy Rebick, interview with the author.

203.5: Lise Corbeil, interview with the author.

205.4: Manning, intervention on GST at the 1991 Assembly.

206.3: Ernest Manning, *Political Realignment, op. cit.* 23.

CHAPTER 10

208.3: Ian Pearson, *Saturday Night op. cit.*

211.1: Miro Cernetig, *Globe and Mail* September 9, 1991.

213.1: *Globe and Mail* April 13, 1991.

214.3: Brian Hay, *op. cit.*

218.3: *Alberta Report* November 6, 1989.

218.6: *Globe and Mail* April 8, 1991.

219.1: Carl Sandburg, *Abraham Lincoln* (New York: Harcourt, Brace and World, 1954).

219.2: *Western Report* November 5, 1989.

220.3: Ron Fisher, *op. cit.*

Note: Preston Manning declined to be personally interviewed for this book and, likewise, did not answer written questions.

INDEX